LEARNING THROUGH READING
IN THE CONTENT AREAS

LEARNING
THROUGH
READING

IN THE CONTENT AREAS

Richard Allington
State University of New York
at Albany

Michael Strange
University of Texas
at Austin

D. C. HEATH AND COMPANY

Lexington, Massachusetts   Toronto

To Maggie, Heidi, Tinker, and Bo

Preface

Learning Through Reading in the Content Areas introduces content area teachers to the processes involved in learning from textual material, specifically content area textbooks. We believe that content area learning is improved when content area teachers understand fundamental aspects of how learners acquire knowledge through reading. This book has three basic themes: (1) understanding learning from textual materials; (2) assessing learners and textual material; and (3) designing more effective content area instruction. It thus provides prospective teachers with a repertoire of skills for assessing the learners' abilities and the difficulty of the textual material. It then prepares them to design and deliver instruction that minimizes the mismatches between ability and demands.

The text is intended for a variety of reading courses in teacher education programs; it can also be used for teaching-methods courses in specific content area disciplines. It is assumed that students have a basic background in human learning. While the intended audience is content area teachers, we feel the text can be profitably used in the training of reading specialists as well. We have, however, delineated quite different responsibilities for these two groups.

In each chapter we have tried to present a balance of theory and practical interpretation. Theory is necessary for understanding why certain procedures or practices are effective, but it needs to be interpreted for practical application. To facilitate this interpretation, we have included a series of "spotlights" in the text. These inserts provide examples of practical application for content area teachers or opportunities for simulation activities. In addition, these spotlight features present strategies for assessing the difficulty level of textbooks, for efficiently estimating learner abilities, for developing key concepts, for selecting specific instructional procedures, and numerous other "real world" concerns.

We, like all authors, are indebted to those who provided our initial training and to the many others who have since influenced our thinking in various ways—including our students, who supplied the impetus for this work and valuable criticism of earlier attempts.

R.A.
M.S.

Contents

LEARNING THROUGH READING
IN THE CONTENT AREAS

Textual Material
and Learning

1

PROBABLY NO INSTRUCTIONAL RESOURCE is more common in American education than the textbook. Although no empirical data exist that adequately document the pervasiveness of textbooks as the primary instructional resource in schools, the popularity of the textbook, particularly in content area classes such as English, American history, and algebra is unarguable. Because most teachers rely heavily on textbooks, developing students' ability to employ textbooks effectively and efficiently becomes central to the role of the content teacher.

Many teachers choose not to employ a single traditional textbook. Some employ multiple textbooks, using a segment of each as the primary resource for a particular unit of study. Other teachers abandon the traditional textbook altogether and employ other forms of text, such as novels, articles, essays, or diaries to communicate content. However, few teachers abandon textual material completely. In all but a few classrooms, the ability to learn from text is a critical part of learning.

Although teachers have been criticized for failing to refine students' abilities to learn from text, few teachers have received any instruction in how they should attempt to achieve this goal. We hope to provide such instruction in this book.

Why Do We Use Text?

Written material is not the only way one acquires knowledge, even in schools, yet textbooks fill desks and lockers and account for a large expenditure of funds annually. One often-leveled charge is that adopting a single text greatly reduces the instructional demands on the teacher. This may be true to some extent, but it seems more likely that most teachers feel the professionally produced textbook provides a more coherent treatment of the desired content than could reasonably

3

be expected from any individual teacher. No teacher or school system could devote the resources to produce a course of study that the commercial publishing company expends in producing a textbook. A textbook, then, represents a type of economy—each teacher does not have to reinvent the wheel, as it were. In addition, a textbook serves as a single repository of information on a subject, allowing both the teacher and the learner to use a single common source for acquiring the desired content.

> The much-touted (educational) reforms appear to have been non-events . . . textbooks predominated as the medium of instruction; telling and questioning, usually in total class groups, constituted the prevailing teaching method; the inquiry or discovery approach was seldom evident; there was little individualization of instruction; and an astonishing amount of time was taken up in control, classroom routines, and what appeared to be scarcely more than busy-work. (Goodlad, 1977)

Although we noted earlier that there are avenues other than textbooks that lead to acquiring knowledge, textual materials are unlikely to be replaced as a primary learning source. Consider, for instance, the economy of text in imparting new information or ideas.

Whereas television and radio allow one to hear a message as it is uttered and, when recorded, at later times, text provides access to the message when it is personally most convenient. A public lecture may provide a better understanding of a topic than reading about it, but we cannot always be at public lectures. An additional advantage to text is that it allows the learner to proceed at a self-selected pace and return time and again to further clarify or evaluate aspects of the message. Finally, text is often a more efficient avenue to learning, because the writer usually pays more attention to the organization and sequence of the message than the speaker does.

> From an economy of goods, which America was as recently as World War II, we have changed into a knowledge economy. . . . Thirty years ago . . . semi-skilled machine operators, the men on the assembly line, were the center of the American work force. Today the center is the knowledge worker, the man or woman who applies to productive work ideas, concepts, and information rather than manual skill or brawn. (Drucker, 1969)

Text, and textbooks in particular, can be efficient and effective avenues to learning. However, we are sympathetic to critics, such as Postman (1970), who decry the prevalence of text-based learning in American education. We are not advocating the rise of text but rather noting that textbooks *are* widely used and that this practice can be defended on a variety of grounds.

What Variables Influence Learning From Text?

Many factors ultimately influence how much, or how little, one will learn from reading particular textual material. Individual learner differences explain some of these factors but not others. We will discuss these factors in greater detail later, but the discussion that follows should serve as a brief introduction to some of the factors that influence learning from text.

Reading Ability

A primary influence on how much is learned from text is simply how well one can read. The most common method of designating a person's reading ability is in terms of a grade-level equivalent. A student enrolled in ninth grade with an assessed reading level of seventh grade has achieved a score on a reading test equal to that of the average seventh-grade student. Such a student would probably experience difficulty with some of the textual material assigned in ninth-grade content area classes. A ninth-grade student with an assessed reading level of fourth grade would be unable to deal with much of the material assigned for reading in content area classes.

Reading ability is a complex skill, and (as we will discuss later in this text) many issues surround its measurement. Most assessments of reading ability consider both word-identification abilities and the understanding, or comprehension, of the message. The most common methods of assessing reading ability are (1) the informal reading inventory (IRI), in which each learner is tested individually by orally and silently reading material to an examiner who notes word identification and comprehension accuracy, and (2) standardized group reading achievement tests, which also typically provide both word identification and comprehension estimates.

Readability

Just as we can estimate a learner's reading ability, we can also estimate the level of difficulty of textual material on a grade-equivalent scale. This estimate is called the readability level. A number of ways exist to estimate the readability level of materials, the most common of which is some measure of word frequency and sentence length (see

Pearson, 1975). Ideally, readability also means "comprehensibility"; but because understanding, or comprehension, is unique to each learner, an estimate of the readability of a section of material is *only* an estimate. Thus readability can be a useful construct if employed properly, but caution must always be exercised because one is dealing with only a general estimate of difficulty, not an exact measure. In any event, if the difficulty of the material to be read generally exceeds the reading ability of the learners, then little will be learned from the textual material.

Writing Style

The style in which an author attempts to communicate ideas can cause difficulty. For example, it is not unusual for English literature students to have problems with the writing style of William Faulkner. Faulkner's use of the English language can prove to be a nearly insurmountable barrier to understanding his work. Thus the author's style of writing can either hinder or enhance understanding of text. For the most part, textbook authors seek to present information in a relatively straightforward manner. This may not lead to great literature or even exciting reading, but the presentation is usually clear. However, sometimes, especially when the conceptual load is heavy, the style of presentation can interfere with understanding.

Learners' Intentions

Often, learners are asked to read a number of pages in a textbook without directions from the teacher about the purpose of reading the material. Some learners adapt to such situations and create meaningful reasons for reading. Many others have no purpose, or intention, for reading other than to comply with the teacher's request. Unfortunately, such purposeless reading of textbooks results in frustration for teacher and learners alike. An intention to "get through" assigned material usually results in little true learning or understanding. Teachers can assist students in establishing purposes and creating intentions for learning by helping them distinguish between the important and the unimportant, by directing attention, and by providing a framework for thinking about what is to be read.

One cannot be sure what a student is doing when he is looking at the pages of a textbook. He may be reading every line or he may be skimming the page. He may test himself on the implication of what he reads, but he may not. He may give selective emphasis to certain sections, as students seem to do when they underline portions of a text. The student's emphasis is not necessarily the empha-

sis that the teacher desires. The student may spend more time on
sections that he has trouble understanding, or he may skip difficult
sections . . . a similar analysis could be made of the behavior of
students confronted with a lecture. (Anderson, 1970)

Teachers' Intentions

Given the same course of study and even the same text, two teachers
could easily develop different intentions for teaching. The primary
purposes of education, according to Collins (1977), are (1) presenting
knowledge, (2) developing skills for applying that knowledge to new
situations, and (3) developing strategies for acquiring knowledge independent of the teacher. Any teacher could easily select a single purpose for instruction (for example, presenting knowledge) or a
combination of several purposes. In addition, the types and applications of knowledge presented can vary from classroom to classroom.
Thus, because teachers' intentions in teaching and for student learning can vary, learners must adapt to these differing demands.

We noted earlier that some learners form their own intentions for
learning but others apparently do not. It may be more accurate to say
that some students form intentions for learning that closely approximate the teacher's and others do not. It is not that some learners have
no intentions but rather that their intentions differ from those of the
teacher. Also, some learners' intentions may be of the "get it over
with" type rather than genuine intentions to learn.

Teachers usually have fairly well-defined areas of knowledge that
they attempt to present. However, they often lack well-defined strategies for encouraging the application of this knowledge, and even less
often do they seem to have goals for teaching that focus on developing
learner abilities for independent knowledge acquisition. Thus a self-
evaluation of instruction might profitably begin by asking "What is to
be learned?" and "Why is it to be learned?" By answering these questions, teachers can begin to discover their intentions for teaching.
Only when they are aware of their intentions can they make judgments about the possible mismatch between teacher and student
intentions for learning. In any event, the greater the disparity between
the intentions of the participants, the more difficult learning becomes.
The teachers' intentions become the basis for decisions about how
they will use text in general or a single textbook in particular.

We frequently fail to recognize that much of the material presented
students in classrooms has, for the student, the same perplexing,
meaningless quality that the list of nonsense syllables has for us

> ... education (then) becomes an attempt to learn material which
> has no personal meaning. (Rogers, 1969)

Vocabulary

Most content areas have a specialized vocabulary that allows the initiated to communicate with economy and precision. For the naîve learner in the field, however, this specialized vocabulary may be extremely confusing and thus may hinder understanding. The term *legend*, for instance, has different meanings in different disciplines. If a learner attempts to apply the meaning appropriate for *legend* drawn from an American literature text to a physical geography class, he or she will undoubtedly experience some confusion. Thus, developing an understanding of a discipline's specialized vocabulary is a primary role of instruction; but it is a role that is too often overlooked by teachers who assume that *everyone* knows the appropriate meaning or, at the very least, that *everyone* will discover the meaning by reading the text.

> Your students have a good chance of being successful if they can
> deal with the language of your subject area. If they can't manage
> the language—write it, speak it, read it, listen to it—with under-
> standing, it is not likely that they will be successful in your
> classroom. (Piercey, 1976)

Previous Knowledge

It probably goes without saying that we are better able to learn from text when we share certain concepts with the writer. A passage on the Civil War may be reduced to little more than a good battle tale if the reader does not have some common understanding with the author (Rystrom, 1977). What we are able to understand is intimately linked with what we already know (Bransford and Johnson, 1973). If learners are unable to establish a cognitive framework for the topic, they have no base from which to test the information presented by the author. All written material is produced by authors who make assumptions about the prior knowledge the readers will bring to the task. When the author overestimates the amount of prior knowledge the reader has, learning is hindered. However, even when the textual material seems appropriate for the majority of students, the teacher should try to ensure a clear understanding of concepts by *all* students.

What Do We Know About Learning From Text?

Unfortunately, although we know that the factors previously discussed influence learning from text, we have no single adequate model of text learning by which we can measure either the effects of the separate influences or how they interact together. This book would have been easier to write if we had had validated, theoretical models of both how people learn from text and how intellectual operations develop during adolescence. Our present state of ignorance in these areas has been aptly summarized by Miller (1976) and Neimark (1975). Currently, researchers from a variety of disciplines are demonstrating great interest in these areas, but there is no reason to optimistically assume that these endeavors will soon produce answers to all the pressing questions. This text attempts to present the available knowledge from which to produce a framework for developing instructional strategies.

What Is the Teacher's Role in Using Text?

Textual learning is a primary facet of instruction in most American schools. Unfortunately, the use of textual material is often approached casually, almost incidentally, by teachers and learners alike. This attitude results in less learning with more difficulty. On the other hand, were the use of textual material to become more purposeful for both parties, then a large step would be taken toward improving the efficiency and effectiveness of text-based learning. Students in any content area classroom exhibit a wide range of individual differences, even on a single factor like reading ability. Because learning to read is a rather complex and difficult enterprise, some learners master it slowly. The typical range of reading abilities encountered in a heterogeneous ninth-grade classroom includes a few students at or below fourth-grade level and a few whose reading achievement is at or above grade twelve. How a content area teacher deals with such diversity is critical to the ease and effectiveness of student learning. However, as we noted earlier, a reading deficiency is only a single factor that, with numerous others, exerts considerable impact on student learning. The student's ability to read the assigned textual material is indeed a critical factor and one that must be addressed if textual learning is an expected instructional strategy.

We do not fully agree with the statement "Every teacher is a teacher of reading." Although reading textual material is a common facet of content area instruction, it does not follow that every teacher should be expected to teach reading per se. To be truly effective, content area teachers who choose to employ textual materials must at least regard reading as an instructional variable. That is, if a teacher chooses even a low-level goal, such as merely imparting knowledge through the reading of textual material, but fails to consider (1) the readability of the material, (2) the prior knowledge of the learners, (3) the clarity of presentation, (4) the learner's intentions, and so on, then learning may not simply be hindered but may be virtually impossible.

Our position is that content area teachers do not have a particular responsibility for teaching reading. Instead, we believe that content area teachers should realize that the ability to learn from textual material is critical for school success and should consider general reading ability an important variable in content area teaching. These considerations should be directed, not at improving general reading ability, but at helping to develop abilities that *allow* successful learning from textual material. This type of assistance recognizes both the individual differences of learners and the purposes of teaching in the content areas. The form of such assistance ranges from preteaching specialized vocabulary to constructing study guides to foster evaluative reactions to the material being read.

Because content area instruction is purposeful, goals must be established, goals that go beyond professional-sounding platitudes. These goals must reflect the purposes of content area teaching. In addition to identifying the content-specific knowledge, concepts, processes, functions, and relationships to be developed, teachers must also foster in learners the ability to apply this knowledge to new problems and to develop autonomy. The effective content area lesson not only produces content-relevant learning but also provides the learner with strategies for applying this knowledge and for learning from text.

> When people ask for education they normally mean something more than mere training, something more than mere knowledge of facts. . . . I think what they are really looking for is ideas that would make the world, and their own lives, intelligible to them. (Schumacher, 1973)

The teacher's role, then, is to tailor textual material to the reading abilities of the learners and to the goals of the content area lesson. To do this effectively, the teacher must understand the basic processes involved in learning from text and the most common barriers to such learning.

Summary

Each topic we have addressed can present a barrier to learning from text. Learning will suffer when:

1. a learner's general reading ability is significantly below the level of difficulty of the textual material to be read.
2. the author's writing style interferes with clear presentation of the content.
3. the reader has no particular intention in reading the given text.
4. the teacher has no particular intention in asking the learner to read a given text.
5. there is a significant discrepancy between the vocabulary used by the author and that available to the learner.
6. the author overestimates the level of sophistication of the learner concerning prior knowledge of the content.
7. teachers do not understand the factors that influence learning from text and cannot modify teaching strategies accordingly.

The
Reading Process

2

BECAUSE GENERAL READING ABILITY is a central factor in learning from text, it seems useful to provide content area teachers with a basic understanding of the reading process. Even though most content area teachers will never be responsible for teaching reading per se, the brief introduction provided in this chapter should enhance understanding of the complexity of learning to read and point to some of the common pitfalls in this developmental process.

What Is Reading?

Most adults who are fluent readers have long forgotten the struggles involved in learning to read. Most also see reading as a decoding process with the reader processing each letter in turn, producing the appropriate sounds, and forming words. Most remember letter-sound instruction as the primary component of reading instruction. Unfortunately, fluent reading is just not that simple.

For at least the last hundred years, the subject of reading has been connected quite directly to the concept of literacy; both reading and literacy, in turn, have been linked with the written word. Learning to read has meant learning to read words, and research into reading has, until recently, been directed toward finding out how people can learn to read words more quickly and effectively.... Recent research has shown that the reading of words is but a subset of a much more general human activity which includes symbol decoding, information integration and organization, and the use of various short- and long-term memory systems.... The reading of words is one manifestation ... but there are many others—the reading of pictures, maps, circuit diagrams, music, or less conventionalized systems found in the natural world (the reading of clouds in the sky or wind patterns on water, for example). (Wolf, 1977)

Reading is an active cognitive process that does indeed require using graphic (letters) and phonic (sounds) information; but for fluent readers particularly, the language-based cues—semantic (meaning) and syntactic (grammar)—seem far and away more important than graphic and phonic cues. In addition, the reader's "knowledge of the world," or the prior knowledge the reader has of the topic, interacts with the text-based and language-based cues to produce efficient reading.

Fluent reading is not simply getting the words right. In fact, fluent readers are likely to make many minor errors that do not substantially alter the intended message (Goodman and Goodman, 1977). Fluent reading is the efficient extraction of meaning from text. To do this, the reader must be actively involved with the reading process—predicting upcoming words, evaluating incoming information, and thinking. Without comprehension, reading does not occur. Yetta Goodman (1973) points out that if reading is the extraction of meaning, "reading comprehension" is a redundant phrase, because without comprehension, reading has not truly happened. The learner may produce the appropriate words, but unless an understanding of the material is present one should not label the act *reading*. Access to meaning in print, then, is neither easy nor automatic upon the words being identified (Olson, 1977).

The silent-reading speed of even moderately skilled elementary school children is so rapid that it transcends the physical ability of the human eye to focus on each printed letter or to be consciously aware of each word. Instead of focusing on individual graphic items, readers make use of a sampling process. They are predicting or anticipating what will be coming up in the text by using selective information. Sampling caused by reading speed is not unique. In conversation, oral language flows so rapidly that listeners, too, must sample from the available oral information. Fortunately, both oral and written language have ready-made cueing systems available to support this selection process.

In written language the three cueing systems comprise grammatical structure of the language, the relationship between sound and graphic symbols, and the semantic system.

Reading as a process will always include a certain number of miscalculations. The effective reader is not the one who necessarily produces errorless or near-errorless performances but the one who is able to gain the greatest amount of information from the written material. . . .

Proficient readers resort to intensive graphic/sound analysis of an entire word only when all other cues have been used unsuccessfully.

Source: Reproduced from *Reading Miscue Inventory* by Carolyn L. Burke and Yetta M. Goodman. Copyright © 1972 by Carolyn L. Burke and Yetta M. Goodman. Reproduced by permission of Macmillan Publishing Co., Inc.

Fluent reading, then, is an extremely complex cognitive process. The fluent reader uses knowledge of graphic and phonic cues, semantic and syntactic cues, and knowledge of the world based on prior experience and learning. The fluent reader constantly predicts the direction of the material from the next word (for example, First there was a tremor and then the volcano ____.) to the final outcome (for example, Who killed Mr. McDonald?). The fluent reader is actively involved in reading, constantly creating hypotheses and evaluating them based on the new information and prior experience. If the reader is restricted to word-by-word reading, comprehension suffers dramatically (Steiner, Weiner, and Cromer, 1971).

But how does one become a fluent reader? And why do some learners never achieve fluent-reader status? To better understand these issues, we need to briefly examine beginning reading and the type of instruction provided in elementary schools.

Skills Used in Learning to Read

No one begins as a fluent reader. At the beginning level, most programs emphasize two types of skills: language and visual. Reading, of course, requires both language and visual skills. Reading is a language process and instruction is usually provided to demonstrate the relationship between reading and the other communicative arts. Simply reading aloud to children demonstrates this relationship. Thus parents and teachers who read aloud and encourage children to follow the printed line help develop this concept. Another technique for fostering an awareness of the relationship between reading and communication is to allow children to dictate stories, which are then written down for the teacher or parent to read later. The importance of developing the reading-communication relationship can be seen in the constant exhortations to parents to read to their children. Other language skills involve developing larger meaning vocabularies for children, encouraging oral language facility, and providing receptive language experiences, such as sequencing a story previously listened to.

Reading is most likely to be a thinking process under the following conditions:

1. When there is a problem to be solved, a story to be interpreted, a question to be answered; under these conditions the reader has a mindset to read in a thoughtful, purposeful way.
2. When the reader has time to review what he already knows about the problem and to think while he is reading.
3. When the reader receives instruction and practice in the techniques of reading critically and determining the precise meanings of words.
4. When pupils have a chance to discuss what they read; group discussion alerts them to the need for critical reading and rewards their effort to read thoughtfully.
5. When pupils are encouraged to relate their experience to their reading.
6. When examination questions can be answered only by thoughtful reading.

Source: R. Strang, "Secondary School Reading as Thinking," *The Reading Teacher,* 13 (1960): 155–161. Reprinted with permission of R. Strang and The International Reading Association.

Basic Visual Skills

The visual skills receive much direct instruction in the typical beginning-reading program. The primary visual skill is visual discrimination, which requires the learner to differentiate between graphic symbols. At the earliest stage, simply learning to differentiate between geometric figures may be taught. From these, the learner moves quickly to differentiating between single graphemes (for example, *b-d, e-f*) in English orthography to discriminating between words. In visual discrimination the learner has to note the differences between visual stimuli. As the discrimination becomes increasingly finer (as between *there/three, meditate/mediate*), the learner must note the changes in the sequence of letters within words as well as fine differences between letters. Learning to detect distinctive features is the teacher's goal in providing instruction in visual discrimination. Even for beginning reading, visual discrimination must be highly developed. Some children experience difficulties in developing this skill and many visual training programs are available commercially. However, teachers should seriously question the worth of many of these programs (Allington, Gormley, and Truex, 1976; Hammill, Goodman, and Wiederholt, 1974).

A second visual skill involves remembering the features of graphic stimuli. Visual memory is necessary in order for the child to learn to

SKILLS USED IN LEARNING TO READ **19**

wrong place for this

top of page

Another criterion for selecting which words to teach by sight recognition is phonic irregularity. Because many high-frequency words do *turn page* associate verbal responses, such as phonemes (sounds) or words, with visual stimuli. After the learner has developed the ability to discriminate between similar letters and words, the ability to remember distinctive features must follow. Visual memory allows the learner to recognize a grapheme or word on presentation.

Sight Recognition of Words

After the learner has mastered the prerequisite visual skills, which occurs by second grade for virtually all children (Allington, 1977), training in sight recognition of words can follow. In nearly all beginning-reading programs, the learner is taught to recognize a particular set of high-frequency words generally called **sight words.** To be an efficient reader, one must recognize some words instantly. The role of sight-word learning, then, is to train the learner to respond instantly when presented certain words. Several lists of sight words exist; the most widely accepted one, prepared by E. W. Dolch a half century ago, contains 220 words of primary importance because of their frequency. The 220 words should be mastered by the end of second grade. Copies of this word list are widely available in texts on elementary reading instruction.

goes here

The content area teacher may at times wish to develop sight recognition of important words in the text. For instance, *Versaille, mesa, abacus, basalt,* and so forth, present some recognition difficulties because (a) they are derived from other languages, or (b) they have more than one feasible pronunciation based on their spelling.

Secondary-school students usually have well-developed visual-perceptual skills, so the teacher's task is primarily one of teaching the association of the correct response, or pronunciation, with the visual configuration. As we will discuss later, this task is facilitated if the word to be taught is meaningful to the student—that is, if the student has some understanding of the meaning of the word.

To teach sight recognition, the content area teacher should simply present the word visually on the blackboard, point out the letter sequence, instruct students to spell the word several times to themselves as they view the word, and repeat the proper pronunciation several times. When combined with using the word in the text and in the lecture, this strategy helps students develop the ability to recognize the target words at sight.

not follow common phonic generalizations, attempting to apply phonic analysis would be a frustrating experience. For instance, in *come, have,* and *give* the vowels do not have the same values as in *home, gave,* and *dive.* A similar situation exists between *the/he, was/gas, to/go,* and *where/here/were.* Thus many phonically irregular words are taught through sight recognition.

Sight recognition requires the ability to visually discriminate between words and to remember specific features of words. Teaching sight words requires directing visual attention to the important features of letters and letter sequence. Two other factors influence learning sight words: familiarity and meaningfulness. To retain any word, the learner must be familiar with its use and meaning. Meaningfulness is a function of familiarity. No word is meaningful unless it is familiar, though many familiar words are not necessarily meaningful. For instance, a child's name is much more meaningful than a word such as *with,* even though both may be familiar.

Word Analysis

Although most beginning-reading programs introduce sight words initially, training in the word-analysis skills or their prerequisites generally accompanies sight-word instruction. Beginning reading also teaches auditory skills, the most common of which is auditory discrimination. As in visual discrimination, in which the learner differentiates between visual stimuli, auditory discrimination involves differentiating between auditory stimuli *(sheaf/chief, blank/plank).* Letter sounds (phonemes) are the stimuli most frequently presented to students for differentiation. For children to develop the ability to use word-analysis skills, they must be able to differentiate and recognize the auditory elements.

Another prerequisite skill for word analysis is grapheme/phoneme association. After the learner masters the visual and auditory discrimination and memory skills, associating the auditory elements with the visual stimuli follows. Acquiring the grapheme/phoneme association skills allows the learner to analyze words, to sound them out. Generally, the sounds of the consonants are introduced prior to the vowel sounds because the consonants are more consistent and more frequent and therefore easier to master. Usually, the vowel sounds are introduced either in isolation or in a phonogram pattern. Phonogram patterns are constructed by a vowel/consonant, vowel/consonant/ consonant, or vowel/consonant/silent-e sequence (such as *it, at, em, og, ick, unt, ate, ime, ore,* and so forth). The learner is taught to construct words by adding and substituting an initial consonant, a consonant blend *(bl, dr, st),* or a digraph *(ch, wh, th, ph).* After mastering initial substitution, the learner is presented with final consonant substitution *(pat, pad, pam),* followed by substitution of vowels *(pat, pit, pot).* As indicated earlier, this substitution ability requires knowledge of the letter-sound association for the consonants. The vowel values in this method are presented in words and the learner is required to generalize individual vowel values from patterns.

To grasp the power of knowing consonant sounds alone versus knowing vowel sounds alone, try to read each of the following sentences:

-o-- -e-- -o --e --o-e -e--e--a-.
J-hn w-nt t- th- st-r- y-st-rd-y.

Mastering grapheme/phoneme association provides the learner with phonic-analysis ability. This is commonly called **sounding out**, though educational literature refers to this ability as **decoding, recoding, phonetic analysis, phonics**, and so forth. Regardless of the label, being able to analyze words provides a learner with the ability to identify previously unknown words. Because English is an alphabetic language, it allows the reader to use phonic analysis. Estimates vary, but it is generally agreed that the majority of English words can be decoded following the most common phonic generalizations. Unfortunately, it is those irregular words that often foil the best-laid plans. However, phonic analysis is only one of the word-analysis skills, and the others, although not as well known, are at least equally useful and perhaps more so, because single-letter phonics is an inefficient word-identification skill at best.

Structural Analysis

Structural-analysis skills include the ability to recognize and analyze compound words, contractions, syllables, affixes, and inflected endings. Structural analysis is generally faster than phonic analysis and is often employed in conjunction with both that skill and sight-word recognition. For example, if the learner recognizes the word *look* at sight or through phonic analysis, a presentation of *looked, looking,* or *outlook* would allow the use of various structural-analysis skills.

Contextual Analysis

Contextual analysis, or the use of context, has received a renewed emphasis in the past decade. Context is provided by the semantic (word) and syntactic (grammatical) elements in a phrase, sentence, or paragraph and, of course, is not available when words are presented in isolation. Contextual analysis requires the ability to use semantic and syntactic cues, as in the sentence "John ＿＿ to work early." Contextual analysis is a form of prediction; rather than attempting to analyze a word solely through its phonic elements, fluent readers use their knowledge of the language and of the world to predict what the unknown word might be. A primary advantage of contextual analysis is that the reader has to be involved actively in the reading process because prediction requires understanding the preceding information. Contextual analysis, then, focuses more on meaning than any other analysis skill. It can also be combined with phonic analysis to produce a rather efficient word-recognition method. As one adds more graphic information (The boy kicked the b＿＿; The boy kicked the b-ll), it becomes easier to prove or disprove an initial prediction based primarily on available semantic and syntactic information. Using context has probably been the least frequently emphasized word-analysis skill, though current beginning-reading programs are now recognizing its importance to fluent reading.

Use of the Dictionary

Another skill often offered as a word-recognition technique, use of the dictionary, seems to have more deficiencies than strengths. The primary weaknesses are (1) the number of prerequisite skills required, and (2) its relative inefficiency. To use the dictionary as a pronunciation guide, the user must be able to use diacritical markings as well as a host of other skills. In fact, skilled readers rarely pick up a dictionary, using it primarily as a last resort, which probably best demonstrates the dictionary's inefficiency.

Summary

Using the primary word-recognition skills puts the learner on the path to becoming a skilled reader. No single word-identification skill can be classified as most useful. Each skill is best used in combination with the others, and programs emphasizing one skill to the neglect of the others should be avoided. Phonics, for instance, has often been touted as *the* remedy for reading disability, but phonic analysis alone can produce an overanalytical, word-by-word reader. Although important, phonic analysis should be combined with the other useful recognition techniques.

Consider the problems that using phonic cues alone can produce. Frank Smith (1971) developed a list similar to that which follows to point out the difficulties in knowing what sounds should be associated with *ho*:

What sounds should one assign to the letters *ho*? Consider these examples:

--use	--t
--ist	--g
--rse	--w
--ok	--ne
--ot	--ney
--ur	--nest
--uston	--rizon

Even the poorest readers in most middle and secondary schools have mastered a host of skills basic to the reading process. These learners are active and capable language users with refined visual-perceptual abilities and, generally, a substantial store of knowledge about grapheme/phoneme associations. Unfortunately, these poor readers have not been able to combine their skills into a fluent reading process that yields meaning from print. They have learned many skills, but too often they have not learned how best to use them. The various skills discussed are important; however, acquiring these skills does not ensure good reading abilities, because fluent reading is much more than well-developed isolated skills.

Theories of the Reading Process

One reason for the multitude of available reading programs is the lack of an empirically validated theory of the reading process. Although several theories are commonly accepted, at this time none has a majority of followers among practitioners in the field. In order to provide a background to current thinking about the reading process, we will briefly examine the several major theories of reading.

Psychological Models

Williams (1973) reviewed existing theories and models of reading ability and categorized the models. Her categories include **psychological, linguistic,** and **information-processing** models, which we will briefly review here. The psychological models include several quite different theories of reading.

The Behaviorist View. One popular early model was the behaviorist view, advocated by Skinner (1957) and Staats et al. (1962). The behaviorist view of reading is similar in many ways to the stimulus-response (S-R) theories of behavior and learning. The models are primarily associative, linking verbal responses to graphic stimuli. Various authors and materials developers have attempted to fit learning to read into the traditional operant-learning model. These authors see developing reading skills as a basically cumulative and hierarchical process. The reading act is broken into logical components, each with separate skills. The learner proceeds through the hierarchy of components, mastering one skill at a time.

Unfortunately, although the behaviorist model provides for learning and recognizing individual words, it cannot account for the behaviors of skilled readers. Word recognition can be taught as an S-R experience, but even the elaborate associative models fail to describe the reading act adequately. Reading is more than associational learning.

The Cognitive View. A second predominant psychological model in the current research literature is the cognitive view. In a recent text, Gibson and Levin (1975) present a rather thorough argument for accepting this model. Their comprehensive model is divided into phases. In the first phase, learners develop skills in language because reading is a communicative act. These skills include acquiring and understanding the phonological, semantic, and syntactic systems of speech. In the next phase, the learner develops familiarity with graphic symbols—scribbles, drawings, graphemes, words, and so forth. In a print-oriented society, this graphic familiarization typically begins before formal schooling, regardless of social level. Once the learner has developed an appropriate conceptualization of the various graphic representations, particularly differentiating graphemes and words, learning higher-order skills can proceed. Analyzing the internal structure of words, abstracting generalizations from words, and other cognitive skills are developed. In the final phase the learner uses the structural principles abstracted to organize information. These include (1) using the correspondence between graphic symbols and phonological (sound) system; (2) using grammatical constraints; (3) predicting words or word meanings, based on context; and (4) using orthographic familiarity to predict words or phrases. The cognitive models point out complex aspects of fluent reading that have often been ignored by researchers, educators, and teachers. However, though probably the most comprehensive model to date, the cognitive view has raised many unanswered questions about how reading is acquired and how it might best be taught. A primary contribution has been to demonstrate that fluent reading is a tremendously complex and little understood skill.

Linguistic Models

The Symbol-Sound View. Early formulations of linguistic models (Bloomfield, 1942; Fries, 1963) dealt primarily with the structure of the correspondence between the graphic system (letters) and the phonological system (sound). Thus, much effort focused on teaching beginning readers about the regularities of symbol-sound correspondence. There was little concern for using semantic and syntactic systems. For instance, beginning materials presented sentences such as "Dan can fan. Nan can fan. The man can fan. Dan can fan the man. Dan can fan Nan." A brief overview of beginning-reading materials developed by proponents of early linguistic models indicates the overwhelming emphasis given the decoding aspect of reading. Difficulty in reading was seen as stemming from the irregularities of symbol-sound correspondence. A primary weakness of this early linguistic view was that it neglected the language aspect of reading; that is, it taught reading more as getting the words right than as extracting information from the print.

The Information-Processing View. Information-processing models of reading, such as that proposed by Smith (1971), emphasize the importance meaning plays in reading. Predictions based on both graphic-phonic cues and context are an integral part of reading. Because the reader has access to both types of information, identification of words is based on both. When using information provided by context, a reader may use graphic-phonic information only to confirm the prediction, if at all. The beginning reader may overuse the visual information and read very slowly, word by word, with little comprehension. The reader must progress to the point where meaning plays an important role in prediction, or word identification. Thus, beginning instruction focuses on meaning and making sense of what one reads. Many traditional strategies for teaching would be eliminated (Smith, 1973); the teacher would provide feedback but allow learners to abstract appropriate generalizations and rules for themselves.

The Psycholinguistic View. Goodman (1967), who sees reading as a constructive process, offers a similar point of view. The good reader is actively involved with meaning and is not a passive word identifier. This psycholinguistic view of reading argues that reading is holistic and cannot be fractionated into component segments. Reading instruction should focus on acquiring meaning rather than on perfecting a rendition of the printed page. The concept of **errors in reading** is reshaped; instead, the errors are **miscues** from which an interested party can deduce which cues (graphic, phonic, semantic, syntactic) the reader was attending to. Psycholinguistic models emphasize the complex nature of reading and put the premium on understanding. The miscue concept has become a powerful influence by demonstrating that errors in reading are neither arbitrary nor random responses, but instead are responses to one or more of the cues available.

Summary

A variety of models of the reading process are available (for detailed reviews and critiques see Davis, 1972). The primary conclusions one can draw are:

1. Reading is a complex behavior, much more so than in the traditional view.
2. Of the several different points of view available, the most comprehensive models see reading as effective utilization of various cue systems, particularly the semantic, syntactic, phonic, and graphic.
3. Reading is a language process in which acquiring meaning is the primary goal.

Reading in Elementary School

The various theoretical models of reading have spawned a wide variety of instructional materials and strategies, though probably more materials and strategies have been the by-product of either common sense or tradition. For instance, Aukerman (1971) reviews over one hundred current approaches to beginning reading and indicates that this is not a complete list of the available programs. Similarly, elementary schools have developed various organizational strategies for reading. Although the variety available precludes any comprehensive discussion here, we will review the two facets of elementary reading instruction just mentioned—approaches to instruction and organizational strategies for instructions.

Approaches to Reading Instruction

The initial stage of learning to read includes a fairly structured reading **readiness period,** usually in the kindergarten year or the early part of the first grade. Various materials and approaches to readiness training are available, and most often an elementary school selects a readiness program congruent with the theory of reading exemplified in the reading series used in beginning instruction. For instance, some readiness programs heavily emphasize various visual-perceptual skills; others include training in letter names and the letter-sound associations. Some provide extensive motor-training experiences; others omit all structured commercial materials and rely on developing many of these same prerequisites by reading to children and writing stories the children dictate to the teacher. Regardless of the particular readiness program used, most emphasize familiarity with the graphic aspects of English orthography.

True reading instruction typically begins in earnest in first grade. The first books in the basal series, primers, have limited vocabularies, though recently publishers have been expanding the number of words introduced. The new series have also broken the "Dick and Jane" tradition stories about "nice" middle-class families and neighborhoods by providing a variety of story types.

Basal Readers.   Basal readers are still the most popular material for reading instruction (Howlett and Weintraub, 1979), though other materials are making significant inroads on the market. Although classed as one approach to reading, the basal series actually represent a variety of theoretical viewpoints. Some basals present reading instruction through a letter-by-letter phonic approach. Others follow the linguistic models or represent a whole-word approach. Most basals, however, present a somewhat eclectic approach combining instruction in decoding skills, whole-word recognition, use of context, and comprehension.

The Language Experience Approach (LEA).   A second popular method of teaching beginning reading is LEA. In this approach the teacher begins with group experience stories—stories developed orally by the class and written on large poster-size sheets of paper. These stories serve to introduce reading as a meaningful language activity as well as to introduce a basic vocabulary. The teacher progresses to longer group stories and to individual stories. As each of the children develop stories, books are often generated—books for a child containing each personal story and books for the class containing perhaps stories on a common subject such as trips, pets, horses, or monsters. Often the LEA is used prior to introducing basal readers into the classroom.

It does seem logical to think that instruction at the elementary level should prepare students for the reading required in secondary schools. However, certain factors qualify this position. At the primary level students are taught basic reading skills—decoding and simple interpretation—principally through narrative material; and this extends through elementary grades. Even though students are required to read expository material in subjects other than reading, they are not taught how to handle exposition. Yet students at the secondary level are required to read increasingly complex and abstract exposition, and teachers assume they are equipped to do

Source: Harold L. Herber, *Teaching Reading in Content Areas,* © 1970, p. 271. Reprinted by permission of Prentice-Hall, Inc., Englewood Cliffs, New Jersey.

Individualized Reading.   Another approach commonly integrated with LEA is individualized reading. The term *individualized reading* is frequently misunderstood, because it has often been linked unwittingly to individually prescribed instruction (IPI) formats. However, Veatch (1959) popularized individualized reading prior to the advent of IPI curricula. Simply stated, individualized reading is an approach based on students self-selecting reading materials, principally trade books. The popular paperback libraries so readily available have made this approach more feasible in many schools with inadequate library facilities. The teachers' primary responsibilities are to see that a wide variety of reading materials are available and to hold regular individual conferences with students to discuss material read. This approach is currently regaining popularity, particularly among those who accept psycholinguistic models of reading, because the underlying theme is that, to become proficient, one must.enjoy reading and read widely.

Individually Prescribed Instruction (IPI).   Another type of reading program is the aforementioned IPI. The primary features of these programs, which tend to follow the behaviorist theories of reading, are their hierarchies of reading skills. IPI programs break reading down into component parts, with instruction provided on each subskill in the hierarchy. These programs are available independently or for use with basal programs. Several recent reviews have identified major weaknesses in philosophical, empirical, and pragmatic bases for programs of this nature (Conklin, 1974; Johnson and Pearson, 1975). The primary risk involved is confusing the means with the end; that is, the skills sheets, skills tests, skills charts, and so on, take on such importance that educators forget the original goal, which was to develop willing, fluent readers.

Programmed Instruction.   Another approach philosophically similar to IPI is programmed instruction. Also behaviorist in format, the programmed-reading materials provide incremental learning, self-checking, self-pacing, and so forth. However, this approach has rapidly lost its appeal, both to teachers and students. When first introduced the materials may generate enthusiasm among students, particularly poorer readers; however, the format of programmed readers makes story-line development difficult, so the task soon has all the excitement of completing spelling exercises.

Summary.   A wide variety of approaches is available and used, but those reviewed above account for a majority of the programs found in elementary schools. Each approach has its advocates, but none has been able to overcome all of its inherent weaknesses, and none has unequivocal data demonstrating its superiority to other programs. Thus, one can argue philosophically, but not empirically, about which approach produces the best readers most efficiently.

Organizational Strategies for Reading

In this section we will present two means of organizing reading: (1) within classrooms and (2) within schools.

Within-Class Organization.   Unfortunately, classroom organization still too often revolves around three group patterns—high, middle and low. There is promising evidence (Allington, 1978) that this trend is slowly disappearing. However, considering that this pattern has been under attack for at least half a century, one can be only somewhat pleased.

No one quite knows why three groups emerged, unless it was because the English language has those three sensible categories. In any event, three groups are generally considered better than one. However, Rist (1970) presented evidence that the low group got the least and worst teaching and argued that groups were differentially treated in a variety of respects. These concerns were supported in a more recent study (Allington, 1978) that found significant differences in the teaching provided good and poor readers. Another disadvantage of the three-group approach is that, although the range of differences *within* groups is narrowed, it can still be so large as to preclude attempts at small-group instruction.

> In addition to the formal separation of the groups within the classroom there was also the persistence of mechanisms utilized by the teacher to socialize the children in the high reading group with feelings of aversion, revulsion, and rejection towards those of the lower reading groups. Through ridicule, belittlement, physical punishment, and merely ignoring them, the teacher was continually giving clues to those in the high reading group as to how one with high status and a high probability of future success treats those of low status and low probability of future success. To maintain within the larger society the case aspects of the position of the poor vis-a-vis the remainder of society, there has to occur the transmission from one generation to another the attitudes and values necessary to legitimate and continue such a form of social organization. . . . It should be apparent, of course, that if one desires this society to retain its social class configuration . . . one should not disturb the methods of education as presented in this study. (Rist, 1970)

The other classroom organizational patterns are more groups, whole class, and individualization. In the trend away from three-group organization, individualization seems to have become the most prominent. The difficulties of individualization are well known to any teacher; in fact, those difficulties are perhaps a primary cause of the extended popularity of the three-group pattern.

Within-School Organization. The two most widely employed within-school organizational patterns are simply homogeneous and heterogeneous ability grouping. However, as school systems move to continuous-progress curricula, open-space architecture, and individualization, the homogeneous ability-grouping, or tracking, patterns seem to pass. Little can be said about the effect either has on whole-school reading ability, though most educators now accept the empirical evidence which suggests that heterogeneous grouping facilitates all types of learning for all children.

Most schools, however, are still organized into heterogeneous, self-contained classrooms, leaving the ultimate decision for within-class grouping to the teacher. Most schools now also offer special remedial-reading classes for underachieving readers, but, unfortunately, many schools limit remedial attendance to students above grade four. In effect, this restriction ensures that most remedial clients will have a rather severe disability by the time they are eligible to receive remedial assistance.

Reading Difficulties

Many secondary teachers argue that if the elementary teachers were doing their job no student would arrive at the secondary level unable to read well enough to cope with the reading necessary in content area instruction. However, even if all learners achieved at the level commensurate with their innate intellectual abilities, half of them would read below their grade-placement level because virtually all the available tests are norm referenced. That is, they report an average grade-level score, and an average, or mean, score by definition requires that half of those taking the tests fall below that score and half fall above. Thus, even with ideal achievement, the content area teacher could expect only half the students to read at or above grade level.

Normal Distribution of Reading Abilities in a Tenth-Grade Population

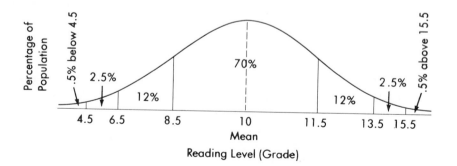

A primary type of reading difficulty is simply that not all learners achieve reading levels commensurate with their abilities. Therefore, virtually all classrooms contain some learners with reading deficiencies. To understand **achieving below potential**, we must recall the nature of the reading process. A popular myth is that learners with reading difficulties simply need more phonic instruction. As noted earlier, however, several other important cue systems exist and poor readers often underuse both semantic and syntactic cues. In fact, learners with reading difficulties often overuse graphic and phonic cues, resulting in reading errors that make no sense, another indication they are not using semantic and syntactic cues. Underuse of these latter cues results in decreased comprehension even if word-identification accuracy remains high.

In a second type of reading difficulty, learners may have a reading-achievement score commensurate with their intellectual abilities but still exhibit a reading deficiency. These are learners whose **intellectual abilities** are **below average**. A learner with an intelligence quotient of 85, for instance, is still in the average intelligence range, but even if achieving at full potential in reading, this learner will be below average. A learner with an intelligence quotient of 70 who is achieving at an expected level would possess a reading-achievement level three or four years below grade placement as a sophomore (Harris and Sipay, 1975).

A third type of reading deficiency occurs when the **difficulty** of the textual material assigned to be read **exceeds the grade level** of the learners. In this case, learners achieving at or below grade level will not be able to read the material. These students can read at their expected grade level, but the assigned material is substantially more difficult than one can expect learners at that grade level to be able to read.

A fourth type of reading deficiency is exhibited by the learner who **can read but does not**. This learner may have a reading ability adequate to deal with assigned textual material but for one reason or another (low motivation, lack of interest, dislike of reading, or dislike of school in general, for example) does not read it.

Reading deficiencies are largely relative. Not every learner can be expected to read at grade level so long as norm-referenced tests are employed. Not every learner can be expected to achieve a reading level commensurate with innate potential, so some will always read less well than expected. Not every learner will be able to read assigned textual materials that are substantially above grade-placement level. Finally, not every learner who *can* read *will*. The content area teacher must realize that, for a variety of reasons, not every learner, nor in some cases even a majority, will be able to read assigned textual materials even if it is at an appropriate level of difficulty. Fortunately, as we will see later, a variety of techniques for circumventing such difficulties are available.

A question often asked relates to the meaning of the term *functional literacy*. The following definition by one of the leaders in this area indicates that there is no such thing as a "fixed" functional literacy level. Rather, this level varies depending on a variety of conditions.

> Functional literacy is possession of those literacy skills needed to successfully perform some reading task imposed by an external agent between the reader and a goal the reader wishes to obtain. (Sticht, 1975)

Weiner and Cromer's Sources of Reading Difficulties

Given our earlier definition of reading as extracting meaning from printed text, one would characterize any learner who exhibits difficulty in extracting meaning as deficient in reading. Using this same definition, Weiner and Cromer (1967) posited four sources of reading deficiencies. Their categories included a **defect** reader, one who exhibits a malfunction of one of the basic systems necessary for typical reading growth. This category includes learners with sensory impairments such as blindness or deafness. A second category is the **disruption** reader. This label assumes something is present in the learner that must be removed for learning to read to occur. Learners with severe emotional difficulties might best exemplify this category. The third category is the **deficit** reader. Weiner and Cromer suggest that this type of learner must be taught some needed skill or that "some function or process is absent and must be added before adequate reading can occur" (p. 6). The final type is the **difference** reader whose reading deficiency is attributed to a discrepancy between the way the reader typically responds and the response pattern that is most appropriate. Examples of this are (1) the learner speaks in a dialect other than the one called for; and (2) the learner knows the words but doesn't comprehend them.

In the past, both defect and disruption readers were the responsibility of the special educator. However, the recent implementation of P.L. 94-142, which mandates providing a **least-restrictive** educational environment, has fostered the creation of a variety of **mainstreaming** plans that integrate exceptional learners into the regular middle- and secondary-school curriculum. These learners may exhibit reading deficiencies that require modifications of content area reading assignments. Fortunately, many content area teachers now have access to special-resource teachers who have the training and experience necessary for altering the regular curriculum to match the abilities of these exceptional students.

The deficit reader is usually given the greatest attention through remedial services. This type of reading deficiency is characterized by a general lag in all processes of reading—word identification, comprehension, fluency, and so forth. These learners perform much like normally achieving readers in lower grades rather than exhibit a single skill deficiency (Guthrie, 1973). Weiner and Cromer suggest identifying these learners by noting whether both word identification and comprehension are significantly below the expected level. On the other hand, the difference learner usually exhibits no word-identification deficiency but comprehends substantially below the expected level.

The content area teacher must remember that selecting reading material that exceeds the appropriate level of difficulty can create a classroom of deficit readers and difference readers. The ability to learn efficiently from textual material depends on the ability to read the assigned material. However, the inability to comprehend the assigned textual material is not simply a matter of not knowing enough words or enough phonics. Content area teachers, who are not reading teachers, have neither the training nor the responsibility for remediating the deficit reader. As outlined later in this text, numerous strategies allow the content area teacher to achieve the imparting-knowledge purpose of teaching. We will present additional strategies that focus on applying knowledge and developing autonomous learners, because refining the ability to learn from the text is a responsibility of the content specialist.

Many college-educated persons have difficulty extracting meaning from the following paragraphs. Typically, paragraph 1 presents relatively few word-pronunciation difficulties, but meaning is not available because of a lack of background knowledge. Paragraph 2, however, poses extreme word-pronunciation problems for most people, and meaning again is not available.

1. There are various unit-types with which a speaker may set out to construct a turn. Unit-types for English include sentential, clausal, phrasal, and lexical constructions. Instances of the unit-types so usable allow a projection of the unit-type under way,

and what, roughly, it will take for an instance of that unit-type to be completed. Unit-types lacking the feature of projectability may not be usable in the same way.

2. The chief source of nutrient vessels to the inferior part of the diencephalon is an arterial trunk consisting of the posterior communicating and the posterior cerebral arteries. This trunk extends from the optic chiasma around the side of the basis pendunculi to the pulvinar. Its nutrient branches are in three groups: two of these—the thalamotuberal and the thalamoperforating—enter the diencephalon in front of the attachment of the midbrain; the third group—the thalamogeniculate vessels—enter the diencephalon behind the attachment of the midbrain. . . . The thalamotuberal vessels leave the posterior communicating artery as it lies alongside the hypothalamus. They enter the tuberal region of the hypothalamus and penetrate into the overlying nuclei of the thalamus, hence their name. They supply all but the anterior end of the hypothalamus, which receives fine vessels from the internal carotid and the anterior cerebral arteries.

Sources: Sacks, H.; Schegloff, E.; & Jefferson, G. "A Simplest Systematics for the Organization of Turn-Taking for Conversation. *Language*, 50 (1974): 702.
C. G. Smith, *Basic Neuroanatomy* (Toronto: University of Toronto Press, 1961), pp. 240–41.

Reading in Secondary School

Learning from text is a popular instructional strategy, but, as we have just noted, many secondary-school students experience difficulty with text-based learning. The impact of reading difficulties is tremendous. Even though anguished cries are often heard about illiterate secondary-school graduates, the more frequent case is that the student experiencing reading difficulties drops out, or is pushed out, of the secondary school (Penty, 1956; Saucier, Wendel, and Mueller, 1975; Hackney and Reavis, 1968).

Although the United States ranks high among nations in the literacy of its people, not all of our problems of literacy have been solved. Estimates of the magnitude of the problems we still face obviously depend on what level of literacy is taken as the indispensable minimum. About a quarter million young adults are estimated to be illiterate even at the lowest level; most realistic definitions lead to higher estimates.

These handicapped persons come from all parts of society. In proportional terms, however, an all-too-familiar picture emerges. Although the schools are managing to teach most children to read and write, disproportionate numbers of the poor, speakers of languages other than English, and members of cultural minorities do not master even the most basic skills—the ability to interpret single sentences, or to follow simple written instructions.

When we ask about the more advanced skills and knowledge required to understand anything beyond the simplest written messages, the success rates of our schools are lower than they should be for all parts of the population. Reading and writing are tools, not goals; they are the tools needed to change the way we think and what we think about. Highly literate people not only can satisfy the practical demands of letter writing and recordkeeping, but also have access to the whole world of written knowledge.

Source: George Miller, ed., *Linguistic Communication: Perspective for Research* (Newark, Delaware: International Reading Association, 1973). Reprinted with permission of George Miller and the International Reading Association.

Only recently have some small strides been made toward both providing appropriate instruction for those with general reading difficulties and continuing to develop and refine reading abilities beyond elementary school. Many secondary schools now attempt to rectify the situation through one or more of the following approaches.

Remedial Instruction Plus

The reading teacher seen most frequently on secondary-school faculties typically provides small-group remedial instruction for the students experiencing the most severe reading difficulties. A second role adopted by many secondary reading teachers is providing instructional support for content area teachers by assisting in identifying the range of reading abilities and the difficulty of materials, preparing differentiated instruction, and so on.

Often a secondary school also offers developmental- and specialized-reading instruction. Developmental-reading instruction is not provided to students experiencing a particular reading deficiency, but rather to students requiring a refining and extending of reading abilities. Virtually all secondary students can improve their reading abilities; but without an instructional emphasis in the secondary curriculum, far too many students stagnate and experience relatively little improvement in reading ability beyond the elementary school.

> Schools are still the principal source of the idea that literacy is
> equated with intelligence. Why, the schools even promote the idea
> that spelling is related to intelligence! Of course, if any of this were
> true, reading teachers would be the smartest people around. One
> doesn't mean to be unkind, but if that indeed is the case, no one
> has noticed it. In any event, it is an outrage that children who do
> not read well, or at all, are treated as if they are stupid. (Postman,
> 1970)

Specialized-reading classes other than remedial are often offered as "short courses," or "mini-sessions," during the school year. These classes focus on a single ability such as increasing reading rate, developing critical reading skills, or refining study skills such as skimming.

The content area teachers role, then, is understanding and acknowledging the role general reading ability plays in learning from text. A learner's inability to identify the words in the assigned material precludes learning from that textual material unless it is presented in nonprint form. The teacher may also choose to select other material that presents the content in a less-difficult manner or to reduce reliance on textual materials for learning. The learner who has no word-identification difficulties but who exhibits comprehension difficulties also needs instructional assistance, though not necessarily the same types of assistance as the deficit reader. All learners need instruction that extends and refines text-learning abilities, instruction that reduces their dependence on the teacher for direction in learning. Imparting the specific content of a discipline is not sufficient; learners must learn how to apply acquired knowledge and how to become efficient and effective independent learners. These, then, are the tasks and goals of the content area teacher in the secondary school.

Summary

An understanding of the reading process and practices is necessary for understanding how to facilitate learning from textual material. Because content area teachers rely heavily on texts to meet the goals of imparting content-specific knowledge, this chapter has provided a brief introduction to learning to read, including the following points:

1. Fluent reading involves the interaction of graphic, phonic, semantic, and syntactic cues with the reader's knowledge of the world.
2. Reading is not simply getting the words right; without comprehension there is no reading.

3. Reading instruction in the elementary school takes many forms, but no strategy for teaching reading works with all learners.
4. The many approaches to reading instruction occur because there is no generally accepted comprehensive model of the reading process.
5. Regardless of the effectiveness of instruction provided in the elementary school, some learners will still arrive at the secondary school unable to learn from their assigned textual material.
6. Reading deficiencies take many forms, all of which are determined subjectively.
7. The content area teacher must consider reading ability when planning instruction. Instruction must be directed toward different types of reading deficiencies.

Barriers to Learning from Text

THERE ARE TWO CLASSES of barriers to learning from text: one based on the learner and the other on the textual material. Of course, learning from text requires both a learner and textual material, so in some respects the barriers are more often an interaction or lack of it between these two classes. However, content area teachers should consider both learner and textual barriers separately in order to initiate instructional changes that can lead to improved learning in the content areas.

Reading Ability

As noted in Chapter 2, general reading ability is a critical variable to learning from text in the secondary school. This is true only if the material is of a difficulty level appropriate for the average secondary-school student, and if a particular learner, or group of learners, has general reading ability substantially below average. If, for instance, the assigned text has a readability level of fourth grade, then deficiencies in general reading ability will not necessarily exclude a significant number of students from learning from that text.

What can the teacher in the typical secondary-school classroom expect in terms of general learner reading-ability range? The best answer is that the teacher can expect almost anything. The best readers will be able to read and integrate the most complicated textual material. They will have little or no difficulty with the words, either in recognition or meaning, and will be able to focus their attention on comprehending the text. It will probably make little difference to these learners whether the assigned textual material deals with history or mathematics because they will have the skills to read both. The limitations on their learning will more often be determined by the expectations and competence of their teachers than their reading ability.

The poorest readers, on the other hand, will have difficulty at the word level, will be unable to identify most of the words in the text, and will derive nothing more than frustration from the typical secondary content area texts. In many cases, these students will be quite reluctant to attempt to read, because it has been their experience that interaction with textual material results in exposure of their reading deficiency and ultimate failure. They will have little confidence in their ability to learn in general, and often will engage in a variety of behaviors to conceal their deficiencies or to avoid interacting with textual material. Often the behaviors, though understandable, will be quite disruptive and will try the patience of even the most concerned teacher.

Do any of these myths seem familiar?

- The Myth of Original Stupidity—Learners are stupid until teachers make them smart.
- The Myth of Stable Knowledge—Believing that knowledge is sacred, stable, and fixed.
- The Myth of the One Best Way—There is always a single correct method for doing anything.
- The Myth of the Passive Learner—Believing that such learners will ultimately develop into creative, constructive, thinking citizens.

Source: M. Jensen, "Humanistic Education: An Overview of Supporting Data," from *The High School Journal*, Volume 56, pp. 341–49, © 1975, The University of North Carolina Press. Reprinted by permission of the publisher.

The remainder of the class will exhibit general reading ability that ranges from that of the worst readers to that of the best. What will happen at any given point in time will depend on their experience and interest in the topic, their need to achieve, whether or not they feel good, and their general reading ability. The students who fall between the extremes, then, are more influenced by a variety of factors than are the students at either extreme.

Guidelines have been developed to aid in predicting the general range of reading ability in content area classrooms. However, there are substantive differences in the amount of text learning in required versus elective courses, vocational versus college-preparatory courses, low-achievement versus high-achievement secondary schools. The combination of these factors makes computing the general range of reading ability difficult and not very useful. However, such a computation may serve the useful purpose of informing content area teachers about this problem—that is, make them aware that many of the students in the typical content area classroom will read below grade level, but also that some will read *substantially* below grade level.

According to Burmeister (1974), the probable range in reading ability will be equal to two-thirds the average chronological age of the students in any given classroom (range = 2/3 chronological age). Therefore, in an average tenth-grade content area classroom, where the mean chronological age will be approximately fifteen, the range of reading levels will be ten years (see the graph on p. 30). To transform this score into grade equivalents, use the following formula:

$$\text{Grade Equivalent} = \text{Grade Placement} \pm \frac{range}{2}$$

(1) For a tenth-grade content area class (CA = 15)

$$\text{GE} = 10 \pm \frac{10}{2}$$

$$\text{GE} = 10 \pm 5$$

GE range = 5 to 15 (college)

(2) For a twelfth-grade content area class (CA = 17)

$$\text{GE} = 12 \pm \frac{11.3}{2}$$

$$\text{GE} = 12 \pm 5.6$$

GE range = 6.4 to 17.6 (college)

The ranges arrived at in the above examples can easily be experienced in any secondary-school classroom. In some classrooms the range will be about the same span but reading ability will be lower or higher. In other words, the hypothetical tenth-grade content area teacher can reasonably expect to have a few students below fifth-grade level. In some schools a majority of students in some content area classes will read below the minimum expected level, according to the Burmeister formula. In any event, the formula does provide the teacher with at least a rough idea of the range of reading abilities that can reasonably be expected. Thus, teachers often find a rather substantial mismatch between the general reading-ability levels of the learners and the difficulty level of the chosen textual material. This, then, is a primary barrier to learning from text. Later chapters present assessment and intervention strategies detailing how the content area teacher can identify such barriers and work to eliminate them.

Many secondary-school students, however, have a specific, and therefore limited, deficiency in learning from text that occurs even in the presence of seemingly adequate general reading ability, or that at times co-occurs with an inadequate general reading ability. One of the most common of these deficiencies is a slow rate of reading.

Reading Rate

The issue of reading rate has inspired vigorous debate over the last half-century (Shores and Husbands, 1950; Tinker, 1965; Carver, 1972;

Greene, 1931). The three most common facets of the debates are: (1) What is the relationship between rate of reading and comprehension?; (2) Can reading rate be significantly increased?; and (3) What is the maximum rate of reading that can be achieved?

A review of existing research suggests that faster readers, up to a point, exhibit better comprehension than slower readers (Harris and Sipay, 1975). Caution must be observed in interpreting this conclusion, because faster readers in the research typically read in the 300–500-words-per-minute range. A primary concern in the relationship between rate and comprehension is whether humans have a maximum rate of information processing. Carver (1977) asserts that there is such a limit. He reviews a variety of studies supporting his assertion that humans have such a maximum rate of processing for verbal material, whether spoken or written. This rate, Carver suggests, is around 300–400 words per minute, a far cry from the rate promised by many commercial speed-reading programs.

A basic difficulty in this area centers on defining and assessing comprehension. One can quickly skim through a textbook and often reasonably summarize the contents. Similarly, if a person knows a great deal about a topic, or if the material to be read is quite familiar, then a very brief perusal of the text is often sufficient for the reader to exhibit comprehension of the material. Research on rate of reading, then, has a dual focus—rate and effectiveness of comprehension. Carver (1977) calls this the **efficiency factor.** However, he believes that generally the most important factor in comprehension is the amount of time spent on the material. The learner who re-reads will have enhanced learning compared to a single reading by the learner. Learning differences between individuals then become more a basic thinking-rate, rather than a reading-rate, difficulty. Carver (1977) also asserts that everyone has a single rate for processing text and seldom strays far from this base. However, his assertions hold only for "typical" reading behavior; he excludes skimming and studying from his model. Of course, those behaviors are just what we would at times try to induce in secondary-school students.

We find untenable the claim that the many secondary-school students who read at a rate of about 100 words per minute are reading at an optimum rate. These learners must spend two to three times as much time completing their assigned textual material as those who read at a 200–300-words-per-minute rate. Moreover, the slower rate generally does not result in superior achievement. The content area teacher must be alert to the possibility of slow reading rates in order to implement instructional intervention to alleviate the problems attributable to rate.

Numerous studies have investigated various strategies for inducing increased reading rate. A highlight of these studies has been comparing mechanical aids, such as the various reading-speed improvement machines, with simple classroom instruction primarily emphasizing making the learners aware of their baseline rate and monitoring this rate while exhorting them to attempt to read faster. The results of such studies have been aptly summarized by Tinker and McCullough (1975, p. 227) who stated:

> In every experiment that has attempted to evaluate the use of machines, it has been found that they are no more effective in increasing rate of reading than are less complicated but sound classroom practices.

Those interested in the actual maximum rate of reading must be concerned with how to define "reading." Returning to Carver (1975, 1977), he asserts that, in order to truly read and comprehend, or encode, each word, a reader must process at a rate of less than 400 words per minute. Both Tinker (1965) and Spache (1962) assert that, considering the mechanics of eye movements, no one can read more than 750–800 words per minute. In any event, claims of 1000+ words per minute cannot be supported by any available empirical data. Persons can skim material, selectively attending to key sections or searching out specific information, at such rates; but given the most commonly accepted definition of reading, the reading rate will normally be limited to around 400–700 words per minute.

Closely tied to this issue of reading rate is flexibility of reading strategies. Many secondary-school students read everything at the same rate—whether fast or slow. They are unable to skim or peruse text quickly for specific information. Nor are some able to read reflectively, weighing the information being processed. Far too many students do not vary their rate of reading as the purpose for reading changes. When asked to locate a particular bit of information in textual material, some students invariably begin at the first line and proceed to read every word rather than skim to find the appropriate item or at least the appropriate section of the material.

Rate of reading, then, can create a barrier to efficient and effective learning from text in several different ways. Maintaining a flexibility of rate that depends on the purpose for reading can be a related barrier to text learning. The better readers are able to adjust their rates to the demands of the task, whereas the poorer readers probably read everything at the same pace—usually slowly.

Word Difficulties

Another specific yet common deficiency among secondary-school students is the lack of effective higher-order word identification. Although most students possess adequate word-identification strategies for dealing with words of up to three syllables, a significant number of students exhibit difficulties with the polysyllabic words common to content area textbooks.

Several factors play significant roles in identifying polysyllabic words. One is the learner's ability to use effective **visual-analysis strategies** on these words (Harris and Sipay, 1975). Visual analysis is the ability to break a word into manageable chunks. It is not identical to syllabication, which is more a matter of printer's convention, because the chunks may incorporate more than one syllable. It is a necessary ability, however, because the limitations of human memory preclude effectively using single-letter analysis on words of more than about five letters. Basically, visual-analysis strategies allow the learner to segment polysyllabic words, pronounce these segments, and then combine these segments to produce a response.

Two other factors play major roles in mediated word identification. Clarity of structure is one of these. Some words present a rather clear and straightforward structure that is easily segmented. *Championship, Waterloo, ordinal,* and *importation* all have rather clear structures, but *pythagorean, hierarchy, prejudice,* and *malleability* are less clear. Other words, particularly those derived or taken directly from other languages, virtually defy identification using the common principles of English word structure (*Versailles, Guiana, radii*).

Another factor of equal or perhaps greater importance is whether the word to be identified is stored in the auditory memory, or internal lexicon, of the learner. Several studies have demonstrated the potency of this familiarity effect (Cunningham, 1976; Menzel, 1973; Walmsley, 1977). Consider, for instance, the word *cupola*. Because the correct pronunciation is obscured by the structure of the word, the learner who pronounces it *cup ō lah* can hardly be faulted for inadequate use of phonic principles. The point is that a large number of polysyllabic words have several possible pronunciations, given common phonic principles.

A final factor operating on identifying an unknown word is the power, or richness, of its context. For this contextual effect to occur, two conditions must be met: (1) the word must be in the learner's lexicon (internal word bank), and (2) the learner must be able to employ the semantic and syntactic cues available in the context. Several studies (Goodman, 1965; Pearson and Studt, 1975; Allington and Strange, 1978) have demonstrated the potent effects contextual information can have on word identification. However, for the effects to operate, the word must not only be available from memory, but the learner must also know enough about the topic to be able to predict the word from the context. Both familiarity and utilization of contextual information facilitate word identification; the content area teacher can effectively use these factors to improve the ability to learn from text.

Secondary-school students can and do have word-level difficulties, but the specific deficiencies discussed above occur with some regularity in all learners, even those with adequate general-reading abilities.

Content area teachers sensitive to such possible difficulties can implement strategies to alleviate such deficiencies with little change in their daily class-room routines.

Meaning Level

Many students in content area classes have no particular difficulty identifying words but still exhibit difficulty in extracting meaning from their assigned textual material. In this section, we present several possible reasons for this situation and discuss them in some detail.

It is logical to begin the discussion at the word-meaning level, even though this particular deficiency often induces undue concern in many content area teachers. No truly clear empirical evidence on the incidence of this specific deficiency exists. Instead, the literature more often offers opinions and techniques for remedying such supposedly existing deficits. However, several researchers (Covell, 1957) have reported that underachieving students in secondary content area classes have an inferior grasp of the technical vocabulary of the given discipline compared to that of high-achieving students. On the other hand, Golinkoff (1975) reports on a series of studies indicating that comprehension difficulties cannot be attributed to deficient word meanings but must lie elsewhere. It may be that both sides are partially correct. A difficulty here is that whenever one compares high- and low-achieving students, the better students are typically more intellectually advanced. This advantage in intellectual ability enhances the likelihood that these groups have a superiority in word knowledge because word knowledge is a primary variable in most tests of intellectual aptitude. Furthermore, high-achieving students by definition must know more about the discipline of study. Tests of word knowledge then become primarily tests of prior learning. Therefore, if groups of subjects with roughly equivalent intellectual abilities are selected and presented more or less unfamiliar material, then those who demonstrate adequate comprehension and those who do not cannot be distinguished on the basis of word knowledge.

Regardless of the importance, compared to other deficiencies, of the role knowledge of word meanings plays in learning from text, a content area teacher can contribute significantly by ensuring the full development of learner vocabularies. A word, whether written or spoken, is simply an agreed-upon label for a concept. The words *casa*, *haus*, and *house* are all labels for a single concept. Developing word meaning, then, is primarily developing concepts.

How does a word have meaning? Simply put, words are composed of semantic features (Katz and Fodor, 1963). For instance, the word *cow* has a number of these features, including *animate, mammal, four-legged, milk producer, rather large, domesticated,* and so forth. A person "knows" the word *cow* if he or she can appropriately classify it by some of its major semantic features. We say a person "really knows cows" if his or her semantic feature list is rather extensive, which means he or she can distinguish cows from bulls, heifers and steers and can recognize the differences between Guernseys, Jerseys, and Brown Swiss. However, before learners understand such issues as the relative butterfat content of Jersey versus Brown Swiss milk, they must have acquired the less complex concept of *cow* (Gentner, 1973).

Although contextual information aids in defining a new word or in developing the concept the word represents, context is often insufficient. Consider the following items:

1. His speech was truly quite *cogent*.
2. We must conclude, then, that a *dyad* represents the most meaningful unit of analysis.
3. Dionne registered his third *hat trick* in as many days.

Unless the reader brings meaning to these words in these examples, little comprehension takes place. The contextual information provided by the sentence frame is simply neither extensive nor powerful enough to trigger the precise meanings of the underlined words.

The mislabelings of a two-year-old provide both evidence and insight into how word meanings, or concepts, are developed. Returning to our earlier example, *cow*, it is not unusual for a suburban child (or adult) to mislabel steers as cows, particularly if the steers have no horns. Many children confuse cows and horses at first, because these objects share some features and therefore are confusable. You will not find a child mistaking a dog for a fireplace, but the child may mislabel a fox.

Secondary students, and many adults, have similar difficulties with words that share several semantic features. Consider the terms *butte*, *plateau*, and *spire*. Most physical geographers have no difficulty with these word meanings; but, although other adults have a general impression (an incomplete feature list), they are typically hard pressed to detail the differences accurately.

Other, more complex concepts are learned in a similar manner, through experience, presentation of examples and nonexamples, and, in some instances, from semantic and syntactic information presented in text. Content area teachers play a crucial role in developing these word meanings because, as the "experts," they know the key features of the word or concept. By providing experiences through various means and presenting examples, the teacher leads the student to discover the appropriate semantic features of new words or concepts. However, expecting the learner to build a feature list by reading text alone causes teachers to contribute unwittingly to erecting a barrier to learning from text. As Lindberg and Smith (1975) point out, concept-carrying vocabulary is often not well developed in text, yet this vocabulary is crucial both to understanding and learning from text. Lindberg and Smith are not necessarily arguing for pre-teaching vocabulary, because a prerequisite to understanding materials with a large proportion of concept-carrying vocabulary is a relevant conceptual background. In other words, the brief introduction to vocabulary that is often recommended cannot be sufficient unless the learner already has a base from which to operate.

Knowledge seems to be stored in humans in a very efficient manner, organized in, for lack of a better word, networks. Thus, the concept *cow* not only has a feature list, but some of the features are superordinate and others subordinate. By way of example, let us attempt to demonstrate this. For our purposes, the feature *animate* is the superordinate one, with the other features arranged in subordinate positions. Under the *animate* feature a person would have an enormous number of items. Moving down the features, fewer examples are found in each class (see figure).

Concept Network for the Word Cow

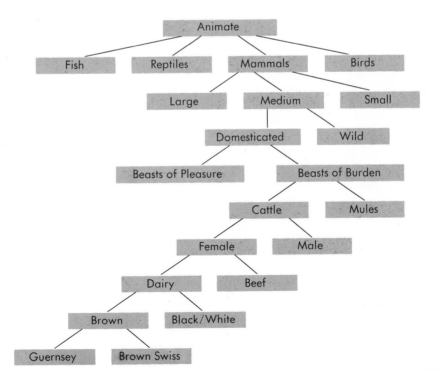

This rather crude attempt at a network serves to illustrate two points: First, because human memory is beautifully organized, learning entails either adding new categories or new features to existing categories. Second, content area teachers should have a rough idea of the level of detail their students have for a word or concept in order to select appropriate content for presentation. The major point is that words are not learned by simple rote memorization of a dictionary definition; learning occurs when a network or feature list is reorganized or refined.

Acquiring word meanings is an important facet of content area instruction. Words, though, are simply labels for concepts. In Chapter 8 we will present a variety of strategies for enhancing conceptual learning.

Text

Even though we know too little to be explicit about the processes underlying the acquiring of word meaning, we are relatively advanced in our understanding of this area compared to our knowledge of the processes underlying learning from text. Only in the last five years have psychologists, educators, and linguists refocused their research on understanding how knowledge is acquired from larger language units.

The greater amount of work to date has centered on the area of sentence comprehension, with relatively few investigators using paragraphs or longer units of text such as stories or chapters. Kintsch (1977) summarizes the most recent literature on sentence learning and notes two major conclusions: First, a learner's purpose for reading largely determines what is remembered from a sentence. Instructions to read a sentence and then recall it verbatim produce different results from instructions to read a sentence for its truthfulness. If left without any specific directions for the type of processing, most persons read for the gist of a sentence. That is, they read to recall the content, or meaning, of a sentence, even though they may paraphrase and not supply the verbatim recall. Second, the difficulty of a sentence is determined not simply by its length but also by its syntactic complexity and concept density. Thus two sentences of the same length that differ in the number of either transformations or concepts will result in different degrees of difficulty of understanding.

Understanding longer textual units is influenced by many of the same variables. Unfortunately, although several investigators (Thorndyke, 1976; Meyer, 1975; Rumelhart, 1976; Mosenthal, 1977) have recently attempted to describe a structure, or grammar, for longer units of text, we currently know little about the effects of textual structure on learning. We do know that stories possess a common structure, and that, if stories that do not follow this normal pattern are presented, learning, or comprehension, is negatively affected (Kintsch and Van Dijk, 1975). In a similar manner, the purpose, or intention for learning affects what is remembered. For example, if learners are given a passage and directed to find answers to specific questions, they apply different strategies and recall different facets of the material than those they use when other types of orienting directions are given (Rothkopf, 1975).

Topic, structure, length, and other variables all have profound effects on what is recalled and with what degree of detail. Unfortunately, two factors limit the rather sparse research in this area: First, much of the written material employed in these studies was quite unlike that found in content area texts—different in content, structure, and length. Second, the task demands of most studies were quite dissimilar to the task demands imposed in content area classes. That is, subjects typically read short selections and were tested immediately for the amount of material they could recall. In most content area classes, assigned textual material often runs into numerous pages with a test of selective information gain following after some delay, often weeks after the material was assigned.

Difficulties in extracting meaning from print can derive from text factors such as vocabulary or text structure. Unfortunately, we know little about how persons learn from text; we have identified some strategies for enhancing learning from text, but usually we cannot adequately explain why these strategies are effective. At some point in the future, someone will put the last piece in place and we will finally have a model of human learning that will not only explain effects but will also suggest alternative strategies for inducing learning from textual material.

Several points do seem clear, though. The learner who picks up a textbook, groans, and then begins to read only because "it was assigned" will not acquire the same quantity or quality of knowledge as the student who reads with a coherent purpose. Listless, passive reading with frequent stops to daydream or to hum along with the radio does not enhance learning from text.

Textual material that presents many unfamiliar concepts will not enhance learning either. To lower this barrier the content area teacher must do more than simply present a brief introduction to the new vocabulary or concepts. To develop word meanings, the concept must be delineated and integrated into existing networks. The student must be able to do more than parrot a verbatim definition.

Summary

In this overview of the various barriers to learning from text we have rather arbitrarily divided the factors into two categories: barriers within learners and barriers within text. As noted earlier, these factors invariably interact, and we know far too little about either of the separate factors or their interactions. We do, however, have a rather general knowledge of the nature of these barriers to learning from text, summarized as follows:

1. If content area learning is to be basically text dependent, the content area teacher must realize that general reading abilities will play a significant role in the desired learning.
2. In virtually all secondary content area classrooms, the teacher will be confronted with learners who range widely (from elementary-school level through college level) in reading abilities. The content area teacher must be sensitive to the demands placed upon the learners when textual material is assigned.
3. The secondary-school teacher who wishes to facilitate learning in the content area classroom will attempt to assess text difficulties in relation to student abilities.
4. Many secondary-school students read at an inefficient rate that interferes with learning from text. Although claims of reading speeds above 900–1000 words per minute are not supported by research, many secondary-school students can develop more efficient reading strategies.
5. Some secondary-school students experience difficulty at the word level but usually only with unfamiliar polysyllabic words. More have difficulties with the comprehension of written material, even when the words are correctly pronounced. This difficulty seems to stem from two primary sources: (a) the lack of individual word meanings, or concepts, for many words important to a specific content area, and (b) the inability to deal with grammatical complexity in sentences and larger linguistic units.
6. A variety of factors influence learning from text, including content, structure, prior knowledge, intentions for learning, and purpose for learning.

Assessing Reading Ability
with Commercial Tests

4

M OST SECONDARY SCHOOLS assess the general reading ability of their students at some point. Many schools concentrate their testing on entering students; but, because of the emphasis literacy is receiving as an educational goal, more secondary schools are implementing rather extensive testing programs, often testing all students every year. In addition, most states have implemented "minimum competency" standards in reading as a necessary requirement for graduation. This normally mandates testing all secondary students for reading ability at some point during the secondary-school experience.

These developments alone make it important that content area teachers understand the basic principles of assessing reading ability. In addition, to assist in making effective instructional decisions, teachers can often profitably employ the commercially produced tests used by most school systems. This chapter attempts to provide the basic information about commercially available tests necessary to develop a strategy for using such information sensibly and sensitively.

The American Federation of Teachers Task Force on Educational Issues (1977) provided the following recommendations concerning testing in public schools:

- Reduce the emphasis placed on standardized tests.
- Develop supplementary measures for evaluating progress.
- Involve the entire teaching staff in planning and implementing testing programs.
- Provide in-service education for all involved in test utilization.
- Assure that whatever testing approaches are used reflect the objectives of the school.

- Provide for an annual review of the system and involve all those who are affected by it.
- Tests should be given for a specific, clearly stated purpose which is agreed on in advance by those who are to use the results.
- Tests should be viewed as only one source of data for decision making.
- Tests should be administered only with the expectation that information derived from them will be helpful in making better decisions than could be made without them.
- Tests should be administered in an atmosphere conducive to learning rather than in an anxiety-producing environment.
- Teachers should be involved with measurement and curriculum specialists in the selection of tests and the interpretation of results.
- Test data should be released to the media only when accompanied by proper background information and interpretation.

Were the above guidelines adhered to, the milieu of standardized testing surely would be improved. Standardized tests must be kept in proper perspective. Rather than lashing out indiscriminately against all such tests, the more sensible route should be to identify specific weaknesses and improve them. That has been the purpose of this survey. In identifying the enemy let us keep in mind that in this case the major one probably is misuse and abuse. Tests should not become so central to the functioning of schools that they become the main reason for existence, but neither should they be totally discarded.

Source: E. H. Brady, "What Do Teachers Think About Tests and Testing," *American Educator,* 1 (1977): 10–12.

In trying to assist student learning from text, one must use all the sources of information available, including commercially prepared tests of general reading ability. Currently, many educators are concerned about the worth and use of commercially prepared tests of all types. Some critics (Goodman, 1975) argue that such tests do not truly assess anything that can be construed as reading ability. Others (Farr, 1969; Brigham, 1972; Masters, 1972) argue more against the uses to which the information from these tests is put rather than the content or structure of the tests themselves. In too many cases the results from a commercially prepared reading test have been used not simply as a primary source, but as the *only* source of information considered in making educational decisions, with far-reaching implications for a student or a group of students. Test and measurement specialists have often been among the first to point out the limitations of their tests and to decry inappropriate and improper uses of tests (Lehmann and

Mehrens, 1969). Commercially available tests represent only one of many sources of information to consider in making most educational decisions, but they do represent probably the single most commonly available source of information on student reading abilities.

The first consideration in using these test data is a decision on whether the information provided is good or bad. The most widely used tests are generally carefully constructed and standardized, with considerable effort and expense expended in attempting to ensure that the test will provide good information when properly administered and interpreted. However, the "goodness" of a test is relative. Several evaluation criteria can be used, depending on the ultimate decisions one wishes to reach with the test results.

Petrosko (1977) presents four broad areas to consider: (1) measurement validity, (2) normed technical excellence, (3) examinee appropriateness, and (4) administrative usability. For a test to be truly useful, several criteria in each of these areas should be met. Furthermore, the content area teacher must have a basic understanding of the processes used to prepare most commercially available tests.

Norm-Referenced Tests

Most commonly used commercially available tests are norm referenced. The basic concept underlying the norm-referencing process is comparing one score to the scores of others who have taken the test. Consider, for example, a score of 88 on a 100-item test. At first glance, that seems like a fairly impressive score. If, however, everyone else who took the test scored 92 or better, the 88 no longer seems so impressive—it was a full 4 points below any other score. For this score to have any meaning, we must know not only how it compares to other scores on this test but also several other crucial points of information.

> Only the vocabulary items were measuring a skill in comprehension (knowledge of word meanings) that was significantly different from the others. This implies that comprehension in reading involves two skills: word knowledge and paragraph comprehension. These results are in harmony with Davis' findings that word knowledge and reasoning in reading account for virtually all of the variance of comprehension.
>
> Source: F. B. Davis, "Research in Comprehension in Reading," *Reading Research Quarterly*, 3 (1968): 508. Reprinted by permission of F. B. Davis and The International Reading Association.

One of the first considerations is information about the population to whom the test was administered. If those who took the test and scored above 90 are all college graduates and the person who scored 88 is in the ninth grade, then that score once again seems quite impressive. If, however, those who scored above 90 were ninth-graders and the score of 88 was received by a college graduate, we would be less impressed. The population used to norm a test, the **norm group**, can theoretically be as large as all persons in the United States or as small as the fourth graders enrolled in public schools in Austin, Texas, or even the fourth-grade students enrolled in a single classroom. For many commercially prepared standardized tests, the norm group is the population of secondary-school students in the United States. To norm-reference the test, though, the commercial producers sample from this larger population in order to deal with a less bulky group. This smaller group is called the **sample population**.

In an attempt to ensure that the sample population is representative of the target population, it is necessary to impose certain constraints on the sampling, or selection, procedure. Sampling according to specified constraints results in what is known as a **stratified sample**. Generally, the constraints, or characteristics of the population, involved are (1) geographic location, (2) socioeconomic status of the community, (3) sex, and (4) racial-ethnic composition. In other words, a test that attempts to provide national grade-level norms will be standardized on a sample considered representative of all students enrolled in American secondary schools. However, test users must be wary, because only the most popular tests produced by the largest companies have followed such elaborate procedures. Far too many of the available tests use norms constructed on quite limited, and often unrepresentative, samples of the population.

After the sampling procedure is completed, test items are evaluated on various criteria. Because one purpose is to be able to rank students who have taken the test, each test item must have some power of discrimination. That is, an item everyone answers correctly does nothing useful in terms of ranking students, nor does an item everyone answers incorrectly. Therefore, items on norm-referenced tests must be directed toward students with different levels of knowledge. Then, the differences in each item's results are indexed statistically. From this index, items are evaluated for inclusion in the final version of the test.

Unfortunately, these procedures have several flaws and limitations. Petrosko (1977) notes that few test makers indicate the source of their items or a rationale for including any particular type of item on their tests. Some test makers draw samples of vocabulary and textual material from content area texts, but others generate these items independent of existing texts. The test-user must examine the content of a test to determine whether the items included assess a needed ability from appropriate content. A basic limitation of these statistical procedures for item selection is that little emphasis may have been given to what

SOME TERMS RELATED TO EVALUATION

Evaluation—refers to assessment of, for example, a performance or a piece of work; it requires judgment by the evaluator but does not necessarily depend on quantitative data.

Measurement—refers to obtaining quantitative information through the use of an instrument.

Standardized Tests—are tests for which the test maker has established expected standards of performance determined by administration of the test to a selected group of students, e.g., by age.

Norm-Referenced Tests—are tests used to determine how the performance of a given student or group of students compares with the performance of a group of students whose scores are given as the norm.

Criterion-Referenced Tests—are used to determine whether a given student has reached a particular level of performance, i.e., the criterion. The criterion is typically a goal defined by the teacher, often in behavioral terms; the test is intended to determine whether the student has achieved that goal. It should not involve comparison with other students.

Validity—refers to whether the instrument measures what it purports to measure.

Reliability—refers to whether the instrument measures accurately what it measures; for example, the instrument should yield comparable results when used at different times.

Achievement Tests—are designed to indicate what students have learned as the result of instruction.

Median—refers to that point in the middle of a range of scores such that half the scores fall above the point and half fall below.

Mean—refers to the *average* among a group of scores; a mean score for a class can be calculated from all the scores of students in that class.

Correlation—refers to whether two or more variables appear to have a consistent relationship, e.g., height and weight are related. This does *not* mean that one variable has a causal relationship to the other.

Source: E. H. Brady, "To Test or Not to Test," *American Educator*, 1 (1977): 4.

is being measured. An item that is incorrectly answered by over half the norming population will typically be included, even if item ambiguity is the primary reason for the incorrect answers. Another concern raised by Tuinman (1974) is that many items on reading achievement tests can be correctly answered without reading the passage. Such items are called **passage independent**, whereas items that cannot be answered without reference to the passage are **passage dependent**. Tuinman found that over one-half the items on many commercially available tests could be answered primarily on the basis of prior knowledge or cues within the question itself. Examples of these test items were: What is the jet stream?; What is the largest state?; and What is the longest American river? The test-user, then, must attend not only to the statistical factors of test construction, but also to the content of items—what is being measured and how.

Norm-referenced test producers are also concerned about the distribution of scores, which underlies sorting items on the basis of an index of discriminability. For norm-referenced tests, the distribution of scores must fit what is called the **normal**, or **bell-shaped**, **curve**. The highest point on the normal curve represents a score in the middle of the distribution; 50 percent of the sample scored lower than this point and 50 percent scored higher. This point is also the **mean score**, or **arithmetic average**. A score below the mean is, of course, below average, and any score above the mean is an above-average score. In Chapter 3 we discussed just this issue, that on norm-referenced tests one-half the population must score below the mean and therefore below grade level.

Two other terms are associated with a distribution of scores: the median and the mode. The **median** is the midpoint in a range of scores. For example, in five ranked scores the median would be the third score—two scores higher and two scores lower. The **mode** is the score that occurs most often. In the hypothetical "normal" distribution (see p. 30), the mean, median, and mode would be the same. In the following example, the scores are rather well distributed on a ten-item test. The mean, median, and mode are all identified.

The mean score is computed by dividing the total of all scores (61) by the number of persons (12) taking the test. Half those taking the test score above the median score and half score below. The mode is 7, the most frequent score. This distribution, however, does not fit the normal curve; that is, the scores are not evenly distributed along the range of all possible scores.

After determining the normal distribution of scores for a test, all other scores are compared to it in order to rate an individual's performance against others who have taken the test. In deciding whether, and how, to use the results of a norm-referenced test, one concern is to satisfy yourself that the norm group bears some resemblance to the

Distribution of Scores

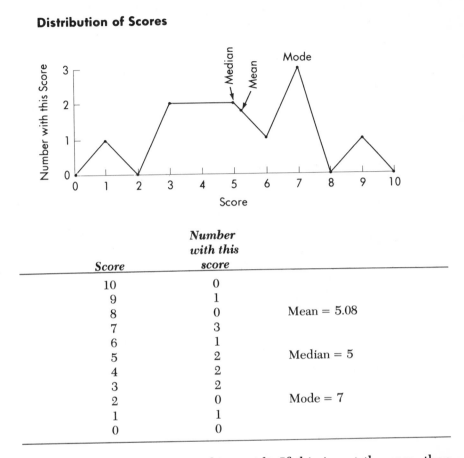

Score	Number with this score	
10	0	
9	1	
8	0	Mean = 5.08
7	3	
6	1	
5	2	Median = 5
4	2	
3	2	
2	0	Mode = 7
1	1	
0	0	

group of students you are working with. If this is not the case, then applying the norms to your students would yield questionable information. The technical manual for the test should contain information about the norming process including a description of the norm group.

Although these factors are important in evaluating a norm-referenced test, they are by no means the only factors to consider. However, the additional factors apply to both norm-referenced tests and criterion-referenced tests, a second type of test that is gaining in popularity. These factors, then, will be considered in a later section of this chapter after the basic concepts underlying criterion-referenced tests have been introduced.

Criterion-Referenced Tests

A criterion-referenced test differs from a norm-referenced test primarily in that it compares a learner's score not with the scores of others, but with a standard that theoretically represents some minimum level of acceptable performance. The philosophy behind criterion-referenced tests is that in many areas it makes more sense to determine whether a person can perform a task at a particular level of competence rather than to discover how well the performance compares to those of everyone else who took the test.

Because the popularity of criterion-referenced tests is quite recent, there are many problems involving test construction and development. One problem associated with reading ability is the lack of any empirical verification of the criteria set by the test developers (Pearson, 1978). Although many criterion-referenced tests set a criterion level of 80–95 percent on a test of reading skill, researchers have yet to establish either minimum or optimum performance levels. Thus, the criterion may be far higher than one could reasonably expect test-takers to score. The development of a criterion-referenced test differs, then, in several important respects from the development of a norm-referenced test.

Another characteristic of most current criterion-referenced tests is greater specificity; that is, they assess a narrower range of skills or abilities. Most criterion-referenced tests attempt to assess mastery of only a single subskill of the reading process. This in itself is a bit risky, because fluent reading is more than a collection of independent subskills. However, if the test-developers wanted to assess a student's syllabication abilities, the test might be constructed of a number of polysyllabic words the student would have to read. The number of items included is important, because more items give a more accurate picture of the subject's abilities. In the interest of efficiency, however, the test-developer will not use all possible words but only a sample. If the developer decides to use ten items, the criterion then might be set at eight or nine correct. The student passes this test only when the criterion is met. If the student scores 5 then the criterion has not been met and mastery of the skill has not been demonstrated. Unfortunately, the test-developer in this instance has no idea whether a score of 8 or 9 is typical or even achievable. Several studies (Stennett, Smythe, and Hardy, 1975; Walmsley, 1978) have demonstrated that some current criterion-referenced tests have just such inherent difficulties. The criteria are far too rigid given the abilities of the population. For example, learners who exhibit no difficulties in learning from text sometimes fail tests that purport to measure a skill or ability necessary to learn from text.

Recently, a procedure has been developed to help solve this particular difficulty. In this case the developer of a criterion-referenced test of reading speed would not arbitrarily draw a criterion speed out of a hat. If the goal were to develop a performance standard, or criterion, for ninth-grade reading rate, then the developer would determine empirically the minimum reading rate of good readers in the ninth grade. This would become the criterion, or performance standard, for ninth-grade students. All students performing at a rate slower than this would be considered deficient. As far as criterion-referenced tests are concerned, it does not matter how far below or above the standard a subject's reading rate is. Unlike norm-referenced tests, the primary information from the criterion-referenced test is whether a level is acceptable or unacceptable.

Another method used to establish a criterion is called the **consensus method**, which involves gathering a group of experts who, based on their experience, set the criterion level. Criterion levels for criterion-referenced measurements of reading abilities are often established using this method (Johnson and Pearson, 1975).

Test Validity

An important consideration for any type of test is whether it assesses what it claims to assess; in other words, whether it is a valid test. This is the most common meaning of **test validity**, although in practice this is a difficult factor to achieve.

Three common types of validity are used in conjunction with tests of reading ability. The first of these is **concurrent validity**, which is achieved by comparing a new test with a test already in existence. By using the statistical procedure of correlation, the test developer can see how closely a score on the new test predicts the score on the old test. If the new test is fairly accurate at predicting the score on the old test, it is assumed that the tests are measuring the same thing. If the old test measured reading ability, then it is assumed that the new test also measures reading ability. It may seem odd that one has to establish what a test is measuring, but several formats for tests claiming to assess reading ability seem in fact to measure something else. One example of this might be the syllabication test discussed earlier. Although syllabication skills are important to fluent reading, the ability to pass that test successfully would not necessarily indicate an ability to extract meaning from textual material. In a similar manner, tests of word-identification abilities do not assess, or necessarily predict, the ability to comprehend written text.

A second consideration is the test's **content validity**. To have content validity, a test should contain items that measure important abilities or knowledge for the subject being tested. To establish this test-developers again often ask a group of independent experts to agree on what the test truly measures. This type of validity is most useful if the construct under consideration is not fully understood, yet a need exists to attempt to measure it.

A final consideration is the test's **construct validity**. To establish construct validity, test developers must show that the test measures some unique ability—for instance, something other than intellectual ability. If subtests purporting to measure an independent skill are used, the developer must also demonstrate that the subtest indeed measures the separate skill. Few current commercial tests have established such validity for their subtests. For instance, reading comprehension tests, which purport to assess various comprehension skills (such as literal recall, inferences, critical thinking, and vocabulary) seldom can demonstrate the validity of such claims. Most research (Davis, 1968; Farr, 1969) shows that current tests of reading comprehension assess only one or, at best, two different abilities.

Test Reliability

Equally important as test validity is test reliability. Simply stated, a test is reliable if it measures an ability or skill consistently.

There are three common ways to establish the reliability of a test. The first is the **split-half reliability** technique in which the scores from half the test are compared to the scores from the other half. The relationship between the students' performances on both halves is expressed as a correlation coefficient and called a **reliability coefficient**. A second method, **test-retest reliability**, involves comparing the scores received on a first administration of the test with scores received on a second administration of the same test. Again the relationship is expressed as a reliability coefficient. A final technique, **alternate-form reliability**, is similar to the test-retest format except that, instead of giving the identical test twice, scores that students receive on different forms of the same test are compared.

Reliability coefficients are expressed in numerical form with a maximum possible value of +1.0. This would mean that, however reliability was assessed, the students' scores were ranked exactly the same on both sets of items or both tests. For a test to be considered reliable, one should find that a student taking the test on Monday and another form of the same test on Tuesday scores about the same on both tests. Students will never always perform exactly the same for a variety of factors, but those with high scores on Monday should still have high scores on Tuesday if the test consistently measures the ability. Thus, one would ideally like to use tests with reliability coefficients as close to +1.0 as possible.

The reliability coefficients of most commercially available tests will probably disappoint the person in search of that near-perfect correlation. Far too many report reliability coefficients below 0.70, a point at which only about half the variance is shared by the test forms. The best advice the test-user can follow is to carefully examine the reliability of the test or tests to be used, aiming for a reliability coefficient of 0.85 or better and considering suspect tests with reported coefficients below 0.70.

Standard Error of Measurement

A statistic directly tied to reliability is the standard error of measurement (SEM). Any instrument of any sort has some error associated with it, and commercially prepared tests are no different. The standard error of measurement represents the range within which a subject's **true score** will likely fall. For example, if a person scores 80 on a 100-item test that has a SEM of ± 10, that person's true score will probably fall in the range of 80 ± 10, or between 70 and 90. Knowing the SEM of a test is important because decisions are often based on test results; that is, the score earned is regarded as an accurate estimation of the subject's ability. Rather than to assume the score received by a student is exactly accurate, the test-user would be much wiser to identify the SEM and consider each score as a score within the range indicated by the SEM.

Errors in measurement exist for a variety of reasons. Subjects may be tired or upset, or the environmental conditions may not be conducive to test taking. Because the test developer is only using a sample of all possible questions, the test may be biased against one curriculum or another. Finally, many of the abilities we try to assess are not well understood. Such is the case with learning from text, and our lack of understanding creates problems in developing adequate measurement tools. Each of these, and other, factors introduces the probability of measurement error.

Interpreting Scores

One reason commercially available tests are so attractive is that they seem to reduce very complex human behavior to easy-to-understand numbers, or scores. Commercially produced reading tests usually report scores in one or more of the following ways: raw score, grade equivalent, percentile rank, or stanine. Each of these has its own meaning and must be interpreted differently.

Raw Scores

Raw scores are the least meaningful scores found on a test report. This simply tells the test-user how many items were correctly answered without regard for comparison to either other scores or a criterion score. However, the raw score must be used to estimate the true-score range from the SEM. The SEM is based on raw scores; if it were ±10, then the true-score range is 10 raw-score points above or below the achieved raw score. After computing this true-score range, the test-user can then go to conversion tables for other types of scores to estimate, for instance, the grade-equivalent range of the subject's true score.

Grade-Equivalent Scores

All scores but raw scores are called **converted scores**, which simply means that, through mathematical manipulations, the raw score is changed to some other type of score. The most frequent type of converted score for tests of reading ability is the grade-equivalent score. Grade-equivalent scores are expressed as numbers that show the grade-level norm for a particular raw score. Grade-equivalent scores are expressed in grade and months; for example, a score of 9.3 would mean ninth grade, third month, and 11.6 would mean eleventh grade, sixth month.

Grade-equivalent scores are norm referenced and are interpreted as follows: Assume a ninth-grade student receives a raw score of 85 on a test of reading ability. A part of the test manual contains a number of conversion tables. By referring to the grade-equivalent conversion table, we find that this raw score yields a grade equivalent of 9.2. In using grade-equivalent scores, it is important to note that a score of 9.2 does not necessarily mean a student is reading at 9.2 grade level. It does mean that the student achieved a raw score on this test typical of students in the ninth-grade norm group. Assuming that a grade-equivalent score of 9.2 indicates the student can read ninth-grade-level material is a common mistake made in interpreting grade-equivalent scores.

At this point it is useful to refer back to the concepts of standard error of measurement and reliability. If this test also had an SEM of ±10, then this student's true-score range is between 75 and 95. By examining the grade-equivalent conversion table for this raw score, we can get an idea about the general-reading-ability-level range of this student. In this case the subject's true reading ability would probably fall in the 7.6 to 10.3 grade-equivalent range. However, if the test is not particularly reliable, we would put little confidence in even this span. Too often, teachers, administrators, and parents place far too much confidence in the results of a single group reading-achievement test. The score received by an individual on a group achievement test must be interpreted with extreme caution. These tests were generally not designed to provide accurate information on individual abilities. Rather, the tests were designed to provide insight into the overall reading abilities of groups of students. As you will remember, if the standard error is in either direction, it may result in over- or underestimating a student's ability. If dealing with a group of students, it is assumed in test theory that these overestimations and underestimations will cancel each other out, and the result will be an accurate depiction of a group mean-achievement level. By comparing group A with group B, we can decide whether one group has a higher reading-achievement level, but it is very risky to attempt to make individual judgments about students in either group. Because group tests of reading achievement were not designed to depict individual reading abilities, attempts to use such results to match individual students with textual material are unwise.

Percentile Rank

Another type of converted score is a percentile rank. A percentile rank differs from a percentage, though they are often confused. A percentage refers to a proportion of the total. In testing this means the number of items correctly answered, divided by the possible number correct. A percentile rank, on the other hand, refers to a score ranking compared to all the other scores from the norm groups. It is obviously a norm-referenced score and is interpreted in the following way: The score of 85 we discussed earlier can be converted to a percentile rank by going to the appropriate table in the test manual. Let us say that in this case the raw score of 85 converts to a 76th percentile rank. This means that a score of 85 is a better score than that received by 75 percent of the ninth-graders in the norm group.

Unlike grade-equivalent scores, percentile ranks change according to the age or grade level of the test-taker. A grade-equivalent score of 9.2 is a 9.2 no matter who gets it. It may be more impressive if the score were received by a fourth-grade student as opposed to a high school senior, but it is still 9.2. The same raw score of 85 achieved by a ninth-grade student may place him or her at the 56th percentile rank of ninth-graders in the norm group; but if achieved by a fourth grader, the 85 would place that student at the 99th percentile rank for the fourth-grade norm group. Because the groups used for developing percentile ranks are more like the students taking the test, percentile ranks can often be more useful than other converted scores. However, the same cautions concerning SEM and reliability apply to percentile ranks.

Stanines

The last type of converted score we will be concerned with is the stanine, an abbreviated form of the phrase *standard nine*. One might choose to use stanines because scores from one test cannot be directly compared with other test scores in any meaningful way. Comparisons cannot be made, because each of the converted scores discussed so far is unique to each test. That is, because both grade-equivalent scores and percentile ranks are based on the particular norming groups used for each test, the comparability of these groups is often in doubt. This makes evaluating student growth using two different tests almost impossible.

Another way of looking at stanines is to examine what proportion of the population falls into each stanine and where the percentile ranks locate in relation to stanines.

Percentile	4	11	23	40	50	60	77	89	96
	lowest 4%	next 7%	next 12%	next 17%	next 20%	next 17%	next 12%	next 7%	highest 4%
Stanine	1	2	3	4	5	6	7	8	9

To overcome this difficulty, the concept of stanines was developed. Stanines simply divide the normal curve into nine equal segments. Returning to our raw score example of 85, for instance, we can again go to an appropriate conversion table and see that this score is in the sixth stanine. Stanines are rankings, just like the other norm-referenced scores, but they lack the seeming precision of grade equivalents and percentile ranks. The range of raw scores in the sixth stanine may be from 70 to 87, but as far as we are concerned all scores in the same stanine are equivalent. Stanines become useful when we administer a different reading-achievement test later in the year from that used earlier in the year. We can compare the stanine achieved on the second test with that achieved on the first to see if progress has been made. Comparing the other converted scores is unwise for the reasons discussed above. A further advantage of stanines is that they provide a range rather than a specific score, which is subject to a greater degree of error and should be considered an approximate score.

Selecting an Appropriate Test

We have discussed several factors important to test selection. In order to use this information, we offer the following strategy for selecting an appropriate test of general reading ability:

(1) *Decide on the purpose for testing.* Commercially produced tests of general reading achievement are not suitable for judging individual reading abilities, but they can be useful as screening devices and do provide substantial information about the reading abilities of groups of students. In other words, these provide useful information about the relative reading proficiency of a single class of students or a larger group. Thus, if one wishes to know whether students in a particular class or grade are reading above or below grade level, then administering a commercially produced test is called for.

(2) *Examine the test as a whole and read through each item to ascertain the test's content.* Do the items measure the type of abilities appropriate to the purpose for administering the test? What types of abilities are assessed and how are they assessed?

(3) *Consider the validity and reliability of the test.* Does the test-producer provide evidence that the test measures what it purports to measure? Examine the reported reliability coefficient. Does it fall at an acceptable level, near or above 0.85?

(4) *Consider the standard error of measurement.* Is it so large as to make the true score range wide and therefore negate the value of the test?

(5) *Decide which type or types of converted score is most appropriate to the purpose of the test administration.*

Following these guidelines will greatly reduce the current epidemic of test misuse. Tests can be used sensibly, but the most important consideration is the ultimate interpretation of the test results.

Using Test Results

Once you have a test that meets both your purpose and the various considerations appropriate from a measurement standpoint, then you can begin the truly important work—using the test results sensibly.

In far too many districts the only data included in a student's folder are the raw score and a single converted score, usually a grade equivalent, for each test. Too often, the results of reading-achievement tests are grossly misused. Some common examples of misuse include using the results of a group achievement test to identify individuals supposedly in dire need of remedial assistance. As noted on several earlier occasions, group tests are neither accurate nor reliable enough to make this type of judgment. The results might profitably be used to screen students for referral for further testing with appropriate individual tests, but group test scores are not appropriate as the only, or even primary, source of information for individual reading abilities. In a similar manner, attempting to use these group test results to select textual material at an appropriate level of difficulty for individual students is an inappropriate application of such information.

Rather than misusing group achievement tests in these ways, we recommend using the results in a manner consistent and appropriate with the test purpose. First, most test developers agree that their tests can provide accurate and reliable information on groups of twenty-five students or more. Thus, to use group achievement-test scores properly, a district must select groups of students for examination or comparison. A content area teacher might profitably compare the general reading ability of, say, the first-hour earth science class with the reading ability of the third-hour class. It is entirely possible that these classes will differ significantly in their overall reading ability, even if they are supposedly heterogeneously grouped. The results of a group achievement test can reliably identify whether discrepancies exist.

Another similar strategy is using the results of group tests to determine whether a large mismatch between a group's reading-achievement level and the difficulty of the assigned textual material exists. To do this, great caution must be observed, because both the tests and measures of text difficulty are sources of measurement error. Discrepancies signal the need for further examination of the issue. For instance, if those earth science classes have mean reading grade-equivalent levels of 7.5 and 9.4 and the assigned textual material has an estimated difficulty level of tenth grade, then the teacher probably has a problem. At this point, it would be fairly safe to assume that most students in the first class will not be able to read the assigned textual material, and that also seems to be the case for many if not most students in the second group as well.

The results of group achievement tests in reading can also be used to compare the reading abilities of different grades of students. Two strategies seem most profitable: First, it is important for content area teachers, as well as administrators, to be aware of general trends in reading abilities among new classes of students entering each year as freshmen. By collecting the data from group achievement tests on an annual basis, one can compare the reading abilities of this year's entering freshmen with those of past and future years. This allows the teacher to note any overall trend of scores to decline, remain relatively constant, or improve. Given the ease of collecting such data, particularly given the time and money involved in administering these tests, it is surprising that such practices are seldom observed in secondary schools. Farr (1969) has suggested that, given the current use of reading-achievement test data, there is probably no greater waste of monetary resources than that spent on purchasing and administering these tests. Unfortunately, we have to agree. Group tests can be used to monitor general reading levels of groups of students, but far too often the results are not used for this; instead, the scores are misused to make decisions about individuals.

A final use of group achievement tests in reading is to determine whether groups of students are continuing to develop reading abilities during secondary school. In some cases, entering freshmen, as a group, have adequate general reading abilities, but by eleventh grade serious mismatches in reading ability and textual difficulty begin to appear. Often this occurs because the reading abilities of many students begin to stagnate or remain relatively constant in the absence of further reading instruction. In such cases, the message is quite clear: some type of instructional intervention must occur if reading abilities are to continue to develop.

Interpreting Test Results

Up to this point, we have presented several basic concepts necessary for effectively using commercially produced tests, along with basic limitations of these instruments and a strategy for using test results. To conclude this chapter, we present several considerations for interpreting group reading-achievement tests.

Interpreting group norm-referenced tests is a difficult task, at best. Several limitations, noted earlier, restrict the test-user as to the type of interpretation that can be safely developed. The most commonly reported converted score is the grade-equivalent score. If a class produces an average score on a group norm-referenced test of 9.5, the appropriate interpretation is that that class's reading abilities are similar to those of the average norm-group class of ninth-grade students at about midyear. Not everyone in the class has a reading ability of 9.5. Rather, half would be below that point and half above, with the majority of students typically falling between 8.5 and 10.5.

If several students in this class have scores below the fifth-grade level, the content area teacher can usually assume a real deficiency does indeed exist. We say *usually* because some students are not interested enough in education to bother completing a test. In this situation a low score cannot be interpreted as an indication of true reading-achievement level. In addition, the teacher cannot assume that a ninth-grader with a score of 4.8 really reads on fourth-grade level. If that student made an adequate attempt to complete the test and still achieved that score, one can be quite sure that his or her reading level is below that of the average ninth-grader, but it may be higher than 4.8 or lower. Furthermore, because guessing is not penalized on most tests, a virtual nonreader can often achieve a grade-equivalent score of 3.0 or better simply by filling in a few blanks on the answer sheet.

The manuals accompanying many commercially produced norm-referenced tests provide good information on test usage and interpretation. Often these manuals indicate both the true-score range and the level of confidence with which one can estimate a student's or a group's reading-achievement level. The other converted scores available from most commercial norm-referenced tests allow the test-user to make different types of judgments. Percentile ranks, for instance, allow one to establish the relative performance of a group compared to other supposedly similar groups. In the case of the ninth-grade earth science class with a grade-equivalent score of 7.5, one can state that this class ranks near the bottom, about the 22nd percentile, of groups of ninth-grade students. The other class, which had an average reading ability of 9.5, would be ranked about average, at about the 56th percentile. In other words, the former class would have many more students with a reading achievement below grade level than the latter, though both groups would have at least one-half of the students in this range.

The primary use of stanines is comparing scores of groups of students on different tests. The entering ninth-graders, for instance, may have been tested at the beginning of eighth grade on reading achievement test X and scored at the sixth stanine. If in ninth grade they are tested on reading-achievement test Y, we can compare the achieved stanine score on this test with that of test X to determine whether the reading ability of the group as a whole has remained constant, improved, or lagged. Rough comparisons can, of course, be made with either the grade-level equivalent or the percentile rank, but to ensure that real differences in achievement exist, stanines are the proper unit of comparison.

If caution is observed, the results of norm-referenced tests can be used to make rough judgments about individual reading abilities. Basically, the important consideration is the measurement error. As we noted earlier, a ninth-grade student with a reading-achievement score of 4.8 on a group test can be assumed to have a rather severe deficit in general reading—that is, if that student did in fact expend a reasonable amount of effort on the test. The measurement error of most tests is not so large as to place a good reader so far below the average. However, the smaller the discrepancy between achievement score and grade level, the less sure one can generally be about the true reading achievement level of the student. Gross discrepancies in subtest scores, such as word meaning and comprehension, can typically be considered significant, but the smaller the discrepancy the less confidence one can have that the differences are real and not attributable to measurement error.

Most group tests, whether norm- or criterion-referenced, can only serve as crude screening devices for individual reading abilities. The appropriate strategy is to use these results to identify students who may possibly have a real deficiency in reading ability for follow-up testing on instruments designed to assess individual abilities. This testing, then, would typically be conducted by a trained reading teacher, a trained guidance counselor, or a school psychologist. Individual achievement and diagnostic tests can provide the necessary information for remedying reading deficiencies, but this is not a role for the content area teacher.

Summary

At this point you may feel as though you know more about tests and measurement than you really need. Because of the widespread misuse of tests, particularly group achievement tests, we feel it is necessary for the content area teacher to have a basic understanding of the purposes, development, conceptual base, limitations, and appropriate uses of these instruments. The information in this chapter, summarized below, should provide the necessary knowledge to achieve these goals:

1. Commercially produced tests of reading achievement enjoy a wide popularity in secondary schools. This popularity stems from these tests' seemingly objective method of reducing complex human behaviors to an easily understood number.

2. Unfortunately, the results of commercially produced reading-achievement tests are often misused. The primary abuse of these test results is attempting to make educational decisions about individuals based on group test results.

3. Neither group norm- nor criterion-referenced tests are particularly appropriate as sources of information for individual decisions, be: :use both the standard error of measurement and test reliability produce fairly wide true-score ranges and low levels of confidence in the scores attained by individuals.

4. Test-users must examine the test items and the test manual to determine what abilities are being assessed and how they are being assessed. Subtest titles do not always provide an accurate indication of the ability being assessed.

5. Because of the nature of the norm-referencing process, one-half the population taking the test must by definition score below average or below grade level.

6. Group achievement tests can be used appropriately and profitably in several ways, including (a) comparing the general reading-achievement levels of different classes or grades of students; (b) assessing group reading achievement; and (c) assessing growth in reading of groups of students.

7. Group achievement-test results can also be employed as rough screening devices for identifying individuals who seem to have a severe deficit in reading achievement. Usually these tests will not provide an accurate indication of either the nature or the extent of the deficiency.

8. Regarding commercially available tests, the primary role of the content area teacher is to know the limitations and strengths of the tests and to use this information for effective instructional decisions.

Assessing Reading Ability with Informal Strategies

Previously we have discussed the strengths and weaknesses of standardized tests as sources of information for the content area teacher. Given the shortcomings of these assessment tools for providing specific information that is useful in instructional planning, we will discuss several alternative techniques in this chapter. These tests, or assessment strategies, are commonly referred to as informal measures because they lack several characteristics of standardized measures. The most significant difference is the absence of the rather rigorous test construction processes, including the item-selection process and the norming and standardization on a large representative population. Usually informal tests are teacher constructed, with little attempt to validate the instrument, though, as suggested later, some rather simple techniques can be employed to refine these informal assessment instruments.

Informal assessments have two important advantages over standardized tests: First, teachers can develop measures that assess specific strengths and weaknesses of their students as these relate to instructional planning. Second, informal assessment instruments can be designed to assess each student's application of these specific abilities to a specific content area textbook. Thus, rather than providing the more general information available from standardized measures, informal tests provide information on each student's particular abilities relative to a specific content area textbook.

> There is a lack of tests on the market which measure reading achievement in specific subjects. If content area teachers desire information regarding student's reading performance in that content area, it would be most useful for them to develop informal inventories designed to measure student's skill in learning from test material. (Farr, 1969)

What Is Informal Assessment?

Informal assessment is simply collecting data in a systematic fashion in order to facilitate instructional decision making. In schools, informal assessment is an ongoing process that takes many forms: observing learners; evaluating learner products such as tests and papers; making judgments about learner background knowledge and interest; and so forth. In discussing informal assessment of the ability to learn from textual material, we are primarily interested in discovering whether learners can read their texts with understanding and, if not, what might be done to modify instructional demands. We will discuss several procedures, all of which can be adapted to suit any teacher's needs.

TYPES OF INFORMAL ASSESSMENT ITEMS

Multiple choice

Advantages—easy to score, requires relatively short amount of time for responses

Disadvantages—guessing correct answer is possible, difficult to assess most skills other than recall

Essay questions

Advantages—provides much information about learner's knowledge and abilities, assessment of more complex abilities possible (for example, reasoning)

Disadvantages—requires much time to complete and score, ineffective writing abilities may interfere with communicating knowledge

Open ended

Advantages—easy to score, response time is relatively short, guessing answers is difficult

Disadvantages—assessing more complex abilities is difficult, poor spelling ability may obscure knowledge of content

Matching

Advantages—easy to score, response time is minimal, analogous relationships can be tapped

Disadvantages—difficult to construct items that go beyond recall, matching may not assess understanding

Cloze

Advantages—easy to score and construct, provides a predictor of learner understanding

Disadvantages —influenced by specific content, can be time consuming for testee, taps broad ability rather than a specific ability

The Informal Content Area Word Test

Perhaps the first aspect of learners' abilities the teacher might want to assess is whether the words representing the specialized vocabulary of the content area present recognition difficulties to a significant number of learners. At this point, we are not assessing whether learners understand the concepts, but rather whether they can recognize the words.

Word-recognition difficulties are usually not the responsibility of the content area teacher, but difficulties at this level are a source of concern. Depending on the general reading ability of the learners and the level of the content presented, the teacher can expect to have virtually no, to virtually all, learners experiencing difficulty recognizing key content vocabulary. If a significant number of learners have difficulty at the word recognition level, then learning from textual material will be difficult if not impossible for them, and other methods for imparting the content will have to be pursued. However, the specialized vocabulary of many content areas would be enough to give even the most competent readers difficulty. Specialized vocabulary such as *diplodocus, orangutan, ichthyologist, butte,* and so forth, do not lend themselves to easy identification, because their pronunciation is not clearly signaled by the graphic representation.

Therefore, the first informal assessment the content area teacher might consider is an informal content area word test. This is an individual test that takes approximately three minutes per individual to administer and has as its primary purpose identifying learners who might need referral to a reading teacher for further evaluation. The informal content area word test is useful as a rough screening device, particularly if data on general reading abilities is either nonexistent or suggests a level of reading ability that may present a barrier to learning from text.

To construct the informal content area word test, the teacher surveys the textual material to select a sample of difficult words used in the content area. These words might range from one-syllable words that are exceptions to common patterns, such as *tongue,* to polysyllabic words and even words derived directly from foreign words. After selecting these words, the teacher simply presents them on cards or in a list to individual students and asks them to read each word aloud. The teacher then marks their pronunciation as correct or incorrect. If no response occurs within ten seconds of presenting a word, the teacher simply marks the item incorrect and tells the student to move on to the next item. However, if the student is actively attempting to identify the word, the teacher may want to provide a few additional seconds. The rationale for the ten-second limit is twofold: (1) it expedites test completion and (2) it can serve to relieve student anxiety resulting from confronting an impossible task. Testing should be terminated after five consecutive errors or after presenting all items. A student who errs on five consecutive items is unlikely to recognize many additional items correctly.

Several considerations must be given to interpreting the results of informal content area word tests. These tests can be characterized as informal criterion-referenced measures. Following instruction, the teacher could realistically hope all learners would be able to recognize all test items, though this may not be true in practice. Prior to instruction, correct recognition might be desired but will generally not be the case. The teacher then must develop appropriate criteria for such informal tests. One method would be to administer the informal content area word test to a number of students enrolled in the content area class and attempt to determine their average score. This score could then be used as an anchoring point for decisions about those who have taken the test. On the other hand, the teacher may feel that students should recognize all the items and be satisfied with nothing less than a perfect score.

In any event, one must remember that the primary purpose of the informal content area word test is to provide the teacher with information about the word-recognition abilities of the learners. Using a perfect score as the criterion does not assume that all students with lesser scores are unable to learn from the textual material. Rather, the teacher becomes aware of the fact that a certain number of learners cannot identify all the words appearing in the textual material, which is an indication that instructional intervention is needed. This may require a referral to a reading teacher, visual introduction of new words by the content area teacher, or a change in instructional materials. Students who correctly identify few of the items generally need referral to a reading teacher, but remedial instruction will not automatically ensure that the learner will soon be able to identify difficult words in content area reading.

If a large proportion of those taking the test receive poor scores, the content area teacher should probably consider selecting different textual material for instructional purposes. If all students consistently miss a few items, the teacher should take care to provide an introduction to such vocabulary items. Words such as *isosceles* or *amoeba* often are incorrectly pronounced because they do not follow common patterns; but even words such as *ecology, recidivism,* or *Montreal* may be mispronounced because several pronunciations are possible given common patterns of English words.

The informal content area word test makes no attempt to assess knowledge of word meaning. The goal is simply to assess the word-recognition skills of learners; however, the content area teacher must always remember that familiarity with a word tremendously enhances the possibility of correct word identification, even if words are presented in isolation. Thus, if items on the test are likely to be unfamiliar to the student both in terms of oral language and visual representation, correct pronunciation probably will not occur. Part of the teacher's task is to develop familiarity with new words and the ideas or concepts represented by the words. Failure to identify all items correctly does not necessarily imply an inappropriate reading-achievement level; instead, it may indicate a lack of knowledge about the content to be presented in the classroom.

WHAT MAKES A WORD DIFFICULT?

Two basic factors influence word difficulty: (1) decoding, or recognition, complexity and (2) semantic, or conceptual, complexity.

Decoding Complexity

Several factors contribute to decoding complexity:

WORD LENGTH: Longer words are generally more difficult to decode; compare *sell/barter, still/quiescent, father/patriarch, Vermont/Versailles.*

WORD REGULARITY: In all of the previous examples, the longer word presents more decoding difficulty because of a structure that is less regular than the shorter word.

WORD FREQUENCY: In the previous examples, the longer words appear less frequently in written language; therefore, learners can be expected to be less familiar with them. Familiarity with a word is virtually prerequisite to pronunciation.

Semantic Complexity

Several factors contribute to semantic complexity:

WORD FAMILIARITY: An unfamiliar word will, of course, present more difficulty than a previously known word.

WORD CONCRETENESS: Words representing concrete concepts generally present less difficulty than words representing abstract concepts.

WORD UNIQUENESS: A word that has familiar or frequent synonyms typically presents less difficulty; for example, *prognosis* has the synonym *prediction,* but the chemistry term *reduction* seems to have no true synonym.

Each of these factors can interact to make a word difficult. By checking the appropriate following boxes, the content area teacher can estimate which words seem likely to present the greatest problems for learners.

	reduction (chemistry)	barter	butte	fortress	fraud
Decoding					
Does word have 3 or more syllables?	yes	no	no	no	
Is word composed of irregular patterns?	no	no	yes	no	
Is the word relatively low frequency?	yes	yes	yes	yes	
Semantic					
Is the word meaning likely to be unfamiliar?	yes	yes	yes	no	
Does the word represent an abstract concept?	yes	yes	no	no	
Is the word unique (no common synonym available)?	yes	no	no	no	
Total number yes	5	3	3	1	

The most difficult words will have scores ranging 4–6.
The least difficult words will have scores ranging 0–3.

Chart the following words using the above criteria: *fraud, onerous, saga, carousel, reclamation, complacent, recidivism, feudal.*

Recognition, however, does not ensure a full understanding of word meaning as is easily demonstrated by the fact that most metric measure words are recognized by a large proportion of the adult population, who, in turn, have great difficulty understanding the relative size and amounts represented by *liter* and *gram.* The informal content area word test, then, can easily provide the teacher with useful information. The results can be used as a screening device to identify (1) students who need referral to a reading teacher for further testing, (2) students who would profit from a visual introduction to new vocabulary, and (3) specific words that may need special attention to ensure learner recognition in general.

Teacher Observation

Content area teachers have often relied on informal observation of classroom behavior to identify learners having difficulty learning from textual material. This procedure can be used rather successfully and requires little teacher time or effort. There are several obvious disadvantages, such as the subjective nature of observation and the problem one has in specifying what might be causing the difficulty. However, we believe teacher observation is a potentially powerful strategy for assessing learner difficulty with textual materials, particularly for several common deficiencies. Its usefulness is also enhanced if the observation is done in a systematic manner.

At the broadest level, observation can be employed to infer which learners have difficulty learning from the assigned textual material. Of course, this is less reliable than several of the techniques discussed in Chapter 4 and is also less reliable than the other informal techniques presented later in this chapter. It is, though, the easiest-to-use technique and may be most appropriate in situations in which the amount of time for assessment is truly limited or in which other services are available for such assessments on referral.

Learners barred from learning by textual difficulty are often characterized by inattentiveness to the textual material when reading is required. They may be doodling, drawing, daydreaming, or engaging in a variety of off-task behaviors. These behaviors may be avoidance strategies employed to cover up an inability to deal with the difficulty of the textual material. However, none of these activities is a sure sign of the lack of an appropriate reading ability. They may signal boredom, poor motivation, or a host of other maladies.

Another sign one might look for is extensive finger pointing during silent reading. This behavior can be induced even in good readers if the difficulty of the material begins to reach the student's frustration point. Finger pointing is not a *cause* of reading difficulty, but rather a symptom. It is a useful relative index because it generally indicates students are processing the material only with great difficulty. The same is true for subvocalization, evidenced by lip movements, which can often be observed in content area classrooms. Most subvocalization is induced by textual difficulty. In both these instances, the learner is processing the printed information only with great difficulty and at a very slow rate.

Rate of processing is a fairly important factor in learning from text. A slow rate can impede learning because the information is being processed too slowly for assimilation. However, as noted in Chapter 2, how fast one can read is limited. The teacher can informally observe the students' rates simply by noting how quickly they turn the pages during silent reading of assigned material.

ASSESSING READING RATE IN TRADE OR CONTENT AREA BOOKS

Speed Drill Record Sheet

Name _____ Date _____

Title   _____

Time started _____   Time stopped _____

Page started _____   Page stopped _____

                                   Words per minute _____

How to Figure Words Per Minute

1. Total number of words on three full lines _____
2. Average number of words per line (divide line 1 by 3) _____
3. Number of lines on full page _____
4. Average words per page (line 2 times line 3) _____

$$\text{Words per minutes} = \frac{\text{words per page} \times \text{number of pages read}}{\text{Time (minutes)}}$$

A final observational emphasis is noting how students approach learning from texts. What do they do if given an assigned material and time to read? Do they forge ahead with little attention to pictorial, typographic, or other textual cues? Some may be underlining or taking notes, but others will do neither. Often the content area teacher can use behaviors observed during such classroom periods to identify learners with poorly developed strategies for learning from text. These same students may have an adequate general reading achievement level appropriate for the difficulty of the textual material.

Teacher observation, then, can be used to gather useful information about learners' abilities to learn from assigned textual material. However, these techniques are less reliable than others and should be employed primarily as screening measures to identify learners for follow-up testing.

Group Informal Screening Test

Koenke (1972) discussed a procedure, the Group Informal Screening Test (GIST), for informal assessment of learner abilities that is appropriate for whole-class administration. The procedure provides the content area teacher with an overview of learner abilities that goes beyond the information available from either readability analyses or informal content area word tests.

The GIST is constructed by selecting one or more passages from the assigned textual material. The selections should be at least 500 words long, but depending on the level of the learners' sophistication, might range upwards to several thousand words. After the material has been selected, ten questions are developed. These items must be given careful attention, both in content and in the specific wording. Koenke recommends developing four questions to assess learner recall of information directly stated in the textual material, but the teacher must be sensitive to what directly stated information is asked for. Questions asking for recall of trivial information, for instance, should be avoided, as should questions asking for recall of information the learner might have known prior to reading the selection.

Three more items should be constructed that require the learner to develop an inference based on information contained in the selected textual material. These items might ask for an explication of a cause-effect relationship implied in the text, or for a chronology or some other logical relationship that could be inferred from the material. Caution must be taken in constructing these items because inference is a delicate process. Often obvious relationships exist that can be inferred; but other, less-obvious relationships, which could be drawn from the same information may also exist. The teacher should attempt to assess the ability to develop inferences carefully, without relying heavily on discovering a simple relationship.

The final three items should attempt to assess knowledge of the specialized vocabulary found in the textual material. These items can ask learners to define vocabulary or to match a term with a synonym.

Administering this test is easily accomplished. The ten items can be presented on a single sheet of paper and given, face down, to the students, who are then directed to read the assigned material. After completing their reading, the learners simply turn the sheet over and complete the items without referring to the material. When the test is completed, the teacher collects and corrects the sheets. Koenke suggests that those who score at or above 70 percent should have no striking difficulty learning from the assigned textual material; for them, enough information has been collected. For those who fall below 70 percent, the teacher should pursue the sources of their difficulty one step further with a Group Informal Diagnostic Test (GIDT). However, before we discuss this procedure, let us further discuss several points about the GIST.

Because using a 70 percent cut-off score is rather arbitrary, the content area teacher should be sensitive to factors of validity and reliability as discussed in Chapters 4 and 5. How one constructs the test is the most important facet in effectively using a GIST. Content validity is achieved if the GIST items reflect the type of information the teacher expects the learners to retain from the assigned textual material. In other words, the GIST items should reflect the type of text-learning abilities the teacher normally requires. If the items differ in either nature or difficulty from the normal demands of the teacher, then the test is not a valid measure of course demands.

The reliability of informal measures is always a concern. The teacher must be particularly concerned about reliability on informal measures because informal tests that over- or underestimate learner abilities provide no useful information. To gain some measure of confidence in the GIST, then, the teacher should carefully analyze the results of the initial administration. In fact, the initial use of the GIST and other such informal measures should be considered a field test.

Dick and Carey (1978) offer several suggestions for group evaluations including how to ensure that the students taking the informal screening test represent a range of abilities. By comparing the GIST results with information already known about those taking the test, the teacher can begin to establish whether the test reliably identifies those who have already-known learning difficulties as well as those who are very able learners. In addition, the teacher can begin to validate the 70 percent cut-off advocated by Koenke. If even the better learners fall below this point, the teacher must adjust the criterion or revamp the test. The same is true if those with demonstrated learning difficulties consistently score above the 70 percent level. By considering the initial administration of a GIST or virtually any other informal measure a field test, teachers can develop insight into the adequacy of the measure and the learning abilities of the target population.

GIST-GIDT Testing Procedure

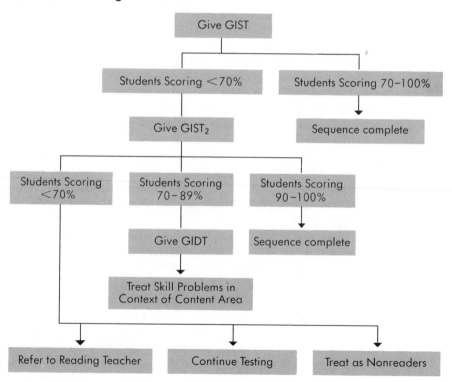

Group Informal Diagnostic Test

For those learners who fall below the cut-off point on the GIST, Koenke suggests administering a second follow-up assessment, the Group Informal Diagnostic Test (GIDT). This group test goes beyond identifying only those who do not seem to have adequate text-learning abilities and attempts to provide some insights into which abilities may be deficient.

To construct a GIDT, the content area teacher would first construct another GIST using material of several grade levels less difficulty. A ninth-grade science teacher might select science material at the sixth- or seventh-grade level for this second GIST. This is then administered and scored, separating the learners into three groups. The first group, composed of all those scoring at or above the 90 percent level, are considered able to learn from more difficult material but will probably need a fair amount of teacher attention. Often, these learners score at the 50–60 percent level on the first GIST and could learn from the assigned material if given specific instructional assistance of the types described in later chapters.

The second group—those scoring 70–90 percent on this second GIST—take a GIDT, designed specifically to help the teacher determine the form of text learning assistance that is needed. The basic procedure is a somewhat modified form of an informal assessment described by Shepard (1961) and differs from the GIST in that learners are given smaller segments of text to read for specific purposes. The teacher might direct the learners to read only a single paragraph to identify a particular item of information or to draw an inference. Rather than dealing with longer selections and a post-reading test, the GIDT provides for sampling learner abilities on relatively shorter selections with the information to be attended to already identified. This allows the teacher to assess whether providing such structure facilitates learning from text.

Many learners who fail the GIST can easily pass the GIDT—they can *find* information once they know what to look for, but have an inordinate amount of trouble if left to their own devices during reading. They can read the material but do not seem to have developed the ability to attend to important information or to draw relationships from text. These may be similar to the different reader described by Cromer (1970); that is, readers who have no inherent word-identification difficulties, but who do poorly on tests of recall, reconstruction, or inference.

The content of the GIDT is important. It, too, should reflect the types of skills necessary for a specific content area. Thus, learners might be directed to read short selections for summarization, to identify specific information, or to infer a relationship.

The third group, those who scored below 70 percent on the second and less difficult GIST, can be handled in at least four distinct ways:

(1) Because they had difficulty even with material substantially lower in difficulty than the assigned material, the teacher might assume a general reading deficiency exists and *refer them to a reading teacher* for additional assessment and possible remediation.

(2) Another alternative is to *continue testing with additional forms of the GIST at even lower levels,* until the learner finally is able to complete the items successfully. The teacher then attempts to identify a level at which the learner is likely to succeed, in order to locate or develop material appropriate to the content area and the learner's ability level. In practice, the teacher would need much assistance from a school librarian or reading teacher in order to provide learners at all levels with material at an appropriate level.

(3) A third alternative is to *treat these learners as nonreaders* for the purposes of learning from the assigned textual material. This approach involves providing these learners with alternative sources for the content area information, sources that do not require the ability to read. This might be accomplished by using cassette-accompanied filmstrips, lectures, audio-tape recordings of textual material, and so forth. This alternative does little to improve the learner's ability to learn from text, but it does serve to provide the information deemed necessary for the particular content area objectives.

(4) A final alternative for this group is for the content area teacher and reading teacher to work cooperatively toward a resolution of these learners' reading difficulties through some other means. The instructional goal would be an improvement in their ability to learn from text, but this instruction would be carried out with textual material drawn from the content areas. Under this strategy, the students receive useful information for content area classes as well as improve their abilities to learn from text.

Group Informal Reading Skills Survey

Whereas the GIST and GIDT are designed to help the content area teacher determine whether textual-intervention strategies are necessary to facilitate learning from text, the Group Informal Reading Skills Survey (GIRSS) is designed to assess more specialized reading and study skills that are appropriate for particular content areas. This procedure, which is similar to one recommended by Niles and Early (1955), involves identification of reading and study skills of particular relevance, using the materials employed in the classroom to create a series of mini tests for each skill. For instance, reading to recognize mood is unlikely to be necessary in a biology or mechanical drawing class. The same is true for skills such as recognizing figurative language or character development. On the other hand, interpreting graphs and tables is more likely to be necessary in the social studies or the sciences. Some specific skills, such as recognizing cause-effect relationships, enumeration, summarization, and so forth, which can be applied in virtually all content area classes, might also be assessed on the GIRSS if these skills are particularly important in a given course of study.

Cloze Procedure

In the next chapter the cloze procedure will be discussed as a strategy for assessing text readability. This procedure, developed by Taylor (1953), derives its name from the psychological construct of **closure**, the tendency to view things as a whole. The cloze procedure requires deleting every fifth word from a passage drawn from the assigned textual material and presenting this "clozed" passage to learners who then attempt to fill in the blank spaces with the exact word that was deleted. The ability to fill in the blanks is an indication of the learner's use of semantic (word meaning) and syntactic (grammatical) cues provided in written language.

Most authorities suggest that a cloze selection should contain at least fifty blanks and that learners falling below a 35 percent correct-completion level will probably find the textual material too difficult (Bormuth, 1975). Learners who fall in a 35–60 percent correct-completion range should find the textual material appropriate for their text-learning abilities. Those who correctly complete over 60 percent of the blanks will find the material quite easy and might be better placed in more difficult material.

As an informal assessment technique, the cloze procedure has many advantages: it is easily constructed, scored, and interpreted. It also provides the teacher with rather reliable information about possible mismatches between learner abilities and textual difficulty. In Chapter 6 where this procedure is discussed in some detail, it is noted that the cloze procedure can be used as a strategy for assessing both textual difficulty and learner abilities.

Readiness Assessment

Often, students having difficulty in content area classrooms are in trouble because they lack the prerequisite knowledge or understanding to learn the new concepts effectively (Gagne and Briggs, 1974). Very little is known yet about learning in humans, particularly the complex sort of learning expected in content area classes. However, we do know that a "readiness for learning" is necessary and that this readiness itself is a complex interaction of a variety of diverse factors including psychological and physiological maturity, motivation, mastery of prerequisite knowledge, and so forth. Readiness for learning is of vital importance in learning from text—it is not enough for a learner to have appropriate general abilities for dealing with textual difficulty. The learner must also have some specific abilities for dealing with the content. We have alluded to this previously, particularly in discussing the limitations of traditional readability indices; what the learner brings to the learning task is as important, if not more so, than the textual variables.

The notion of providing learners with assistance in relating what is already known with what is to be taught is hardly a recent idea. Note the advice offered to teachers nearly three-quarters of a century ago:

> (The teacher) will announce and recapitulate beforehand what is going to be said, and also going to be read . . . in popular language, avoiding the use of too many new and technical words. Thus the intellect of the pupil inclined in the right direction, will be disposed to listen, and the instruction, thrown onto a well-prepared soil, will bear the fruit which he expected. (Compayre, 1907)

Readiness for New Concepts

There are really two different types of readiness for learning from text. The first is readiness for new concepts, which is necessary because human learning depends largely on what is already known. To comprehend new information, it is often necessary to have specific prerequisite knowledge available as both a source of assimilation and a means of testing the new information. Recall the feature list for a cow from Chapter 2. It would be virtually impossible to comprehend the relative merits of a Brown Swiss compared with a holstein without knowledge of size, function, purpose, and so forth, to say nothing of the basic knowledge of cows and their function. A similar situation exists if learners are asked to understand the economic hardships of the Civil War on the population of the Confederacy when they have no prerequisite knowledge of a society's ability to allocate resources; or if multiplication is taught to learners who do not understand addition; or if acceleration is taught to those who do not understand inertia. The point is, prerequisite knowledge not only facilitates learning but also learning often will not take place without it.

Informal assessment for this first type of readiness can be accomplished in several ways. As a group screening activity, the content area teacher might write several key words on the chalkboard and ask learners to free-associate with each item, that is, to respond with as many related words as possible. A word such as *inertia*, for instance, might elicit associations such as *still, stable, motionless, inactive, force, fixed*. The teacher sorts through these with the learners, attempting to pinpoint the depth of their understanding. Some groups will have learners who cannot provide a single association; other groups will supply inappropriate associations for the content-specific meaning of a word (consider the possible responses that might be elicited from *mass, run, redress, civil,* and so forth).

This technique can also be adapted to a paper-and-pencil task in which the learners simply list their associations with the specified words. However, we feel that the teacher can generally get quite a good feel for learner prerequisite knowledge of new concepts simply by regularly employing the group on-board presentation strategy. Johnson (1967) found that the number of associations students could provide was a reasonably accurate measure of their prerequisite knowledge. Thus, for assessing a learner's, or a group's, readiness for learning a particular concept, the teacher need not design extensive or complicated informal measures but can simply attempt to tap the number of words the learners can associate with the new concept.

Motivation Readiness

The second type of readiness is often described as **psychological set, intention to learn,** or **motivation**. In other words, does the learner seem interested in acquiring the knowledge the teacher has identified for learning? Some learners, as we have noted, cannot learn from textual material because of a mismatch in achievement and difficulty levels. Others are barred from learning because of ineffective or inefficient text-processing strategies, although no mismatch is obvious. Still others have great difficulty knowing what is to be learned. However, for some, none of these barriers exist. These learners could learn but do not; they seem to have no interest in the content. We are not sure the teacher truly needs any strategies for identifying these students other than the process of elimination. In other words, if students have the necessary abilities but are not evidencing the acquisition of knowledge, then a good guess is that they have no motivation for learning.

Oral Reading Testing: Not Advised

There are several reasons why we have *not* suggested the content area teacher use oral reading of textual material to any degree in informal assessment. The first is that oral reading performance can be deceptive. Some learners, for instance, just are not meant to be oral readers. These learners, who are often skilled silent readers, seem to have a short circuit in the oral reading mechanism. That is, the oral reading is filled with errors, miscues, repetitions, and so forth. Thus false inferences about silent reading will be drawn from oral reading performance.

Second, oral reading is different from silent reading. These two aspects of reading are somewhat separate processes, and often in oral reading the goal is to sound good rather than extract meaning.

Third, correct interpretation of oral reading processes requires specialized training. Oral reading errors or miscues can be good or bad, depending on the source of the error. No marginal number or percentage of errors is allowed. Some readers make relatively numerous errors or miscues but could be considered rather effective readers; others will make fewer errors and be considered less effective readers.

Finally, by the time a learner reaches the middle- or secondary-school level, oral reading is not a particularly useful skill and typically has not received much instructional emphasis. By this point the learner should be receiving instruction that exclusively focuses on the development of silent reading abilities. The only defensible purposes for oral reading are for assessment by qualified reading teachers and for some instructional goals in areas such as theater, poetry, chorale, and public speaking.

Content area teachers need not be entertainers, but they should attempt to entice students to learn. Invoking the "because I say you will learn it" rule usually inspires few students to new heights of understanding; instead, the teacher can ask introspectively whether any attempt has been made to demonstrate how the knowledge to be learned is applicable to daily decisions.

We are suggesting that assessing the second type of readiness is pretty well accomplished if the content area teacher can rule out the textual and learner factors discussed thus far and still find learners who are not achieving. At this point the assessment should be of the instruction, not of the learner.

Informal Study Habits Inventory

In most content area classes the majority of the instructional time is spent listening to a presentation or participating in a learning activity of some sort. The textual material is used primarily to reinforce or extend the concepts presented in class. Little time is spent in guided reading; instead, the learners are expected to read the assigned textual material in out-of-class time, usually working independently. Therefore, it is important for the teacher to consider conducting an informal study habits inventory (ISHI).

INFORMAL STUDY HABITS INVENTORY

1. Do you generally take schoolwork home? <u>sometimes</u>
2. Do you study at home? <u>yes</u> How long? <u>1 hour</u>
3. Where do you usually study outside of school? <u>my home</u>
4. How many study halls do you have a day? <u>one</u>
5. Do you usually study alone? <u>yes</u> or with friends? <u>no</u>
6. Do you take notes when you study? <u>not usually</u>
7. Do you take notes in class? <u>no</u>
8. Do you underline as you study? <u>yes</u>
9. Do you try to answer the study questions? <u>yes</u>
10. Do you review before tests? <u>most of the time</u>

Fill in what you usually do during the following times.

8:00— 9:00	watch TV	eat breakfast	
9:00—10:00	science class		
10:00—11:00	study hall	go to library	go to school
11:00—12:00	mechanical drawing		
12:00— 1:00	eat lunch	horse around	play basketball
1:00— 2:00	history class		
2:00— 3:00	geometry call		
3:00— 4:00	phys. ed./ football practice		
4:00— 5:00	football practice		
5:00— 6:00	football practice	go home	
6:00— 7:00	eat supper	talk to friends	
7:00— 8:00	do homework	talk to friends	go down to Kelly's
8:00— 9:00	watch TV	read sports mag.	talk to friends
9:00—10:00	watch TV	read sports mag.	talk to friends

Basically an ISHI asks learners to respond about their particular study habits for a specific content area class. Of primary concern are the type, place, and duration of study behavior learners engage in. The questions, which can be multiple choice or open ended in format, are most easily administered if typed and distributed to each student in a group. The teacher can also include a time schedule for the average day and ask students to indicate what they are generally doing at various points in the day. This added feature assists the teacher in understanding the learners and any real time obligations they may have. For instance, no study-hall period, a part-time job, sibling-care responsibilities, athletic participation, and so forth, all serve to reduce the number of hours available for study. A second feature of such a chart is that it allows the teacher to both assess the validity of study habit statements and also offer suggestions on where to reallocate time if necessary.

A word of caution: There is often a disparity between what students *report* as study habits and what they actually *do*. To minimize this, the content area teacher should encourage truthfulness in responding, remind the learners that no grades are given on the survey, and be aware of classroom study habits so that these observations can serve as a validity check on the behaviors reported on the ISHI.

Guidelines for All Types of Informal Measures

In order to gain the most useful information from informal assessments, the content area teacher must keep in mind two primary considerations for any type of assessment: effectiveness and efficiency. The teacher must always be concerned with the *effectiveness* of the informal assessments. However, *efficiency* is equally important, because sometimes instruction makes better use of time than continued assessment. Each teacher must decide how much information is necessary for instructional decision making and then, using any or all the strategies discussed, develop the most effective and efficient informal assessments for gathering that information.

EFFICIENCY VERSUS EFFECTIVENESS

Guidelines for Constructing an Informal Assessment

EFFICIENT

- a single item
- multiple-choice format
- group administration
- selecting a commercial test
- testing once per year
- same instruction for all

EFFECTIVE

- several items
- essay format

- individual administration
- developing an informal test
- testing on numerous occasions
- complete individualization

In the real world of public schools, battling over efficiency versus effectiveness issue is constant with teachers as the final arbiters in the classroom. General reality, or common practice, falls somewhere between the extremes listed above.

Summary

This entire chapter has been devoted to procedures for informal assessment. It is our opinion that the information gained through informal means is more useful than that gained from standardized assessment instruments. The major reason for this is that informal assessment techniques are for specific purposes with particular target populations and restricted context—the content area curriculum. Standardized tests do, however, have one significant advantage—the rigorous construction and standardization criteria they are subjected to.

Measuring human abilities is a tremendously complicated enterprise, and we ought to try to do it in the best way we know of. To this end we have posed the following guidelines to help in developing informal instruments.

1. *Quantity of Items:* The easiest way to improve the reliability and validity of an informal test is to ensure a sufficient number of items per skill to accurately reflect a student's capability. Having four items per skill is much better than having one. The likelihood of a student achieving a satisfactory level of performance by chance is greatly reduced as a function of the number of items. However, there is an optimum ratio between effectiveness and efficiency. This means that although there should be enough items to make a valid judgment, there should be few enough that the instrument is efficient to administer, score, and interpret.

2. *Ambiguity:* In order to get the most useful information, it is imperative that learners understand completely what is being asked. If learners misinterpret the questions, then the chances of getting accurate information are reduced. It is not as simple to reduce ambiguity as it is to increase reliability and validity. The best that we can offer is that if students ask questions about an item, it ought to be discarded or reworked.

3. *Item Inspection:* After you have designed an assessment instrument, put it away for a couple of days and then look at it again to ensure that the items assess what you originally thought they did.

Another good idea is to get a colleague's frank opinion on the quality of the items.

4. *Set Appropriate Performance Criteria:* All the informal assessment techniques we have discussed are criterion-referenced tests. A continuing issue with criterion-referenced tests is establishing appropriate criterion levels (see Chapter 4). It would be easier if we could settle this issue, but, alas, we cannot. We can, however, make a suggestion based on current practice. There is some agreement that an ability to perform a given task about 80 percent of the time represents minimum competence. We feel this is a reasonable standard; therefore, we recommend setting criterion levels in the 75–80 percent range with the caution to keep the arbitrariness of these figures in mind.

5. *Interpreting Results:* Whatever the type of assessments, the data are only as good as the person who interprets them. Take care in drawing inferences about learners' abilities; even more importantly, remember that discovering what learners *can* do is as important as finding out what they *cannot* do.

6. *Instructional Decision Making:* All the testing in the world makes no sense if no one pays any attention to the results. If a teacher goes to the trouble of developing and administering informal assessments, then that teacher must be prepared to modify instructional practices based on the results. Informal tests should be used as instruments that provide information about how one can adapt instruction so that learning is facilitated.

Evaluating
Textual Materials

6

In THE PRECEDING CHAPTERS, we discussed a variety of factors that can be barriers to learning from text. Chapters 4 and 5 focused on identifying learner deficiencies that impinge on the ability to learn from textual material. However, a number of factors in textual material can effectively bar learning. These factors are the focus of this chapter.

Text Readability

As noted briefly in Chapter 1, many factors interact to make textual material difficult. This has led to much controversy over the issue of readability. Ideally, we should be able to make a straightforward assessment of textual difficulty, but the number of contributing factors make this virtually impossible. Current readability indexes, then, do not consider all the factors and are, therefore, limited in many respects. However, readability indexes do provide an estimate of textual difficulty and can be sensibly used in the instructional decision-making processes.

Two characteristics of textual material considered in most readability formulas are word and sentence difficulty. Word length typically is the measure of word difficulty because longer words are usually more difficult to read and less frequent or less familiar than shorter words (Coleman, 1971; Carver, 1976). Sentence difficulty is usually estimated simply by establishing average sentence length.

Neither of these two procedures is wholly adequate. The conceptual difficulty of a word is not simply a reflection of its frequency. Less frequent words are generally less familiar and therefore create more difficulty in understanding meaning than more frequent words. However, the conceptual difficulty of a relatively frequent word like *own* can be quite high, and a less frequent word like *mongoose* can be conceptually quite simple. With these words, *own* and *mongoose*, note that the concept represented by the first is abstract, whereas that represented by the latter is concrete. Unfamiliar, concrete words or concepts are typically easier to learn than unfamiliar, abstract words or concepts. None of the commonly used readability indexes uses this variable to differentiate words as more or less difficult.

Many readability indexes simply use word length, usually assessed in terms of the number of syllables per word. Although word length does provide a fairly stable measure of word difficulty and frequency or familiarity, English is resplendent with single-syllable words that are conceptually very difficult. Several examples drawn from second-ary content area texts include: *mass, force, tax, sum, law, sphere, ohm,* and *bog*. Similarly, many polysyllabic words are neither wholly unfa-miliar nor conceptually difficult. Consider, for example, *elephant, America, Indian, arithmetic, temperatures, and triangle*.

A second limitation of using word length, and even word frequency, as an estimate of difficulty is the multiple meanings many words have, particularly in the technical vocabulary of a content area where a word with a common meaning may be used differently. Neither word-frequency tabulations nor familiarity ratings typically take this factor into account. The secondary-school student may be familiar with the most common meaning of a word but not the technical, or less com-mon, meaning of words like *run, bear, article, sap, current, charge*, or *stock*.

The second factor in most readability indexes is sentence difficulty which is assessed simply by sentence length. In general, longer sen-tences are more difficult to understand than shorter sentences. Again, however, other variables play a role in determining the difficulty of a sentence. Pearson (1975) demonstrated that, if one group of subjects is given two short sentences such as (1) and (2) in the following list and another group a single longer sentence presenting similar information such as (3), the group given sentence (3) finds the cause-and-effect relationship easier to extract:

(1) John watches television every night.
(2) His grades in school are poor.
(3) Because John watches television every night, his grades in school are poor.
(4) John watches television every night, and his grades in school are poor.

However, simply combining (1) and (2) as in (4) does not clarify the cause-and-effect relationship in (3), nor does it make (4) significantly more difficult than (1) and (2).

Therefore, the difficulty of a sentence is also affected by the content of the sentence. Short sentences about unfamiliar content are more difficult to extract meaning from than longer sentences about familiar content. This is in part, but not fully, accounted for by the word-difficulty variable. Consider the following sentences, which present several combinations of unfamiliar and familiar content and short and long sentences:

(5) The din was more than he could bear.
(6) The concepts that schemata represent are not restricted to concepts for which there are simple lexical items in the native language.
(7) The boy went home to see his father.
(8) One day after school John went to the grocery store and bought eggs, milk, butter, bacon, orange juice, and English muffins.

Most readers find (7) easier than (5) and (8) easier than (6), even though the pairs have the same number of words. In fact, (8) seems less difficult than (5) even though (8) has more than twice as many words. Both (5) and (7) are not only equivalent in length, but also have similar grammatical structures. The complexity of (5), however, stems not only from using an infrequent word *(din)* and less-common meaning of a frequent word *(bear),* but also because it uses the passive voice rather than the more frequently used active voice. Active sentences like (9), which follows, are typically more easily comprehended than the equivalent sentence in passive voice (Fraser, Bellugi, and Brown, 1963).

(9) The girl kissed John.
(10) John was kissed by the girl.

Sentences containing semantically complex or unfamiliar content can present difficulty, but syntactic complexity also exacts a powerful influence in the extraction of meaning from sentences.

Some researchers (Carver, 1976) have argued that sentence length is a fairly good indicator of syntactic complexity because, as the number of clauses increases, so do the number of words in the sentence. Again, as with semantic complexity, sentence length by itself does not always provide an accurate measure of syntactic complexity.

The Fry Graph

A primary problem facing the educational practitioner, especially the content area teacher, is estimating the readability of textual material. Although we are aware of many limitations to the current readability indexes, these do not render them totally useless. One of the most popular readability indexes is the recently revised **Fry graph** (Fry, 1977). This index of readability uses number of syllables as a measure of word length, or semantic complexity, and sentence length as the measure of syntactic complexity. Although the Fry graph suffers from the limitations discussed previously, it does provide the teacher with a relatively straightforward and uncomplicated means of predicting the difficulty of textual material.

THE FRY GRAPH FOR ESTIMATING READABILITY

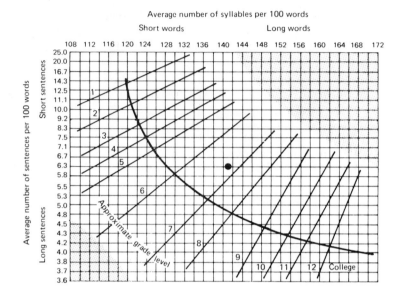

Directions:

Randomly select three 100-word passages from a book or an article. Plot average number of syllables and average number of sentences per 100 words on graph to determine the grade level of the material. Choose more passages per book if great variability is observed and conclude that the book has uneven readability. Few books will fall into the gray area, but when they do grade level scores are invalid.

Example:

	Syllables	Sentences
First hundred words	124	6.6
Second hundred words	141	5.5
Third hundred words	158	6.8
Average	141	6.3

Readability 7th grade (see dot plotted on graph)

Additional Directions for Working Readability Graph

1. Randomly select three sample passages and count exactly 100 words beginning with a beginning of a sentence. Don't count numbers. Do count proper nouns.
2. Count the number of sentences in the hundred words, estimating length of the fraction of the last sentence to the nearest 1/10th.
3. Count the total number of syllables in the 100-word passage. If

you don't have a hand counter available, an easy way is to simply put a mark above every syllable over one in each word, then, when you get to the end of the passage, count the number of marks and add 100.

4. Enter graph with average sentence length and number of syllables; plot dot where the two lines intersect. Area where dot is plotted will give you the approximate grade level.

5. If a great deal of variability is found, putting more sample counts into the average is desirable.

The Fry graph allows the user to place textual material on a graduated continuum from primary-grade to college level of difficulty. Basically, textual materials with short sentences composed primarily of single-syllable words are placed at the primary-grade level of difficulty and textual materials with longer sentences and polysyllabic words placed at higher levels on the graph.

Numerous other readability indexes are available for estimating the difficulty of secondary-school-level material, but most are either more time consuming to use or less reliable than the Fry graph. The Fry graph also correlates rather well with the estimates made by the more complicated and time-consuming readability indexes such as the **Dale-Chall formula** (Dale and Chall, 1947). Given the limitations of all readability indexes, and particularly the Fry graph, the teacher must keep in mind that the level of difficulty is only an *estimate.*

Several other considerations must be noted for the use of any readability index: First, the longer the samples of textual material from which the readability is estimated, the more reliable the results. Simply selecting more than a single 100-word sample increases the reliability, but selecting three 500-word samples produces a relatively reliable estimate of difficulty. The Fry graph, like many other procedures, can be used to estimate the difficulty of as long a sample as one wishes, even though the illustrations provided often employ 100-word samples for ease of computation. In addition to using longer samples of text, one can also increase the reliability by selecting from seven to ten samples of the textual material. As noted in Chapter 4, an element of error is associated with all measurement techniques; assessing readability is no different. Taking as many measures as feasible reduces this error and thereby increases reliability.

Teachers employing the Fry graph or any other readability index are usually surprised if different readability levels are obtained for different samples from the same textbook. Because differences of several grade levels are not uncommon, multiple samples are encouraged. In virtually every textbook, some sections will be more readable than others. Many teachers know this intuitively, based on the difficulty students seem to have with a particular chapter year in and year out. Whereas some textual materials, particularly anthologies, often contain selections of a difficulty level estimated to be several grade levels above the average learner's ability, other selections are placed several grade levels of difficulty below the average learner's ability. Much textual material, however, is written at a fairly constant level of difficulty. The difficulty level of the samples typically ranges ± 1 grade level; for instance, three samples may be rated eighth, ninth, and tenth grade levels for an average difficulty of ninth grade level.

Most readability indexes are developed in a manner similar to the norm-referenced test. Numerous materials from several grade levels are selected and, in the case of the Fry graph, examined for word and sentence length. The mean, or average, word and sentence length for textual material at each grade level is computed and charted. Validity is established by comparing the predicted difficulty level from the new index with that provided by established indexes. Although resulting ultimately in a grade-level designation of difficulty, this process does not necessarily result in difficulty levels directly comparable to reading-achievement test scores. In other words, readability indexes predict the difficulty level of material in terms of average difficulty of textual material used in particular grade levels. Norm-referenced tests, on the other hand, establish reading levels by assessing the average reading ability of students in particular grade levels. The comparability of these two products, then, rests on the assumption that the average text in a particular grade is of an appropriate level of difficulty for the average learner. A further difficulty is that the error of measurement associated with both readability indexes and reading achievement tests makes trying to match learners and materials simply on the basis of these two scores tenuous at best.

> Readability formulas are best thought of as guides or general indicators of a possible range of materials. . . . They are not absolute. If they are regarded as general indicators, they can be quite useful. . . . a teacher who regards the formulas as guides and who is aware of the experiences, interests, and aspirations of the various children in his/her charge almost automatically overcomes the . . . deficits of readability formulas. The various formulas cannot take interest and previous experience into consideration. But the teacher can—and should. (Standal, 1978)

Using readability indexes can be profitable for the secondary content area teacher, particularly when selecting textual materials for instructional use. Applying a readability index such as the Fry graph provides the teacher with a rough estimate of textual difficulty. If the material is rated several grade levels above the ability of the average student in the class, then the teacher must decide whether to include it. The same is true if the material is ranked several grade levels below the ability of the average student. Other considerations, such as desired content of instruction and the way the textual material is to be employed, all must come into play here. Textual material should not be automatically rejected because the readability level appears to be above student ability; but the teacher must be aware of this factor and plan instructional strategies that will circumvent or alleviate the difficulties fostered by presenting difficult textual material.

Constructing a Cloze Passage

1. Select a sample of written text about 250 words in length from the assigned textual material.
2. Begin with the first sentence in a paragraph.
3. Leave this first sentence intact—that is, delete no words.
4. Beginning with the first word in the second sentence, delete every fifth word.
5. The blanks for deletions should be of equal length and large enough for written responses.
6. Continue deleting every fifth word until you have fifty blanks.
7. Leave the remainder of the sentence containing the fiftieth deletion intact.

The Cloze Procedure

The cloze procedure (Taylor, 1953; Bormuth, 1963), which was mentioned briefly in Chapter 5, is another technique for determining readability of textual material. This technique is quite different from the other readability indexes discussed so far. In the cloze technique one simply deletes every fifth word from textual material, replacing the deletion with a standard-length blank. This material, with the deletions, is then presented to the student, who completes the task by attempting to fill in each blank with the deleted word. The ability to provide the deleted word is claimed to assess the learner's ability to comprehend the material (Bormuth, 1975).

The cloze, then, might be considered a "personalized" measure of readability. It assesses each individual learner's ability to comprehend a particular section of text. Unlike other readability indexes, which offer grade-level designations of difficulty, the cloze procedure attempts to predict whether a given learner will be able to extract meaning from a specific text.

More subtle and, consequently, more difficult to teach and learn is the internal organization of material. Authors generally follow some _____ structure as they write. _____ writers evidence little organization _____ that, in itself, is _____ type of structure which _____ be discerned by students _____ to look for such _____.

Several authors concerned with _____ and study skills have _____ organizational structures characteristic of _____ material. Though there is _____ a common agreement on _____ which are of greatest _____, the following appear with _____ in text materials used _____ content classes: cause/effect; _____/contrast; time order; enumerative _____. "Main idea" also is _____ by these sources as _____ organizational pattern. True, it _____ a pattern—but it _____ of a different magnitude _____ the others. Its construct _____ so broad that it _____ each of the other _____. For example, a _____ might be the "main idea" _____ a paragraph and the _____, the "details," or a _____ might be the "main _____" and contrasts, the "details," _____ a stated objective might _____ the "main idea" and _____ enumeration of steps leading _____ that objective, the "detail;" _____ so on. There are _____, however, when the relationship _____ the statement of the _____ topic, or "main idea" _____ supporting information, "detail," does _____ subsume one of these _____ basic patterns. In such _____, the broader label, "main _____/detail," is applied.

It _____ helpful, at this juncture, _____ recall the interpretive level _____ comprehension. Reading at _____ level, the student searches _____ relationships within the text _____ as to form "intrinsic _____."

Source: Harold L. Herber, *Teaching Reading in Content Areas*, © 1970, p. 271. Reprinted by permission of Prentice-Hall, Inc., Englewood Cliffs, New Jersey.

In order to meet the criteria established for readable material, a learner must supply between 35 and 60 percent of the exact words deleted. Achieving a score in this range means that the material "fits" the learners and should be appropriate for instruction. Scores above 60 percent of the exact words usually indicate that the learner will not gain much new information from the selection. Scores below 35 percent indicate that the material is too difficult for the learner and, hence, should not be used (Bormuth, 1975). These levels were established by correlating scores on cloze tests (Bormuth, 1969) with more traditional comprehension-assessment procedures. This strategy has led to the criticism that, to accept the cloze procedure, one must accept the assumptions of the traditional assessment of reading comprehension. These assumptions, as noted in earlier chapters, have been vigorously challenged, primarily on the grounds that, although traditional comprehension assessments measure something, they do not adequately tap the ability to learn from text. However, because cloze tests have been quite highly correlated with traditional comprehension assessments, a number of educators have suggested substituting cloze test as comprehension assessments because they are easier to construct and provide a more "personal" predictive index (Bormuth, 1969; Jenkinson, 1957; Rankin, 1965).

SCORING AND INTERPRETING A CLOZE PASSAGE

1. Scoring is facilitated if students have transferred words from the blanks to a separate sheet of paper.
2. Score only exact word replacements as correct.
3. Compute the percentage of correct responses. If a standard fifty-deletion selection is used, then simply multiplying the number of correct responses by two provides this percentage.
4. Arrange students by scores into the following four groups:

   - 60 percent or above correct—text is predicted to be quite easy.
   - 35– 59 percent correct—text is predicted to be of appropriate difficulty.
   - 20– 34 percent correct—text is predicted to be very difficult.
   - 0– 19 percent correct—text is predicted to be inappropriate, far too difficult.

5. Begin to plan instructional differentiation based on results.

Note: If at all possible, at least three cloze passages should be constructed and administered from a text, with the results averaged across all passages for placement into groups. As noted in Chapter 4, several measures are more reliable than a single measure. With the cloze procedure the same is true—using three passages reduces the risk of drawing an unrepresentative sample from the text—one that is either too difficult or too easy.

A primary battle line was then drawn between (1) those who felt that the concept of readability was primarily one of estimating structural aspects of textual difficulty disregarding idiosyncratic learner abilities, and (2) those who used readability in the sense of "comprehensibility" for individuals. Those holding the latter view saw the cloze procedure as a better tool for estimating whether a particular learner would be able to learn from a given text. Critics soon pointed out that one could often fill in an acceptable percentage of cloze deletions without being able to generate a main idea or theme for a selection. Carroll (1972) reported that subjects could sometimes produce adequate cloze scores on textual material that was syntactically correct but meaningless. Others argued that, although the cloze procedure seemed to test one's ability to deal with the language of a passage, it was sensitive only to intrasentence constraints and did not tap understanding of longer textual units such as paragraphs or stories (Horton, 1975; Tuinmain, Blanton, Gray, 1975). Other efforts (Fleming, Ohnmacht, and Niles, 1974) demonstrated that cloze performance was affected by the types of sentences encountered (such as active versus passive), and that preceding context seemed a more powerful information source than the information following the deletion. Ramanauskas (1972) was able to demonstrate that the cloze procedure was, in fact, sensitive to between-sentence context, though no claim was made that the cloze procedure tapped understanding of story themes or textual relationships. Filling in cloze deletions, then, seems to be a measure of a learner's ability to deal with the language structure of the textual material or to deal with the redundancy in written language. The fact that learners can often achieve an acceptable cloze score without truly understanding the textual material does not invalidate its utility as a predictor of a learner's ability to learn from that material. Rather, such performances suggest that learners can effectively deal with the structure of the material and can learn if presented the material with no deletions.

Some have argued that the cloze procedure really does not tap comprehension. Fill in as many blanks as you can in the following passage and then go to the text following it.

> The procedure is actually quite simple. First you arrange _____ different groups. Of course _____ pile may be sufficient _____ on how much there _____ to do. If you _____ to go somewhere else _____ to lack of facilities, _____ is the next step, _____ you are pretty well _____. It is important not _____ overdo things. That is, _____ is better to do _____ few things at once _____ too many.

Most adults can easily fill in half the blanks with the exact word used in the original of this passage. It could be argued, though, as the authors (Carpenter and Just, 1976) of this selection did, that, even if the original passage, without deletions, is read, the reader often cannot identify the routine activity being described. Readers can answer questions such as (1) or (2) but not (3). Thus the cloze seems to be a good predictor of whether or not a person can read a text, but achieving the cloze criterion does not ensure the learner truly comprehends the content.

(1) What do you do first?
(2) Is it better to do a few things than too many?
(3) What is this passage about? (see below).

Answer: The topic is "washing clothes."

Although we have presented a number of concerns about the cloze procedure, we see it as a very useful tool, if used appropriately, by content area teachers. If one wishes to estimate how effectively the students in a class can deal with assigned textual material, constructing a cloze assessment is both efficient and effective for the purpose.

Several considerations in developing and administering cloze procedures can ensure better use of this instrument. A first consideration is the typicality of the sample of textual material supplied to the learners in the cloze format. Just as with estimating readability from one of the formulas, the teacher must be concerned that the sample is representative of the whole text. In most cases the easiest way to ensure this is to select a number of passages randomly from the text, prepare each in a cloze format, and administer these to a single group of students. From these cloze passages, the teacher would select two passages on which the learners' scores were near the average score for all the samples. For example, if a biology instructor selected four samples at random from the assigned biology text, administered these in a cloze format, scored the tests, and then computed the average, the results might look similar to the following examples:

Sample	Pages	Average Score	Percent
1	17	33	66
2	178–79	22	44
3	381	12	24
4	444–45	18	36

The results indicate a general trend for the text to be more difficult toward the end. Because samples 2 and 4 are most representative of average textual difficulty, the teacher then should employ these two samples to estimate the difficulty other classes of students will have with the text. The first sample is quite easy; perhaps it was written as a general introduction to the text, with few concepts introduced in a rather straightforward writing style. Using this sample would under-estimate the number of learners who would experience difficulty with this text. On the other hand, sample 3 is the most difficult, with the average score quite a bit below the generally accepted cut-off score of 35. It may be that the author introduced a number of previously unknown concepts and employed not only a significant number of unfamiliar words but also fairly complex grammatical constructions. In any event, using this sample alone would overestimate the general level of difficulty most learners would experience with this text.

Differences in cloze performances on samples from a single text will often vary as widely as the previous example because it is virtually impossible to write material at a consistent level of difficulty. Even considering only sentence length and word length as in common read-ability formulas, predicted difficulty levels vary. Cloze scores will vary even if the materials have equivalent difficulty levels based on read-ability formulas, because the cloze procedure is more sensitive to indi-vidual abilities with the written language structure and the content. Using four sample passages is an attempt to ensure that the cloze tests constructed are indeed representative of the textual material. In our example, samples 2 and 4 are fairly representative of average textual difficulty, but if the teacher had selected a single sample, there would have been a 50 percent chance of selecting a sample from the text that would have either over- or underestimated average textual difficulty. However, it must be noted that sometimes the average scores are all above the suggested cut-off points, at say 70 percent or better, which indicates that the textual material is in general quite easy for the learners. At other times the average scores will all be below the cutoff, suggesting the textual material is too difficult for the majority of stu-dents. Using a number of samples is an attempt to ensure general-izability for future uses of the selected samples in the cloze format—not to find passages that are of appropriate levels of difficulty given learner abilities.

Simplifying Administration of the Cloze Procedure.   Several con-siderations can ease the administration of cloze-format assessments:

1. Prepare students for such assessments by introducing the general format of the cloze procedure and presenting a brief lesson on how one might go about filling in the blanks.
2. Assure students that this is not an achievement test and grades will not be based on performance; in fact, try to avoid using the words *cloze test* by substituting *cloze procedure.*
3. Show students how *following* context can be used to fill in some blanks.

4. Indicate that no one can ever fill in all the blanks correctly and that filling in at least half the blanks with the correct word is a good performance.
5. Assure students that exact spelling is not necessary for an item to be scored as correct.

These considerations will go a long way toward lessening the level of anxiety that can often accompany the evaluation of textual material in a cloze format.

Scoring learner performance on cloze passages is quite simple—the teacher scores only exact word replacement as correct. This is done because it is the technique used to establish the suggested cut-off points. Scoring synonym replacement as incorrect may seem unfair; but had synonyms not been scored as incorrect during the establishing of the cut-off scores, they would undoubtedly have been higher. Another problem with synonyms is that it is hard to get scorers to agree on what is an acceptable synonym. For a variety of reasons, then, only exact word replacement can be considered correct.

To facilitate scoring, the teacher can prepare an answer sheet for the learner to transfer responses to, as in the following example. This eases scoring, but learners should be encouraged to jot answers directly onto the cloze passage first and then transfer responses to the answer sheet. This allows the learner to reread sections with deletions filled in.

1._____
2._____
3._____

    .

    .

    .

    .

50._____

The cloze procedure allows the teacher to estimate quite accurately the difficulty students will experience in learning from a particular text. Constructing cloze passages is as easily accomplished as scoring them. These advantages make the instrument an unusually efficient and effective technique for practical application in content area classes. Although the cloze procedure may not truly tap students' full understanding of the content of textual material, it does appear to be an effective predictor of their ability to learn from a particular text.

So far we have only considered evaluating the difficulty of textual material from the standpoint of readability, albeit readability formulas and the cloze procedure define this concept somewhat differently. However, other features of textual material contribute to the learner's ability to learn from text. These are considered briefly in the following section.

Structural Features of Text

Although content and the prose style used to communicate content are the most important facets of text suitability, several other aspects should also be taken into account. Among these other aspects are the structural features of textual material, particularly typographical clues. These features can facilitate learning from text by assisting in identifying both major concepts and the overall organization of the content.

Probably the most common typographical feature is boldface print, which is larger and darker than the standard type used. These boldface headings cue the reader to the topic at hand by presenting a statement of the main idea developed in a particular segment of the text. In many cases the boldface headings alone provide an outline, or summary, of the material presented. These headings can aid the learner in several ways: (1) as a means of previewing material prior to study, (2) as a guide for review, or (3) to expedite a search for specific information.

Italicized type is another common typographical feature in textual material. Whereas boldface type is used primarily as an organizational key, italics are often employed to highlight important concepts or information within the text or to cue the reader to the introduction of a new word or phrase. In most content area textbooks, key vocabulary is italicized when it is initially presented. By simply attending to such typographical cueing, the learner should be able to immediately sort the important information from the mundane. Quotation marks are used in some texts in lieu of italics, but they perform generally the same function.

Let us see what our model looks like now. If an object has the same number of electrons and protons, then the amount of negative electric charge would be equal to the amount of positive electric charge. We say such an object is **electrically neutral**. It has **zero electric charge**.

Neutral atoms or molecules have zero electric charge. They have *equal numbers of electrons and protons*. The following examples will illustrate this point.

Some recent texts have also begun to employ adjunct questions or comments either as marginal glosses or as questions at the beginning of a chapter. For many years teacher editions of textbooks provided similar information to guide the teacher in identifying important segments of text or as an aid for developing pre- or post-reading questions to be presented to the learners. This practice always struck us as a bit odd, because one would assume that the teacher should have less difficulty with the textual material than the learners; but the teacher was the only one provided with this type of organizational assistance. These cues can facilitate learning from textual material by actively engaging the learner in an evaluating frame of mind. We will present more about such strategies in Chapters 9 and 10.

What functions does dating serve in modern society?

When and how are marital selection norms applied in the United States?

How can we account for this statement made frequently to husbands and wives: "You look enough alike to be brother and sister!"?

What are the forces that lead a man and a woman mutually to commit themselves to marriage?

The purpose of these various structural or typographical features of text may seem obvious to the content area teacher. Unfortunately, their purpose and utility is too often unknown to students. By presenting instruction on the use of these features, the teacher can provide students with useful strategies for enhancing learning from text.

Although boldface headings, subheadings, and italicized type can key the reader to organizational patterns and ease locating specific information, there are two other features commonly found in textbooks that facilitate organization or location of information:

1. *Table of contents.* A brief perusal of the table of contents can provide an overview of the text's content and organizational pattern. Though not particularly useful for locating specific information, a discussion of this feature can provide information on locating a general topic.
2. *Index.* Although it is useful for locating specific information, an index typically provides no help in identifying the organizational pattern of the text. Several types of indexes are available; those most commonly found in content area texts are subject index, name index, map index, and in some social studies texts, an annual chronological index. The content area teacher should not assume that learners are aware of these features, much less that

they can use them. Of final note is the structure of indexes: Typically, only the major topics in indexes are organized alphabetically; to find subordinate topics, the learner has to have a script, or schema. Many indexes also consolidate subject, name, map, and illustration indexes into a single index. Point out special features such as these to learners (that is, show them the abbreviations indicating the presence of a map *(m.)* or illustration *(il.).*

In summary, an evaluation of textual material should include an assessment of the utility of its typographical features. In other words, does the material appropriately use such devices to identify key concepts, new vocabulary, main topics, or important questions?

Illustration in Text

Another feature of textual material to consider in an evaluation is the presence and quality of the various types of illustration. There are two primary functions of illustrations: (1) to impart information and (2) to create a more interesting visual appearance. A high-quality text uses illustrations that accomplish both simultaneously.

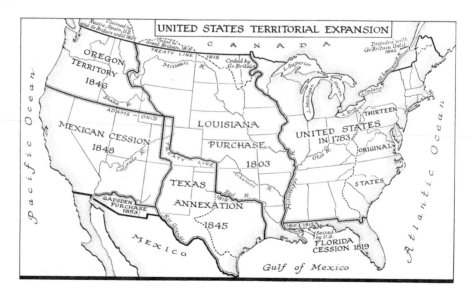

Four illustrative cues are commonly used: maps, pictures, figures, and tables. Each is employed to communicate a different type of information. Maps appear in content area texts of all types. They can be used to depict geographical, geological, economic, sociological, and so forth, information that enhances or clarifies similar information in the text. At the simplest level, maps are an economical method of presenting physical information about a geographical entity. Imagine trying to communicate even the shape of the state of Texas through written information. At more advanced levels, maps can be used to communicate much more complex types of information, but to do this the learner must be able to understand the information presented. In an evaluation of textual material, the teacher should consider whether maps are included where appropriate and whether these will serve to enhance learning from the text.

Pictures, whether photographs, full-color art, or line drawings, serve primarily to present information that is difficult to represent in written words. Consider, for instance, the difficulty of attempting to describe a brontosaurus, a fez, or an octagon in words alone. A picture can often truly "be worth a thousand words." Pictures can serve to communicate an event, an emotion, an object, or an interaction. The value of pictures lies primarily in developing an understanding of concrete objects—abstract concepts cannot usually be represented in pictures, although emotions may appear on the faces of those pictured. Again, to be useful, pictures, regardless of type, must be relevant to the content. Pictures must also clearly and accurately represent the content; blurred, ill-focused, poorly designed pictures will add little to the communication of content. Thus the teacher should evaluate pictures in text on the basis of appropriateness and clarity.

Figures are represented by graphs, diagrams, and charts. The primary purpose of these illustrative cues is to communicate information efficiently and to demonstrate the relationship between two variables.

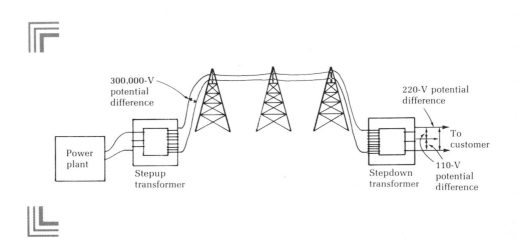

Bar graphs, circle graphs, line graphs, scattergrams, and so forth, all attempt to depict large amounts of data in a small space. As with pictures, the well-designed figure can enhance learning from textual material by graphically displaying important data illustrating selected trends or relationships the author wishes to highlight.

Diagrams generally are employed to graphically illustrate the steps in a process, the components of an object, or the subsystems of a larger system. A diagram might be used to identify the components of a cell or to illustrate social stratification. As with figures, diagrams serve to reduce the verbal description to a minimum, relying instead on simplified graphic representation. As with other types of illustrative cues,

ASSESSING STUDENT ABILITIES IN INTERPRETING FIGURES, GRAPHS, TABLES, CHARTS, AND MAPS.

Although many content area texts include a variety of nontext sources of information (for example, maps, charts, tables, and so forth), students may not have the abilities necessary to correctly interpret information presented in such devices. The teacher, then, should assess whether students are able to use these sources of information. Such assessments can be relatively straightforward, as in the following:

1. Select a figure, graph, table, chart, or map typical of those present in the assigned textual material.
2. Identify several bits of information contained in the figure, graph, and so forth, and develop questions requiring the students to identify this information. These questions can be either open ended or multiple choice as illustrated below the accompanying figure.
3. Present the students with copies of the figure, graph, and so forth, and the question(s) requiring extraction of the information.
4. Students who cannot extract the desired information will need instruction in interpreting such information sources.

Number of Automobile Tires Produced by ACME Tire Company

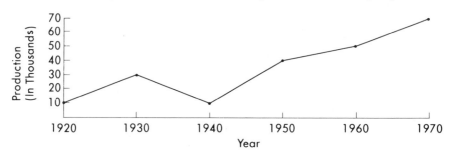

a. In what year did ACME first produce more than 50,000 tires? _____

b. In which decade did tire production decrease?
    1. 1920 – 30
    2. 1930 – 40
    3. 1940 – 50
    4. 1950 – 60
    5. 1960 – 70

diagrams within text should be evaluated in terms of their appropriateness and clarity of communication—in other words, whether they effectively facilitate learning from text.

The final illustrative cue, tables, simply present a wealth of numerical information in a single unit. Tables are useful in this regard, but it is often difficult to derive any understanding from them. Consider the

WHAT AUTO LOANS COST

The table below shows the monthly payment and total interest cost of auto loans at annual percentage rates of 9 to 14 percent and loan durations of one to four years.

Annual Percentage Rate	Loan amount	1 YEAR		2 YEARS		3 YEARS		4 YEARS	
		Monthly payment	Total interest	Monthly payment	Total interest	Monthly payment	Total interest	Monthly payment	Total interest
9%	$3000	$262	$148	$137	$289	$ 95	$ 434	$ 75	$ 584
	4000	350	198	183	386	127	579	100	778
	5000	437	247	228	482	159	724	124	973
	6000	525	297	274	579	191	869	149	1167
10%	3000	264	165	138	323	97	485	76	652
	4000	352	220	185	430	129	647	101	870
	5000	440	275	231	538	161	808	127	1087
	6000	528	330	277	645	194	970	152	1305
11%	3000	265	182	140	356	98	536	78	722
	4000	354	242	186	475	131	715	103	963
	5000	442	303	233	593	164	893	129	1203
	6000	530	363	280	712	196	1072	155	1444
12%	3000	267	199	141	390	100	587	79	792
	4000	355	265	188	519	133	783	105	1056
	5000	444	331	235	649	166	979	132	1320
	6000	533	397	282	779	199	1174	158	1584
13%	3000	268	216	143	423	101	639	80	864
	4000	357	287	190	564	135	852	107	1151
	5000	447	359	238	705	168	1065	134	1439
	6000	536	431	285	846	202	1278	161	1727
14%	3000	269	232	144	457	103	691	82	935
	4000	359	310	192	609	137	922	109	1247
	5000	449	387	240	762	171	1152	137	1559
	6000	539	465	288	914	205	1383	164	1870

Note: Dollar figures are rounded off to the nearest dollar.

tables often found in educational research articles. For most readers the information presented does not truly facilitate learning from the textual material. The tabled information does allow other researchers to analyze or reanalyze the data, or to evaluate the strength of the author's conclusions; but in general, tables do not seem to add to an understanding of text. They do provide an easy-to-locate source of specific information, which is their primary virtue.

In general, then, the various illustrative cues can serve to enhance learning from text. The content area teacher should consider these when evaluating the difficulty or appropriateness of textual material. Illustrations can also serve a second purpose—providing a more interesting visual appearance. Textual material that has made effective use of illustrations facilitates learning.

Summary

1. "Readability" of textual material can be defined in one of two ways: (a) The structural definition emphasizes the difficulty of one compared to another, commonly comparing variables such as word difficulty, syntax, and so forth. (b) The other definition focuses more on "comprehensibility" and strives to predict whether a given material will be comprehended by a particular learner.
2. Word length and sentence length are the two most commonly measured variables in readability indexes such as the Fry graph.
3. Readability indexes such as the Fry graph can provide a rough estimate of the difficulty of a text, but accurate judgments about appropriateness of textual material for individual learners are hazardous.
4. The cloze procedure attempts to predict whether an individual will understand a particular text. Although providing a more accurate estimate of this than other readability indexes, the cloze procedure still provides only an estimate.
5. Regardless of which method one selects to estimate text difficulty, the validity and reliability of the information increases as the number of samples of textual material increases.
6. Typographical cues such as headings, italics, and boldface type can facilitate learning from textual material by drawing learner attention to new information or by providing organizational assistance.
7. Illustrative cues such as pictures, figures, and maps can facilitate learning from textual material by communicating features of objects, concepts, or data that do not lend themselves to written description.

Goals and Plans for Teaching and Learning

C<small>ONTENT</small> <small>AREA</small> <small>TEACHING</small> is typically purposeful, as opposed to incidental. For this purposeful teaching to occur, however, instruction must focus on clearly established goals—goals that go beyond the vague generalities and professional-sounding platitudes too often associated with education. These goals must reflect the dual role of the content area teacher; (1) to identify the concepts, processes, functions, and relationships relevant to the content area; (2) to ensure that the content area lesson not only produces content-relevant learning but also provides the learner with generalizable skills and strategies for learning from text. We will not go so far as to advocate goals that meet strict behavioral criteria; but, for a variety of reasons, the teacher must know what to teach and how it is best learned.

Alice:	Where I come from, people study what they are *not* good at in order to be able to do what they *are* good at.
Mad Hatter:	We only go around in circles in Wonderland; but we always end up where we started. Would you mind explaining yourself?
Alice:	Well, grown-ups tell us to find out what we did wrong, and never do it again.
Mad Hatter:	That's odd! It seems to me that in order to find out about something you have to study it. And when you study it, you should become better at it. Why should you want to become better at something and then never do it again? But please continue.
Alice:	Nobody ever tells us to study the right things we do. We're only supposed to learn from the wrong things. But we are permitted to study the right things *other* people do. And sometimes we're even told to copy them.

121

> *Mad Hatter:*   That's cheating!
>
> *Alice:*   You're quite right, Mr. Hatter. I do live in a topsy-turvy world. It seems like I have to do something wrong first, in order to learn from that what not to do. And then, by not doing what I'm not supposed to do, perhaps I'll be right. But I'd rather be right the first time, wouldn't you?
>
> Source: Lewis Carroll, *Alice in Wonderland*. (Italics added.)

The nature of conceptual learning is a tremendously complicated topic and will be dealt with in Chapter 8. This chapter focuses on identifying what is to be taught and learned and how various aspects of instruction and instructional texts can enhance or impede learning.

The Dual Role of the Content Area Teacher

If we attempt to define education in general, we typically depict a process that results in the acquisition of knowledge and/or competence for the participants. Although one may learn many things incidentally, the generally agreed-upon objective of schooling is to provide planned, or purposeful, educational environments for the acquisition of knowledge. Thus, content area teachers do not begin an instructional episode without planned educational experiences, goals, and outcomes in mind. However, they do have varying expectations of what is to be learned.

Consider these five points about the nature of the human brain and individual learning:

1. The brain was long thought to be passive, a tabula rasa, a blank on which instruction could be inscribed. This notion gave rise to the structure we try to employ—of subjects, courses, and curriculum—all expressions of the belief that if X and Y are taught, X and Y will be learned. Mountains of evidence tell us that doesn't happen. Now we can see more clearly why: the human brain is intensely *aggressive*. Each brain is highly individual, unique; it seeks out, demands, and will accept only what *it* needs next to "make sense" of surrounding reality, as *it* perceives reality. This fact means that group instruction in an elementary subject is certain to fail: it is grossly brain incompatible.

2. The brain is now seen to be by no means the stimulus-response device presented in various behaviorist theories. We now know beyond question that it is elaborately "gated." That is, it will

admit only those inputs it decides to admit, and each brain processes what it does admit in its own individual way. . . . *The
processing depends little on what or how the teacher has presented,
and greatly on the total, previous, stored experience in that particular
brain.* Thus the standard presentation, lecture, recitation, and
discussion that take up most of the instructional time in
classrooms cannot be expected to produce learning in any reliable way.

3. The neocortex, the newest part of the brain and in humans
   nearly five-sixths of the whole, does not function well under
   pressure, or what is called "threat". . . . When students see
   classroom activities as threatening, the learning that should
   occur in the neocortex is inhibited.

4. Young students in particular must *talk* to learn well and rapidly,
   for a great portion of the human brain is devoted to language—
   particularly the neocortex. Yet in most classrooms *teachers* talk
   constantly and the students are told not to.

5. We are obsessed by "logic," usually meaning by that term tight,
   step-by-step, ordered sequential (linear) effort in verbal or symbolic form. Educators try to make the curriculum, the schedule,
   and teaching "logical." But the human brain has little use for
   logic of this kind. It is a computer of incredible power and sub-
   tlety, but far more analog than digital. It works not by precision
   but probabilistically by great numbers of often rough or even
   vague approximations.

Source: L. A. Hart, "The New 'Brain' Concept of Learning," *Phi Delta Kappa,* February, 1978,
50, 393–396. (Italics added.) (See also *How the Brain Works,* © 1975 by Basic Books, New
York.)

From our point of view, content area teaching involves developing
two types of educational goals. The first and most generally agreed
upon can be considered **content area goals.** These goals include
learner acquisition of knowledge and competence specific to any
given discipline. For instance, typical content-specific goals include:
purposefully attempting to lead learners (1) to acquire an understanding of the technical vocabulary of a discipline; (2) to develop skill in
the use of a tool or instrument, say in mechanical drawing or home
economics; (3) to attain a set of conceptual relations; or (4) to memorize specific information. The importance of these types of goals gen-
erates little dispute among content area teachers, although disagree-
ment may exist on which content-specific goals are appropriate for any
particular group of learners.

A second general category of goals necessary for content area
instruction, a set too often overlooked or at least too infrequently ac-
knowledged, consists of **process goals.** These are goals that identify

the types of learning strategies to be developed. Another way of looking at them is to acknowledge that the purpose of education is not only the acquisition of specific knowledges and competencies but also the acquisition of a set of processes, or strategies, for enhancing independent learning. In other words, an important facet of education is learning *how* to learn.

Process goals, then, are designed to facilitate the acquisition of particular learning strategies. From the content-specific goals, the teacher identifies what learning strategies are most appropriate for attaining the desired product, the content-specific knowledge and competence. Rather than leaving it to the learner to identify and discover the appropriate strategy, the teacher makes a purposeful attempt to develop the appropriate learning strategy in the learner. The content-specific goals are not the sole determinant of the process goals, however; characteristics of both the textual material and the learners can contribute to the decision about which process goals are appropriate for a given teaching situation.

The Interaction of Goals, Plans, and Learning

Unfortunately, one cannot design a perfect model of teaching or learning. The complexity derives from the tremendous number of variables that affect both teaching and learning and from the fact that these variables interact or influence one another. In an attempt to sort out some of the most important features of the teaching-learning act, we have decided to focus on goals, plans, and learning.

Goals, which may be explicit in varying degrees, are the desired result of teaching. **Plans** are the teaching acts and materials chosen to facilitate reaching the goals. **Learning** is the intended final outcome, mediated by plans from goals.

All content area teachers must have goals for their instruction; they must intend that something be learned as a result of their teaching. These goals, however, are not always explicit or objective. That some goals are not well defined is defensible, but it is indefensible not to have any goals for instruction. This is not to say that the teacher must necessarily state goals in a strict behavioristic sense (Mager, 1962) or even to suggest that behavioristically stated goals are more desirable than other explicit statements of instructional goals. However, to teach effectively and to assess the impact of teaching effectively, the teacher must identify what is to be learned.

A useful analogy is a journey. If one leaves on a journey with no destination in mind, it will be difficult to say when the journey is over. On the other hand, stating the goal or final destination makes it much easier to identify the end of the journey. Specifying the final destination does not limit us to a single route to that goal. This is where plans come in. If it is our intention to arrive at the destination as soon as possible, then we have defined a second facet of our goal and thereby limited our plans accordingly. However, if we have an indefinite period of time to reach our destination, we would have available a number of routes with several modes of transportation. In any event, we would still know when we had reached our goal or final destination. Our initial evaluation of the journey would consist of determining whether we had reached our goal. But it would also go beyond that to evaluate other aspects of the journey, such as the reliability and comfort of the chosen mode of transportation. So it is with teaching. Setting goals does not necessarily limit the teacher to a single plan. Like the traveler, the teacher can decide whether the journey to the goal is to be the most efficient, the most enjoyable, the most memorable, the most difficult, and so forth.

A small book entitled *Preparing Instructional Objectives,* by Robert Mager (Palo Alto: Fearon, 1962) had a tremendous impact on the educational community. In his book, Mager delineated the components of measurable instructional objectives and advised all teachers to rework their objectives into his format. Thousands of teachers have been trained in his approach, but gradually, attention to preparing objectives along Mager's lines has decreased. We are not so interested in measurable objectives from a psychometric standpoint as we are interested in clear goals that provide a clear direction for teaching and learning. In Mager's defense, however, we must note that he neither condoned nor suggested that we attempt to fractionate the learning act as completely as some have done. The following are sample objectives drawn from Mager's book:

    (a) The student must *be able to correctly* solve *at least seven* simple linear equations *within a period of thirty minutes.* (We would simply eliminate all underlined elements which seem either redundant or excessively specific for goals.)

    (b) The student must *be able to* write *three* examples of the logical fallacy of the undistributed middle.

    (c) Given a list of 35 chemical elements, the student must *be able to recall* and write the valences of at least 30.

    Goals for instruction vary, depending largely on learner characteristics. This has been a topic of much recent debate (Rosenthal and Jacobson, 1968; Brophy and Good, 1970) because teachers' perceptions of learner characteristics, in some instances, have been viewed as prejudicial. However, this "teacher expectancy" effect operates in a number of seemingly appropriate ways as well as in some possibly detrimental ways. For instance, teachers respond to age–developmental level differences, expecting fewer higher-order cognitive abilities from younger learners (such as grade three) than from older learners (such as grade eleven). This is not seen as detrimental but rather as excellent professional judgment. On the other hand, some have argued that teachers also generate differential goals based on social class, perceived intellectual deficiencies, race, sex, and other factors. These lowered expectations create a discriminatory educational environment in which some learners are penalized because of either lack of instruction or different instruction based on goals generated from factors unrelated to the "teachability," or learning ability, of the learners (Rist, 1970). The dilemma here is that individualizing the instruction can indeed become discriminatory if the teacher develops differential goals based on learner characteristics unrelated to learning ability. However, given the range of human abilities, it is also discriminatory to assume one set of goals is appropriate for all learners.

Many content teachers reject the teaching of vocabulary because they associate the process with teaching general vocabulary, a task they rightfully attribute to the English teacher. They say, "I'm a science (or history, or math) teacher, not an English teacher. My job is to teach science, not vocabulary." When shown a list of technical words for a unit of study in their subject and asked if students should know those words, the reply is, "Most certainly. That's the unit! But it's not vocabulary—it's my subject!"

Source: Harold L. Herber, *Teaching Reading in Content Areas,* © 1970, p. 153. Reprinted by permission of Prentice-Hall, Englewood Cliffs, New Jersey.

When setting goals for instruction, then, the content area teacher should be sensitive to learner characteristics such as age-developmental level, prerequisite abilities, learning rate, and so forth, but should exercise restraint in the inferences drawn from stereotypes based on factors such as social class or race. Later in this chapter we will present some strategies for identifying both content-specific and process goals for instruction. Our point here is to forewarn—goals for instruction are rooted in a maze of factors the teacher carries in his or her head.

As noted in our earlier analogy of a journey, setting goals does not necessarily provide us with a plan. The teacher must first select the goals for instruction and then consider the alternative plans available for attaining those goals. Here again, however, we stumble across several important possible interactions. For instance, although setting a goal does not delineate our plan, it can severely restrict the types of plans to be implemented. Given a geography class, the teacher might choose as a goal memorizing the names of the states and their capitals (though one could, and should, wonder why). This goal then serves to eliminate numerous plans that might focus on developing an understanding of the interdependence of the states in terms of energy, natural resources, economics, transportation, and so forth. The goal, however, does not limit the teacher to plans that will ultimately fulfill the goal. Thus, the teacher could use simple choral recitation repeatedly, flash cards, unlabeled maps, lists, a fancy audiovisual presentation, a programmed text, a cassette with script, team competition, self-study, or any number of formats or plans to reach the goal. Whatever plan is selected, the teacher will be able to assess the success of the plan because the goal was clear. The point is, goals and plans do interact, they do not operate completely independently of one another.

The discussion to this point has focused primarily on content-specific goals and the alternative plans one might use to facilitate their attainment. The process goals are similarly influenced by many of the same factors. For instance, taking our previous example of a goal (learning states and capitals), we can readily determine that a number of process goals are eliminated from consideration by the very task demands required for the content-specific goal. Because the primary process involved is simple memorization, an appropriate process goal would be developing a strategy in learners to ease memorization, say a mnemonic, or imagery, strategy, or something of that kind. Setting the identification of geographical similarities in state capitals as a process goal would be inappropriate because memory is all that is required to reach the content-specific goal. The primary point is simply that the content area must have congruent content-specific and process goals. Furthermore, the plans selected for attaining both sets of goals must also be congruent, for efficient learning to take place.

The design of instruction is the crucial aspect of content area teaching. Gagne and Briggs (1974) list the following steps as the core of instructional design:

1. State and inform the learner of the objective of the lesson.
2. Stimulate recall of related existing knowledge.
3. Guide learning
4. Provide verbal definition.
5. Provide a variety of examples.
6. Present problem and elicit performance.
7. Provide feedback.
8. Assess attainment of objective.

A matter of final concern is the learner's goal, or at least the learner's impression of the teacher's goal. Because the learner is the third major component of teacher-text-learning interactions, the teacher must be concerned with what goals the learner sets or selects as a guide. If learner goals match teacher goals, learning is facilitated—at least learning the desired knowledge and competence. Probably the single most effective means of meshing these goals is for the teacher to be quite explicit in explaining the goals that have been set and the plan selected to facilitate such attainment. Learners who do well at "psyching out" the teacher are simply those who are able to infiltrate the maze and identify what the teacher wants. Rather than leave this goal identification to chance and ingenuity, the teacher can improve learning by identifying what is to be learned and providing a strategy to facilitate such learning.

Teaching, Testing, Talking, and Practice

One problem seldom dealt with in most textbooks on teaching is defining teaching. Rather than present the various philosophical viewpoints on this topic, we have chosen to attempt to define teaching simply by exclusion. That is, by presenting examples of testing, talking, and practice activities, we hope to eliminate a number of activities often mislabeled as teaching.

The easiest nonteaching activity to identify is **testing.** For instance, if a teacher were simply to assign a certain number of pages to be read and then to administer an examination covering that material, then it seems obvious to us that no teaching has taken place. In this instance the teacher has simply turned all responsibility for learning over to the learners. No goals or plans for content-specific learning were identified, nor were any strategies or processes presented to facilitate attainment of content-specific goals. Basically, the teacher has defined the teaching act as one of monitoring independent learning—neither facilitating nor seriously hindering the learning act. A similar situation occurs with the teacher who presents a text assignment to be read and follows with oral questions on the content during the following class session. If no explanation of goals is present, the teacher turns the learning act into a game of chance, a variation on "Twenty Questions," if you will. The student reads but cannot attend to everything in the assigned chapter of textual material. If the student is lucky or ingenious, what is retained will match the stated goals set by the teacher. If the student is neither lucky nor ingenious, then it may well be that what is retained will fail to match the unstated goals, and the teacher will decry the laziness or intellectual ineptitude of the student. The key point is that in neither of the preceding examples did the teacher do anything to facilitate learning other than to identify the material to be read.

A second activity often mislabeled teaching is simple **talking.** Observation of content area classrooms leads one to recognize that often a substantial amount of time is spent on noninstructional talking: talk about the weather, the baseball game, an administrative mandate, an upcoming event, and so forth. Although these behaviors are not necessarily negative, they are not teaching.

From my standpoint what is called teaching in some content area classrooms is too often only testing or telling. To support this contention let me present two brief scenarios which one can observe in virtually any school on any day. In the first, the teacher simply assigns pages to be read with no further guidance and follows this with a test covering the material assigned. Or the teacher may simply use class time to question students on the assigned material. In the second scenario the teacher tells students a number of pieces of information and then also follows with a formal test or perhaps with the in-class questions. Both of these scenarios recur endlessly in the schooling process, and seem plausible methods for ensuring students have read assignments or attended to the lecture, but we need to examine whether either is truly teaching.

If the teacher simply writes "Read pp. 108–123" on the chalkboard and then later assesses student knowledge of this material, then it would seem that instruction has not occurred, neither has telling really, for though a general idea has been identified to be read, the teacher has not specified what is to be learned (unless one assumes everything contained on pages 108–123 is to be learned). Now suppose the student fails these tests. Has the teaching failed? Perhaps it failed by omission but in the strictest sense teaching cannot be evaluated. How, then, should the failure be construed? If no teaching has occurred, what type of inadequacy is indicated?

It could be that the student has not read the assigned material, or perhaps *could* not read the material. It is also possible the student completed the assignment but did not have adequate experiences, or previous knowledge, to fully assimilate all the concepts presented. Then again, the student may have completed the assignment and understood the material but failed to retain the specific information presented on the test. The point is, the student failed the test but without a teaching component it is difficult to assess the relevance of this behavior.

Source: R. L. Allington, "Teaching, Learning, and Reading in the Middle Grade Content Areas," in D. W. Welle, ed., New Directions in Meeting Special Needs in Reading (Union, N.J.: Kean College), 1976.

A third activity often confused with teaching is **practice**. For instance, consider the English class where a majority of the time is spent completing the diagramming of twenty-five sentences on a practice sheet. In this situation, the activity is a practice activity if the teacher presented instruction on diagramming sentences prior to handing out the practice sheet. If no such teaching occurred, then the activity is, for all practical purposes, a test. If instruction did occur, then a practice activity is in effect—but it is not teaching.

At this point, it should be clear that we have a rather narrow definition of teaching, one that differentiates between the general description of teaching as what teachers do all day and a specific instructional interaction. Using our definition, few teachers teach more than a third of the time, and many teach little, if at all. We included this segment because too often we see teachers who have relegated all responsibility for learning to the learner, teachers who view their role as a monitor or gatekeeper, rather than facilitator, of learning. Although this is particularly true for process goals, at times it is true for content-specific goals. That is, the teacher makes assignments and then assesses whether the students were able to sort out what the goals were. This, then, is neither teaching nor the role of the content area teacher.

> The question of what is to be taught is usually answered, at a general level, by the guidelines set forth by State Curriculum Committees. At a more specific level, the issue is settled by commercial publishers. The curriculum materials *in use*, to a large degree, define the knowledge to be acquired by students and, thus, define for the teacher what it is that is to be taught. (Berliner and Rosenshine, 1977)

Identifying Content-Specific Goals

Perhaps the ideal method for identifying content-specific goals is for the teacher to begin by simply asking: "What is it I wish these students in my American history (or any other) class to learn?" and then selecting the important knowledge and competence to be learned in a specific class. From this list of goals the teacher would then develop plans for attaining the goals by selecting experiences, textual materials, films, simulations, and so forth, to facilitate attainment. In the real world, however, content area teachers are seldom allowed such liberty in the design of instruction.

A general constraint often imposed on teachers is a state and/or local curriculum guide that suggests what others have decided should be taught in a particular discipline at a particular level. Some states further define the curriculum by administering statewide achievement tests for various disciplines, with the schools that produce students who score well considered better schools, in which students learn more. In any event, factors such as these serve to constrain the teacher's free will in selecting goals for instruction.

A second and more prevalent constraint is the adopted, or approved, textbook. In fact, many teachers are textbook dominated. At the worst, the teacher gives up all goals save one—get through the book. These teachers are easily recognized. Simply ask, "What are you studying in American history (or any other) class?" and they respond, "We're just about through the Civil War (or Chapter 13)." In these cases, all authority for setting goals has been relegated to the learner and the text.

There is a commonly practiced but little-known theory of learning called appropriately the "Vince Lombardi" theory of instruction. The approach is typified by what its proponents affectionately label "covering ground." Operationally, the theory is simple: you begin on page 1 and forge ahead until you have reached the goal line—the end of the book. Not unlike the late Green Bay Packers coach whose football teams were satisfied with the same approach—covering ground until they reached the goal line.

Other teachers relegate much goal identification to the authors of the teachers' guide. In this case, the book is covered sequentially, and the teacher follows the directions in the guide quite closely. This is not to belittle the effective use of a guide, but rather to point out that following such a path removes the goal-setting responsibility from the teacher. It is our belief that an individual teacher is the best judge of appropriate goals. Selecting goals from the guide is quite different from accepting the guide as the determiner of the goals.

In most instances the teacher has some sort of goals statement available from external sources (state education departments, curriculum committee, departmental chair, teachers guide, and so forth). The presence of such guides can be a positive factor in identifying content-specific goals, but those sources must be used with some care. The strategy we find most acceptable is one in which the content area teacher uses such guides as resources from which to draw some of the content-specific goals. Using these resources in such a manner allows the teacher to retain control of the goals of instruction, to tailor the instruction to meet the needs and interests of the learners, and to build on the individual activities of both the students and the teacher.

WRITING CLEAR GOAL STATEMENTS

Whether you choose to set goals and then select materials or to analyze a mandated text, there are several strategies you can use to facilitate developing clear statements of goals:

1. Remember that words such as *understand, know about,* and *learn* are ambiguous. Although you may know what you mean by *understand*, it is not a verb that clearly depicts what the learner will be required to do to demonstrate understanding. Try to use verbs such as *list, select, identify, sequence, defend,* and so forth, which clearly communicate what the learner must do to attain the goal.

2. Avoid setting goals that are too trivial. One of the major sources of dissatisfaction with the behavioral-objective format advocated by Mager (1962) is the tendency to focus on minute and often irrelevant detail. It is perhaps less work to write a goal statement that asks for listing the dates of major conflicts in the Civil War, for instance, than to write one that requires the learner to list the major economic and political repercussions of the first Battle of Bull Run. However, the former seems a more trivial aspect of history than the latter.

3. Remember that the easiest way to write a clear goal statement is to ask yourself what exactly it is that you wish the learner to know, to be able to do, or to understand. Many content area teachers get caught up in the format of the goal statement rather than the content. The goal statement should simply reflect the type of knowledge or ability to be attained and the manner in which to assess the learners' knowledge of it.

Basically, then, the teacher confronted with a year of teaching should develop both long- and short-term goals. Prior to attempting this, however, the teacher should consider several important learner variables that could be placed under the general heading of prerequisite abilities, that is, where one is starting from. To do this, the several informal procedures discussed in Chapter 5 can be adapted to assess the background of learners in the content area. Standardized achievement instruments typically have less value in these matters than informal procedures because the former seldom tap specific knowledge or competence.

Once a general notion for learner prerequisite abilities has been established, then identification of beginning goals can begin. From these beginning content-specific goals, the teacher builds longer-term goals considering various learner and instructional variables.

If the teacher is further constrained by the requirement to employ a particular text, then the task becomes a bit more complex because the entry level has already been established as has the scope of the goals. This is true, of course, only if the teacher decides, or is required by mandate or fiscal constraints, to employ a single-test strategy. If this is the case, the teacher can still retain some control over the goals for instruction, primarily by selective assignment and selective emphasis. Teachers should keep in mind that everything printed in a textbook is not necessarily an important goal for instruction.

Even if a single text is mandated, the teacher can set content-specific goals that cannot be met within the framework of the required text. Goals of this sort simply mean developing plans that use other sources and other possible mediums. Another point by which to guide goal identification is that not all learning is based on text.

Identifying content-specific goals is a responsibility of the individual teacher and should not be wholly turned over to authors of texts and accompanying teaching guides or to curriculum committees. After first identifying learner prerequisite abilities, the teacher should form beginning content-specific goals and long-term goals. The teachers' guides, curriculum guides, and so forth, can be a useful resource, but the ultimate responsibility for what is taught and learned resides rightfully with the individual content area teacher.

Identifying Process Goals

As noted earlier, process goals stem primarily from the content-specific goals selected. There are several types of process goals, depending on the types of cognitive processes required to attain the content-specific goals. Our earlier example required only memorization, and although we indicated less than complete satisfaction with that goal, a goal of memorizing information can often be defended in virtually all content areas. It is important to remember, though, the limited usefulness of stores of facts unrelated to problem solving. Rather than attempt to induce learners to memorize the names of states and their capitals, teachers might set as a goal an ability to list three reasons why major cities such as Detroit, Chicago, New York, Los Angeles, and Dallas are *not* the state capitals. Whereas the earlier goal requires simple memory, the latter requires a more sophisticated cognitive strategy.

Consider these two examples of direct experience, or involvement, in the learning and application of knowledge.

> **Item:** A Spanish class meets in a building in Spring Garden, the Spanish-speaking section of Philadelphia. After an hour or so of classroom instruction, the students walk around the neighborhood, practicing the language by striking up conversations with store-keepers or passers-by. "It's really amazing because you realize how many flaws you make in your speech patterns much better than any record could give you," one student, who had been failing in Spanish in his former school, observes. "You don't have to sit in the classroom and fold your hands and say you will not learn. You learn by experiencing, by doing different things, by really going out."

> **Item:** A geometry class learns "by really going out," too. The students meet in the teacher's apartment for formal instruction, then go about the city, trying out what they've learned. "We had one class in Logan Circle, where we tried to figure the diameter of the circle itself," a student reports. "That's something new; you know you have to get certain measurements and everything—not just that you're told you have a circle of such and such a distance. You couldn't waste your time finding irrelevant facts, because you were going to get soaked by the big fountain there if you did. You actually learn by going out and doing what you're learning in theory, which is something I never did before."

> Source: C. E. Silberman, *Crisis in the Classroom: The Remaking of American Education* (New York: Random House, 1970).

The process goals, then, should reflect the type of cognitive strategies required for attaining content-specific goals. These strategies can range from memory, to inference of cause-effect relationships, to identification of chronology, to evaluation of conclusions, and so on. The process goal, then, identifies the type of cognitive strategy the teacher will try to develop or enhance through instruction.

Process goals relate directly to the assignment of textual material for reading. Once the teacher has identified the content-specific goal and decided to employ text as a source of information, then the process goal is translated not only as a cognitive strategy but also as a reading strategy. That is, one goal is to develop in learners the ability to employ different cognitive strategies, or processes, when reading. If the teacher is unsure of learner abilities to employ an appropriate process strategy, then, again, the informal assessment procedures described in Chapter 5 should be used. If the ability is lacking, the teacher must plan instructional sequences to model not only the cognitive strategy but also the utilization of such strategies while reading text.

It is certainly difficult to develop process strategies, because we know so little about thinking itself. We can identify some logically separable strategies, but logic is not always the most reliable source of information. Just as we noted earlier in our discussion of reading comprehension, the research is tremendously fragmented and incomplete. Nonetheless, what follows is an attempt to clarify the nature and to list some of the types of process goals. However, we must caution that these categories have little empirical basis and more often than not appear to be inseparable components of thinking.

The following process goals are ways in which the learner must deal with information:

- Locate—find a specific fact, detail, or object from an array, either within text or some grouping of objects; basically identification.
- Recall—simply a memory process; can be quite complex, however, and, although memory is facilitated by understanding, it does not ensure it.
- Classify—abstract salient features from the items to be classified.
- Infer—infer relationships that are not explicit; recall and classification involve inference at some points.
- Evaluate—look at an opinion, a statement of fact, or a conclusion, make a judgment as to its validity, and defend that judgment.

These five categories of processes are quite simplistic, but they are purposely so. To create process goals the teacher needs a starting point, and for that reason, we provide the stem from which teachers could develop an infinite number and variety of goal statements. It must also be noted, though, that each process seems to incorporate all of the previous processes. For example, to recall one must have located, to classfiy one must recall, and so on. Another factor is that some items can be misleading. For instance, if the goal in an American history class is to understand the cause-effect relationship between the issue of states' rights and the Civil War, then that particular goal could be interpreted several ways. If the text makes such a relationship explicit, the teacher might simply require a recall of that relationship or an evaluation of the author's basis for such a conclusion. Only if the relationship is implicit, can the *infer* stem be used, and then the teacher might also wish to follow the *infer* goal with an *evaluate* goal.

The process goals of content area teaching are related directly to the content-specific goals, but they go beyond these to identify the learning strategies necessary to attain the content-specific goals. A primary reason for the explicit statement of process goals is to remind everyone that the major aspect of schooling is supposed to be learning how to learn, not simply acquiring specific bits of knowledge from a limited set of disciplines.

Developing Plans from Goals

Once the teacher has identified both the content-specific and process goals for a lesson, developing a plan for attaining those goals begins. At this point the teacher knows what content-specific concepts, processes, functions, or relationships to teach, and which cognitive strategies appear most necessary for attaining the content goals. Ideally, at this point the teacher would begin by identifying an array of possible materials to facilitate attaining both sets of goals. However, as noted earlier, most teachers operate within the constraints of a mandated text and fiscal limitations. In this case, then, the teacher should reflect on learner abilities as depicted by the informal assessment procedures. If the teacher has a rather homogeneous class with adequate abilities to deal with the available textual material, then the process is fairly straightforward: (1) The teacher should explain the content-specific goals to the students so they know what is to be learned. (2) The teacher should identify, explain, and model the learning strategy that follows from the process goal. (In later chapters, discussions focus on using a number of techniques for developing learning strategies, particularly strategies for learning from text.) (3) The students are left to apply the learning strategies and acquire the knowledge and competence identified in the content-specific goals.

Unfortunately, few teachers have homogeneous classes of able learners. Instead, the group may be tremendously heterogeneous, particularly in their learning activities. This is where the difficulties begin, or, as Doyle (1976) has suggested, where the "practicality ethic" comes into play. This practicality ethic is simply the notion thatteachers cannot do everything, cannot meet every demand. Doyle suggests that the reason so much of the touted educational innovation never gets implemented or is dropped after a trial run is that too often it is seen as "impractical" or "un-do-able" by teachers. So, before going any further, we would like to note that, if the teacher follows our advice even this far, we will be happy. Simply knowing what is to be learned, what types of learning strategies are most appropriate, and informing learners of these are giant steps toward facilitating learning in content area classes. In addition, if the teacher has identified the general range of abilities and the relative difficulty of the assigned textual material, then we feel confident instruction will be improved, simply from such awareness. On the other hand, although the remainder of this text, particularly the final chapter, attempts to acknowledge the practicality ethic and the reason for its existence, we feel teachers can go even a few steps further relatively painlessly.

These few final steps will allow the teacher to begin to meet the needs of learners and to deal effectively with the diversity of ability found in most content area classrooms. However, before one can begin to differentiate instruction, the content and process goals must be identified as must the abilities of the students.

> Much of the problem in leading a child to effective cognitive activity is to free him from the immediate control of environmental rewards and punishments. That is to say, learning that starts in response to the rewards of parental or teacher approval or the avoidance of failure can too readily develop a pattern in which the child is seeking cues as to how to conform to what is expected of him. (Bruner, 1961)

Tests as Goals

We must discuss one final aspect of the teaching-learning process—the tremendous influence of tests or, perhaps more accurately, test content on learners' goals for instruction. In other words, the teacher must develop assessments that reflect the content-specific and process goals. Tests are powerful shapers of learning strategies; for example, to identify *evaluate* goals but assess *recall* of information is to mold learners into a memory strategy. Assessments of learning must be congruent with the content-specific goals and the process goals.

> One way of unobtrusively determining the content-specific goals and even the process goals from which a teacher is operating is to examine the items found on the tests she or he prepares. Each of the following items was drawn from such tests. Consider each and identify the nature of both types of goals:
>
> 1. How tall was the grass on the prairie? _____
> 2. Which of the following is the longest river in Africa?
>   a. Amazon
>   b. Congo
>   c. Nile
>   d. Euphrates
>   e. Mississippi

3. How old are redwoods? _____ how tall? _____
4. Rats and pigeons are of the same genus. T/F
5. A 10-5-5 mixture provides more nitrogen than a 10-8-3. T/F
6. What is the capital of Wyoming? _____ Idaho? _____
7. Which planet has the lowest gravitational pull? _____
8. Most babies walk by six months of age. T/F

Summary

In order to deliver instruction effectively, the teacher must not only have an awareness of learner abilities and textual difficulty, but must also assess the instruction provided. This assessment of instruction should focus on what is to be learned and how it is best learned. The major points covered in this chapter include:

1. The content area teacher has a dual role in instruction: (a) to develop content-specific knowledge and competence; and (b) to develop, extend, or refine the ability to learn.
2. To fulfill this dual role the teacher must develop both **content goals** and **process goals.** The former identify the content-specific concepts, functions, and relationships to be developed, and the latter delineate the learning strategies to be developed.
3. Neither of these goals must be written in a behavioristic manner, but without explicit goals instruction lacks direction, continuity, and congruence.
4. A first step in improving instruction, then, is to identify and explain both types of goals to the learners. This simple act improves learning by reducing the uncertainty about what is to be learned.
5. Although teaching, testing, talking, and practice are all components of instruction, they should not be confused with one another. Most teachers spend only a small portion of their instructional time teaching and generally greater amounts in the other activities.
6. Identification of content-specific goals begins by asking, "What should be learned?" These goals are influenced by curriculum mandates, materials available, fiscal constraints, learner abilities, and so forth.
7. **Process goals** define the learning strategy most appropriate for attaining the content-specific goals.
8. **Plans** are developed to facilitate the attainment of both types of goals. The teacher works within a practicality ethic, realizing no one person can solve all the problems. The plans, then, must be congruent with the goals and learner abilities but must also be practical for the teacher.
9. **Assessments** of learning must be congruent with goals and plans.

Conceptual Learning

A PRIMARY DETERMINANT in understanding textual material is the reader's knowledge of the concepts contained in the passage. In this chapter we attempt to briefly describe concept attainment and then to present several alternatives for enhancing it. As noted earlier, correctly pronouncing the words in text does not ensure understanding, because word identification can be accomplished without a full awareness of word meaning. One important method of improving content area learning, then, is to help learners develop the word meanings, or concepts, presented in assigned textual material.

Concepts and Vocabulary

A beginning point for the content area teacher is to realize that a printed word is little more than a graphic representation of an oral-language symbol for a concept. The word *lamb* is simply four letters that convey some information on appropriate pronunciation of the item; in oral language, *lamb* is simply the agreed-upon label for a small, fuzzy, four-legged creature otherwise described as an immature sheep. *Lamb* in either its oral or printed form is simply a label; its structural qualities offer no clue as to what the symbol represents, which is true in all alphabetic languages.

Humpty Dumpty:	When I use a word it means just what I choose it to mean—nothing more or less.
Alice:	The question is whether you can make words mean so many different things.
Humpty Dumpty:	The question is which is to be master—that's all.

Source: Lewis Carroll, *Alice in Wonderland.*

There are different types of concepts and different types of vocabulary. Concepts can differ in complexity, abstractness, familiarity, and usefulness. Each of these factors plays a role in attaining a concept. **Complexity** is the amount of prerequisite information necessary for attainment. *Castling* in chess, which is not complex if you understand the basic rudiments of chess itself, is often difficult to explain to the naïve participant. Although an understanding of castling requires some prerequisites, it is a relatively concrete concept. That is, it involves the movement of chess pieces rather than a recombination of existing knowledge. On the other hand, *gravity* is a more **abstract** concept, whereas *sin* and *justice* are *purely* abstract concepts. However, the concepts *sin* and *justice* are relatively more **familiar** than the concept *gravity*; in fact, they are common items in the vocabulary of most adolescents. The final feature, **usefulness**, is highly individual. If one has a burning desire to play chess, then understanding *castling* would be quite useful, whereas knowledge of *gravity* might be judged less useful.

> Reading for concept development may be defined as making one's way through printed and written language in such a manner as to seek out a number of relations and to put this growing set of relations into a tentative structure. (Henry, 1976)

The difficulty of a concept, then, is not easily objectified. The complexity of a concept, for instance, is related to each of the other features—abstractness, familiarity, and usefulness. That is, not all simple concepts are concrete, familiar, and highly useful. Likewise, not all complex concepts are necessarily abstract, unfamiliar, and of little utility. Confounding all this are the prerequisite knowledges, abilities, and interests of the students who are to "know" the concept. Rather than attempt to weight concepts as to complexity along these dimensions, we would suggest that teachers simply acknowledge these factors and realize that all concepts are not of equal complexity. Some concepts will be rather easily attained by students, and others will present major instructional difficulties.

The teacher must recognize not only the importance of concept attainment to content area learning but that words, whether printed or spoken, are simply agreed upon labels for concepts. At this point, then, the content area teacher must consider (1) how to identify the concepts that are necessary for the intended learning, (2) how to assess learner concept attainment, and (3) how to facilitate attaining unfamiliar concepts.

Identifying Key Concepts

As Herber (1970) notes, many teachers fail to understand the relation-ship between developing a conceptual base and developing vocabu-lary, because they associate the latter with drills on word meanings in general. Along lines similar to Herber, we argue that the key vocabu-lary in content area texts is the basic set of concepts the teacher wishes learners to attain. With that in mind, then, identifying a set of key concepts is primarily a task of identifying the vocabulary or the words that represent the concepts.

For the teacher who relies primarily on a single text, identifying key concepts is relatively straightforward. In this instance, the teacher would carefully review the unit of study and list as many major con-cepts as possible using the teachers' manual and professional exper-tise. Remember, these items may be (1) single words (for example, *erosion, capital, mass,* and *emancipation*); (2) phrases (*per annum, unicameral legislature, central tendency, subsistence income, birds of prey*); and (3) proper names, titles, or locations (*Industrial Revolution, Bay of Pigs, Eric the Red, Magna Carta*). Some concepts are concrete and some are abstract, some familiar, some unfamiliar, and some are more useful than others. But once the major concepts have been iden-tified, the teacher then decides whether the number seems manage-able, given the time allocated for the unit. There is no magical number of concepts that can be taught in a given period of time, for two rea-sons: (1) The complexity of the concepts must be evaluated in terms of the amount of prerequisite knowledge necessary for concept attain-ment. Two aspects are of concern here: the innate complexity of the concept and the maturity of the learners in terms of prerequisite knowledge. (2) Not only concepts, but also learners, vary in their "tea-chability." Some groups of learners can move along at a relatively fas-ter pace than others. Thus, after the major concepts are listed and the teacher has evaluated the list, some paring may be necessary. Again, these decisions must be left to the individual teacher, but the goal is to arrive at a list of concepts that can be thoroughly developed in the available time.

Concepts as public entities are defined as the organized informa-tion corresponding to the meaning of words. These meanings are put into dictionaries, encyclopedias, and other books. Thus, the meanings of the words comprise the societally accepted, or public, concepts of groups of persons who speak the same language. (Klausmeier, Ghatala, and Frayer, 1974)

The teacher who has decided to use multiple textual materials in the course of study goes about identifying key concepts in a similar manner, except that the various texts must be reviewed and perhaps only key concepts that appear in all texts need be identified for assessment and instruction. If this teacher must differentiate instruction for learners of various abilities (see Chapter 10), then the key concepts must also be differentiated.

Identifying key concepts or vocabulary, then, is a task that relies heavily on the ability of the teacher to decide what is important and should be taught. The teacher with complete control over the curriculum would identify the key concepts *prior* to selecting textual materials and, in fact, would base selection of these materials largely on their adequacy in facilitating concept attainment. However the textual material is obtained—by mandate or by selection—identifying the key concepts is crucial to effective instruction. This step can and should mesh with the goal-setting activities described in Chapter 7. The teacher must also consider whether concepts not presented in the textual material are either necessary for attainment of text-based concepts or desirable in addition to those presented in the assigned text. If either seems true, then instruction must be provided for these concepts, and they should be added to the list developed from perusing the textual material.

Assessing Learner Knowledge of Concepts

Because each teacher individually selects the key concepts for each unit, assessing learner attainment of the concepts must be accomplished through informal assessment procedures such as those described in Chapter 5. No standardized tests can be used. The basic guidelines for informal text construction were presented earlier, but in attempting to assess concept attainment, the teacher must realize one thing: A brief informal assessment will be more useful if viewed as a general survey of abilities rather than as an instrument that will identify which learners have attained the concepts and which have not.

At the most informal level the teacher can simply list the concepts on the chalkboard and ask whether students have general knowledge of them. For instance, students may have a general familiarity with some of the key concepts but will not have the specific or in-depth awareness desired by the teacher. Along the same lines the teacher can ask learners to write synonyms, examples, or short explanations of the concepts listed on the board. The use of even such an informal procedure will typically bring out ambiguities in understanding, lack of familiarity, or simple lack of depth of understanding.

THREE STRATEGIES FOR THE QUICK ASSESSMENT OF EXISTING CONCEPT KNOWLEDGE

1. Write a key concept on the blackboard and ask learners to respond with synonyms or related words. List these responses after each word and assess both quality and quantity of responses. Note also whether participation is limited to only a few pupils or more nearly full participation.
2. List key concepts on the blackboard or a handout and ask learners to write down all the synonyms or related words they can think of. Review these lists to assess quantity and quality of responses.
3. List key concepts, with examples (or synonyms) and nonexamples, on a handout. Ask learners to simply cross out the unrelated words.

Assessment strategies 1 and 2 might provide an outcome like that illustrated below. Note though that this could also serve as an item for assessment strategy 3 if a correct response were added. These responses suggest that the learners have no familiarity with the concept *puree*.

Concept: *puree*
Responses: a place in France
clean
kittens
water
boil

At the next level, the teacher can present the key concepts as a paper-and-pencil pretest. Learners could be asked to write a brief statement on what they know about each concept, or the task could take the form of multiple-choice or matching items. Rather than use instructional time, these pretests could be sent home to be completed. Remember, the primary focus of these assessments is for the teacher to develop an awareness of learner background knowledge. We cannot overemphasize the importance of implementing these assessments—they allow the teacher to instruct more effectively. Because the focus is on developing a general awareness of learner abilities, the level of effort expended should be commensurate with the information desired. There is no need to use valuable energy and instructional time attempting to construct airtight assessments for this task.

Sample of an informal pretest for concepts using a matching format. Vocabulary for a unit in a secondary biology text.

1.____food vacuole   a. transport of materials
2.____mitochondria   b. protein synthesis
3.____lysosome   c. covering of only a plant cell
4.____endoplasmic   d. governs activities of cell
        reticulum
5.____nucleus   e. energy ("powerhouse of cell")
6.____ribosome   f. self-destruction of old cell
7.____chloroplast   g. inside nucleus
8.____cell wall   h. food broken into soluble material
9.____centrosome   i. covering of only animal cell
10.____nucleolus   j. found only in animal cells
                                 k. contains chlorophyll

Facilitating Concept Attainment

Before proceeding to the operational aspects of facilitating concept attainment, we must consider (1) what a concept is and (2) how concepts are attained.

Many educators and psychologists use the term *concept* as though everyone were aware of, and agreed on, the meaning of the word. However, some use the term in a relatively narrow way—to describe various types of knowledge. We have chosen to follow a more general meaning proposed by Nelson (1977): A concept is "organized information that is not dependent upon the immediate perceptual array and is at least potentially nameable." The notion of a concept, then, is one of organizing information but not necessarily at the appropriate or highest level of organization. The small child who calls horses *cows*, for instance, has developed a concept even if we consider it primitive, naïve, and incorrect. This is not to argue that concepts are not categorized, classified, and organized in other ways, but rather that single objects or instances are sufficient for concept formation. Later in this chapter we will discuss how these higher-order organizational operations work. A concept, then, is not necessarily logically organized, totally correct (in an adult sense), or completely understood. It *may* be all of these things, but it does not *have to have* each of these features.

The pattern of decisions involved in attaining a concept is affected by a host of factors. Without doing too much violence to this diversity of determinants, it is possible to group them under several broad headings:

(A) The definition of the task. What does the person take as the objective of his behavior? What does he think he is supposed to do?

(B) The nature of the instances encountered. How many attributes does each exhibit, and how many of these are defining and how many are noisy? Does he encounter instances at random, in a systematic order, and does he have any control over the order in which the instances will be tested? Do instances encountered contain sufficient information for learning the concept fully?

(C) The nature of validation. Does the person learn each time an instance is encountered whether it is or is not an example of the concept whose definition he is seeking? Or is such validation only available after a series of encounters? Can hypotheses be readily checked or not?

(D) The consequences of specific categorizations. What is the price of categorizing a specific instance wrongly and gain from a correct categorization? What price is attached to a wrong hypotheses?

(E) The nature of the imposed restrictions. Is it possible to keep a record of instances and contingencies? Is there a price attached to the testing of instances as a means of finding out in which category they belong? Is there pressure of time to contend with, a need for speedy decisions?

Source: J. S. Bruner, J. Goodnow, and G. Austin, *A Study of Thinking* (New York: John Wiley & Sons, 1956).

Differentiation and Generalization of Concepts

There are two basic competing theories concerning the acquisition of concepts. The first, **differentiation,** assumes that the learner begins with very general bits of data that become more detailed, refined, and organized as the concept is developed or attained. The basic process, then, is differentiating, or sorting out, relevant features from irrelevant ones and correctly identifying examples of the concept being learned. The second theory holds that the learner begins with a specific instance or object and proceeds to generalize from this one example to the more general. This **generalization** process, for instance, seems to be operating when a young child goes from calling the father "DaDa" to labeling all males as such, to developing categories for father, familiar males, and all other males. Unfortunately, neither theory adequately explains concept attainment in all cases because there seems to be an abundance of examples of both in studies of concept attainment.

Formal Operations

Up to this point in the discussion, the examples have been of young children, although students in content area classes are adolescents or at least approaching adolescence. This is important to note, because at age 11–15 learners generally shift into what Piaget (1971) calls **formal operations.** When the student enters this stage of cognitive development, operations can be based on "pure" abstractions rather than simply on abstractions based on experience or empirical evidence. This **deductive reasoning,** which is based on logical necessity, is a new method of thought. Prior to this stage, **inductive reasoning,** which moves from a specific event, through additional events, to a general rule, was the normal thought process. Using deductive reasoning, the learner can manipulate information in ways not possible before. The teacher can, however, facilitate the development of this new ability by requiring deductive reasoning in classroom problem solving.

Examples of formal operational concepts indicate the importance to content area learning of reaching this stage of cognitive development. Consider the importance of each of the following concepts developed from formal operational thought: *inertia, correlation, valence,* and *equilibrium.* A basic characteristic of concept attainment in the formal-operations stage is that it frees the adolescent from the need for direct physical experience in concept attainment. However, although this stage of cognitive development is typified in adolescents, it must be noted that not all individuals attain the formal operational stage. This appears to be related to the fact that there seems to be a minimum level of intelligence necessary for achieving this level of cognitive development.

Thus the teacher must keep in mind this basic difference between adolescents and younger learners. The middle-school student is just developing the preliminary abilities associated with the formal operational stage, whereas intellectually advanced secondary-school students are well into this developmental stage. The teacher must remember, though, that students can still learn from direct and vicarious experiences, even if they have moved into formal-operational thought. In addition, learners at this stage of cognitive development benefit from instruction that forces the use of developing abilities.

Teachers must remember that *having* the cognitive abilities, and *knowing how* to use these abilities does not mean that students will actually *employ* them. Instruction could, then, profitably focus on developing strategies for using routines characteristic of formal operations and requiring that students use them.

Klausmeier, Ghatala, and Frayer Model

A perhaps obvious, but nonetheless important, characteristic of concepts is that they *are* learned and do not simply *emerge* with maturation. Learning concepts is a complex cognitive activity. A relatively clear model of concept attainment has been proposed by Klausmeier, Ghatala, and Frayer (1974). Their model of concept attainment proposes several levels of learning: At the initial level, which they have labeled **concrete,** a concept is formed when an individual **cognizes** an object that has been previously encountered. This entails the learner attending to an object, event, or a set of circumstances. From this attending, the learner must sort out the relevant features that distinguish this one thing from all others and remember these features. An example might be noticing the *aurora borealis* and distinguishing this from lightning, fireworks, or the horizon glow given off at night by the lights of a large city.

The next level is to **identify,** which requires that the learner recognize ("re-cognize") an object, event, or set of circumstances as the same as that encountered before when viewed from a different perspective. Learning to identify John's truck from the front, back, and side is an example of this stage.

The third level requires the learner to **classify.** That is, after learning to identify John's truck from different perspectives, the learner begins to note other similar-looking vehicles and labels these also as trucks. However, at this level one can still not be sure that the learner has developed the concept of truck fully, because even treating two examples of the same class as equivalent is accepted as evidence that this level has been attained.

The final level, the **formal,** incorporates all preceding levels and, in addition, requires that the learner be able to label the concept, list the defining attributes, classify examples and nonexamples, and list the reasons for including or excluding examples based on the defining attributes. Returning to our truck example, the learner must be able to label trucks, sort them from buses, wagons, trains, automobiles, and so forth, and list the attributes true examples have and those the nonexamples are lacking. The learner may acquire the label in any of the three earlier levels and may also discover the defining attributes or at least the more general properties. However, labeling and definition of attributes must occur at this formal level.

Model of Conceptual Learning and Development

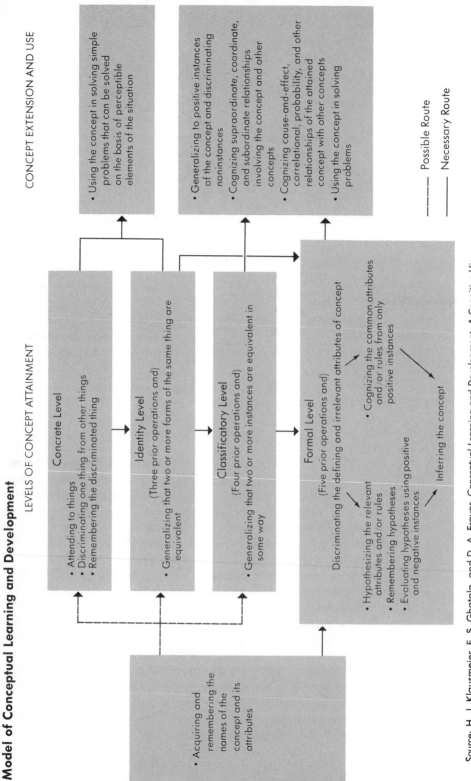

CONCEPT EXTENSION AND USE

LEVELS OF CONCEPT ATTAINMENT

Concrete Level

- Attending to things
- Discriminating one thing from other things
- Remembering the discriminated thing

Identity Level

(Three prior operations and)

- Generalizing that two or more forms of the same thing are equivalent

Classificatory Level

(Four prior operations and)

- Generalizing that two or more instances are equivalent in some way

Formal Level

(Five prior operations and)

Discriminating the defining and irrelevant attributes of concept

- Hypothesizing the relevant attributes and/or rules
- Remembering hypotheses
- Evaluating hypotheses using positive and negative instances

Inferring the concept

- Cognizing the common attributes and/or rules from only positive instances

- Using the concept in solving simple problems that can be solved on the basis of perceptible elements of the situation

- Generalizing to positive instances of the concept and discriminating noninstances
- Cognizing supraordinate, coordinate, and subordinate relationships involving the concept and other concepts
- Cognizing cause-and-effect, correlational, probability, and other relationships of the attained concept with other concepts
- Using the concept in solving problems

- Acquiring and remembering the names of the concept and its attributes

-------- Possible Route

———— Necessary Route

Source: H. J. Klausmeier, E. S. Ghatala, and D. A. Frayer, *Conceptual Learning and Development: A Cognitive View* (New York: Academic Press, 1974), p. 13. Reprinted by permission of the authors and the publisher.

Truck may seem to be an elementary example because attainment of this concept is typically complete prior to middle school. However, although the concept *truck* may seem elementary and straightforward, consider the following:

1. List relevant attributes of trucks.
2. Distinguish trucks from automobiles.
3. Distinguish trucks from buses.
4. Distinguish trucks from vans.
5. Distinguish trucks from jeeps.

In each case, list the attributes that differentiate the items. Size is not a real criterial attribute because trucks vary considerably in size. The point is that, even for a relatively familiar, concrete, and useful concept such as *truck*, the learner must identify attributes that are not particularly obvious on first glance. In this case, the primary attribute might be one of function rather than size, color, or number of wheels.

Now think of several concepts from your content area that are less concrete, familiar, and useful (in real-world terms) and attempt to list primary attributes. Consider *evaporation, vilify, accrual, negotiate, fodder, tangent, vituperative, melancholy, prosody,* and *modifiers.*

Teaching activities that facilitate concept attainment follow directly from the four levels and the abilities required in each. Even with the initial or *concrete* level, it is useful to supply the learner with relevant attributes. Often at this point, if the learner cannot clearly differentiate the object, event, or set of circumstances, irrelevant attributes are selected for the learner to attend to. The father who says, "See that red thing? That is a truck." directs attention to a nondefining attribute of trucks, because not all trucks are red. The teacher should consider what attributes are relevant and direct attention accordingly. This step facilitates concept learning, because it helps to limit the number of irrelevant features, or attributes, the learner attends to. The teacher can also provide a second type of cueing by prompting the student to recall information from earlier levels. The learner must remember the identified attributes of the object, event, or set of circumstances in order to decide which are relevant to the specific understanding of the concept. In our truck example, the learner must disregard *redness* because it is a nondistinguishing attribute.

Finally, the teacher would ask the learner to name the concept, state the distinguishing attributes, and perhaps also note the nondistinguishing attributes.

According to the Klausmeier, Ghatala, and Frayer (1974) model of concept attainment, what levels would each of the following students be identified with?

- John sees a *stalactite* while on a tour of the Hidden Caverns and asks, "What's that? I've never seen one of those before."_____
- John points to a chameleon and says, "That looks like a lizard."_____
- John asks Bill for a ball-peen hammer in metal shop class but rejects the one offered saying, "That's a claw hammer, Bill. A ball-peen hammer has one rounded, ball-shaped head and one flat head."_____
- John says, "I hate trying to write sonnets. I can never make the words rhyme."_____
- John says, "I forgot what you call it, but it has water on three sides of it but remains contiguous to a larger land mass on the fourth. Like Michigan, Florida, and Baja California."
_____
- John says, "If you have to puree a vegetable you just mash it into juice."_____

Developing Concepts and Vocabulary

A primary area on which the teacher may profitably focus instruction is the rich and full development of concepts, functions, and processes represented by the specific or technical vocabulary of the content area. Developing an understanding of this vocabulary is necessary for learning because, as Preston (1969) and Elkind (1975) noted, words do not *have* meanings nor do learners *get* meanings from a word. Rather, the learner *gives* meaning to words, and this meaning can only be given in terms of individual experiences, whether direct, vicarious, or abstract.

Given that meaning is not inherent in words but rather must be supplied by the learner from experience, the development of vocabulary or conceptual learning must involve experience at some level. If a teacher wishes to achieve learner understanding of vocabulary, then experience, whether vicarious or direct, is a more effective instructional strategy than presenting the rather empty, experientially barren definitions so often found in glossaries. We note this because far too often at the middle- and secondary-school level, students are presented with workbooks, worksheets, and board drills that purport to increase vocabulary. Typically, these strategies increase the number of learners who can match a word with a definition or synonym—an indication of attaining the concrete level—but seldom do such strategies move learners to the formal level. An additional deficiency of such experientially barren instructional strategies is that often no teaching, as we have defined it, occurs. The teacher simply distributes the workbooks, worksheets, and so forth, and asks the learners to match, select, or write the appropriate definitions. No instruction is evident, just plain and simple testing. Although such exercises might profitably be employed as a preinstructional assessment, they are among the least effective strategies for developing an understanding of concepts or vocabulary.

The effectiveness of other strategies in part depends on the prior experiences or background knowledge of the learners. The type of concept to be developed also exerts constraints on the strategies to be employed. However, the teacher should attempt to identify the strategy for most effectively and efficiently developing the understanding desired. Dale (1969) attempted to rank various types of experiences on an effectiveness scale. His **cone of experiences** ordered various instructional strategies on a continuum from direct to abstract experiences.

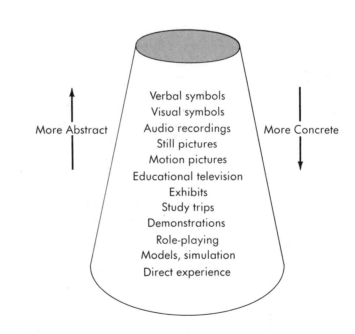

More Abstract

Verbal symbols
Visual symbols
Audio recordings
Still pictures
Motion pictures
Educational television
Exhibits
Study trips
Demonstrations
Role-playing
Models, simulation
Direct experience

More Concrete

Source: From *Audiovisual Methods in Teaching*, 3d ed., by Edgar Dale. Copyright 1946, 1954, © 1969 by Holt, Rinehart and Winston, Inc. Reprinted by permission of Holt, Rinehart and Winston, Inc.

Dale's (1969) Cone of Experiences is an attempt to roughly list the most useful types of experiences for learning. According to Gagne and Briggs (1974), a good rule to keep in mind when using Dale's Cone of Experiences is: "Go as low on the scale as you need to in order to ensure learning, but go as high as you can for the most efficient learning."

Direct Experience

The most powerful learning strategies are direct experiences. If a teacher wishes to develop an understanding of phenomena such as the *aurora borealis, erosion,* or *butte,* then direct experiences are potent facilitators. No picture or written definition can ever quite capture the essence of such events. However, the direct experience must be structured in such a way as to allow the learner to engage in analysis or identification of features central to the concept. In other words, the teacher might want to present a variety of examples of erosion in an attempt to facilitate the development of generalizations. In addition, the teacher should have clearly in mind the level of learning to which the concept is to be developed. Is the objective simply to be able to recognize eroded geographical features? Or should the learner be able to list positive and negative facets of erosion? Not all levels of concepts can be fully developed simply through experience. The point is that to facilitate higher-order learning the learner should be provided with direct experience whenever possible. This direct experience allows for the development of a cognitive schema or network into which later facets of understanding can be incorporated.

The specialized language of mathematics differs from social English in that it has a high conceptual density factor, reflected by limited, if any, redundancy. This factor requires that the exact meaning of every concept (word) and logical-syntactic relationship must be discerned accurately since interpretation is not facilitated by the presence of additional semantic-syntactic cues (redundancy). Aiken also stresses that adjectives are more unimportant in mathematical than in regular English and that common words are used with a limited rather than a generalized meaning. These observations immediately suggest that youngsters with learning disabilities who experience difficulties in processing auditory language . . . may experience associated reductions in solving verbal mathematical problems. (Wiig and Semel, 1976)

Direct purposeful experience requires contact with the physical objects and is perhaps characterized as "learning by doing." Such instructional strategies have a long tradition in various disciplines. In most schools, for instance, art, mechanical drawing, metal shop, physical education, typing, and so forth, are based on learning by doing. Students have direct experiences within the learning environment. Other disciplines, such as chemistry, physics, and biology, also have traditions requiring a laboratory setting, which provides direct purposeful experience within the learning environment. Unfortunately, the social sciences, literature, and to some extent mathematics curricula have no such tradition. Recent "innovative" curricula in these areas often attempt to integrate "hands-on learning" with text learning but there has been no discernible revolution in these disciplines toward experience-based curricula.

One might argue that in order to be experienced directly, a concept must necessarily be concrete. Although it is true that concrete concepts such as *tree, erosion, granite, butte, squid,* and so forth, lend themselves more easily to direct experience, the fact that a concept is abstract does not necessarily exclude the teacher from presenting direct experiences. For instance, in one rather widely publicized lesson, a teacher provided students with direct experiences with the concept *bias.* The students were white and lived in the rural midwest. The teacher felt quite sure that they had not reached the formal level of understanding *bias* or *prejudice* and therefore were developing less than an ideal understanding of the nature, purpose, and necessity for civil rights legislation, their topic for study. In order to develop a deeper understanding of this concept, the teacher segregated the class based on eye color and allowed students with a certain eye color various privileges and denied privileges to others. After only a session of this contrived caste system, those discriminated against became unruly and demanded the experiment be terminated. The teacher then switched the basis of discrimination and continued. In the end, each student had experienced bias directly, even if in a rather contrived format. If the concept is not represented by a concrete object, it becomes a bit more difficult to present direct experiences of it, but the creative teacher can develop instructional strategies that take advantage of the potency of direct experience.

Abstract and Vicarious Experience

Although many concepts can be experienced directly, others can only be experienced vicariously or abstractly. Dale (1969) presents a variety of options for vicarious experience, including models, pictures, movies, simulations, and so forth. Although it is possible to have direct experience with a butte or erosion, it is more probable that the teacher will be restricted to vicarious experiences because of budget and time constraints, not to mention the fact that only a few regions of the country have buttes. Vicarious experiences attempt to provide the learner with the next best thing to direct physical experience. Textbooks rely heavily on pictures to facilitate concept attainment by using photographs of examples of various concepts. The effective teacher will seek to expand on those pictures of erosion, a butte, or the aurora borealis through judicious use of additional pictures, scaled models, simulation, films, or filmstrips.

The abstract level, which is least facilitative for concept attainment, is characterized by visual and verbal symbols—written and spoken language. A primary difficulty is that most concepts are very difficult to describe without the description becoming circular. It is often even more difficult to convey any notion at all about the concept if the learner is truly naïve. Consider, for instance, the often-suggested strategy of using a dictionary or a glossary to learn the meaning of a word or to develop the understanding of a concept. Most written definitions rely heavily on synonyms to communicate understanding. The learner is told that *lunacy* is equivalent to "great folly" or a duck is a "swimming bird with a flat bill, short neck and legs, and webbed feet." In the first example, one must previously know the meaning of *folly;* in the latter the description is basically correct, but one would have a difficult time drawing a realistic picture that is based only on that information.

To illustrate the difficulty of relying on dictionary definitions or the visual symbolic level, consider each of the following, which were drawn from *Webster's New World Dictionary:*

- *aurora borealis:* luminous bands or streamers of light sometimes appearing in the night sky of the Northern Hemisphere.
- *shrimp:* a small, slender, long-tailed crustacean, valued as food.
- *cathode-ray tube:* a vacuum tube in which cathode rays are produced.
- *erosion:* an eroding or being eroded.
- *butte:* a steep hill standing alone in a plain; a small mesa.
- *mesa:* a small, high plateau or flat tableland with steep sides and, often, a layer of rock covering it.
- *plateau:* an elevated tract of more or less level land.
- *bathos:* false pathos.
- *pact:* a compact, covenant, or agreement.

A primary difficulty for many learners is that too often teachers assume the learner will acquire concepts simply by reading the text and, if necessary, by searching out definitions in a glossary or dictionary. This assumption that abstract visual symbols will be sufficient to develop a concept fully can become a barrier to content area learning. This is not to suggest that meaning cannot be developed by using semantic and syntactic cues in text, but rather that the technical vocabulary of content areas presents a particular problem for the naïve learner because most text authors assume that a minimal introduction to a new concept is sufficient. Perhaps these authors assume that teachers will provide appropriate instruction to develop these concepts. For whatever reason, the typical content area text does provide a written description or explanation, in text or in a glossary, and often presents pictures or other in-text aids in an attempt to facilitate concept attainment. Unfortunately, these efforts are often inadequate, making additional instruction necessary for many, if not most, learners.

The most common instructional strategies employed outside the text are verbal abstract descriptions, or talking about objects, events, concepts, and so forth. Dale (1969) ranks this only a step above written explanations. The primary benefit of verbal descriptions is that they are easily tailored or modified, depending on the feedback from the receivers. This assumes, of course, the teacher is attending to both verbal and nonverbal feedback and tailoring the message appropriately. In any event, although talking has advantages over print, it still is far from the ideal instructional strategy for facilitating concept attainment. Talking is a necessary component of virtually all instruction aimed at developing concepts, but talking in an experientially barren environment is less effective than talking combined with experience.

The following activities were drawn from Wiig and Semel (1976) and might be used when attempting to develop concepts and vocabulary in content area lessons:

1. Association between the name of a class member with the label for the semantic class, using a multiple-choice format (subordinate-superordinate association):
   Is a lion an animal or a bird?
   Is an armadillo a mammal or amphibian?
2. Association between the label for a semantic class and the name of one or more class members, using a multiple-choice format (superordinate-subordinate association):

Which is an animal—a table, a dog, or a car?

Which is a crustacean—a horseshoe crab, a chameleon, or an armadillo?

3. Identification of names of members that do not belong to the class in question (deletion of false subordinates):

Which of these does not belong?: apple, pear, shoe, banana.

Which of these does not belong?: class, caste, sect, rank.

4. Selection of names of class members belonging to a specific category from among a list of choices (matching subordinates to a superordinate):

Listen to these: red, white, and blue. Are they colors, toys, or foods?

Listen to these: wheat, corn, and beans. Are they annuals or perennials?

5. Categorization of the names of members of different classes according to the appropriate class descriptions (subordinate categorization by function):

Listen to these: bread and butter, shoes and socks. Which are things to eat? Which are things to wear?

Listen to these: shield and anti-aircraft battery, a sword and a long-range bomber.

Which do you use to attack an enemy? Which are used to defend against an attack?

6. Categorization of the names of different class members on the basis of shared attributes (subordinate categorization by attribute):

Listen to these: candy, lemons, and cookies. Which are sweet? Which are sour?

Listen to these: solar and hydro-energy, nuclear and fossil fuel energy. Which are "hard" technologies? Which are "soft" technologies?

7. Categorization of names of class members belonging to different classes according to the appropriate class names (subordinate categorization by class label) :

Listen to these: apples, marbles, checkers, oranges. Which are games? Which are fruits?

Listen to these: weasels, wolves, deer, lynx, and squirrels. Which are carnivorous? Which are herbivorous?

8. Abstracting and formulating similarities between objects, events, etc.:

How are apples and oranges alike? How are cars and trains alike?

How are whales and whooping cranes alike?

How are Gettysburg and the Battle of the Bulge alike?

9. Abstracting and formulating differences between objects, events, seasons, ideas, feelings, etc.:

What is the difference between Halloween and Thanksgiving?
What is the difference between indifferent and callous?
What is the difference between Roosevelt's New Deal and John-
son's Great Society?

Source: E. H. Wiig and E. M. Semel, *Language Disabilities in Children and Adolescents* (Columbus, Ohio: Charles Merrill, 1976), pp. 178–79.

Planning for Concept Development

Prior to presenting the textual materials to be employed in the instructional sequence, the teacher should identify the key concepts deemed necessary and appropriate for attaining the goals set forth. Once these are identified, the teacher can begin a sort of readiness instruction. This phase of teaching is designed to prepare the learner for the text assignment—to develop the concepts necessary for comprehension of the written material.

The initial decision concerns finding the most effective and efficient level for developing the concept. We have already noted that not all concepts can be experienced directly, and many of those with this feature cannot be easily experienced. The teacher working in an eastern urban center will be hard pressed to provide a direct purposeful experience with a butte. Although this teacher might be able to provide a direct experience with the concept of ghetto, direct experience may be inefficient or unnecessary. This is where the weighing process comes into play. Is the concept central to the lesson? If so, at what depth of understanding does the teacher wish to develop it? A bus trip through a ghetto may provide an adequate base for a concept of the physical characteristics of a ghetto, but will not develop the deeper understanding of a ghetto as a functioning social organization. Nor will a bus trip provide an understanding of the political-economic underpinnings of urban ghettos in general.

The types of experiences that can be provided are virtually limitless. Following are two lists of experiences that one might provide for learners in a science or social studies unit. These ideas are from "Incorporating Language Experiences into the Content Areas," by Dianne Seim, which appears in Braun and Froese (1977).

Topic: *Snow*

1. Take learners into school yard after providing training and materials for observation. Have learners describe snow, either on the ground or falling.

2. Observe snow more closely by measuring depth, measuring temperature of snow on ground and comparing with air temperature, or viewing through magnifying glass; learners can describe, draw, etc., as methods of recording observations.
3. Take snow into classroom and melt to determine water content or length of time it takes to melt specified amount. Have learners filter water to identify impurities. Compare samples of freshly fallen snow and older fallen snow for impurities.
4. Record the weather over a period of time to identify when it snows. Observe whether different conditions produce different types of snow.
5. Investigate patterns of drifting snow through observation. Experiment with different areas, types of obstructions, and types of snow to observe effects on drift pattern.

Topic: *Land Use*

1. Have learners record land use in specified neighborhood areas. Map single-family dwellings, apartments, industry, roads, parking lots, agricultural and recreational usage, etc.
2. Study transportation networks for getting various products to community.
3. Identify new construction and analyze whether buildings which seem appropriate for a particular land usage are being built or whether the land would be better suited for other purposes.
4. Study land formations in the community and attempt to make a three-dimensional model. Analyze land usage as it relates to land formations.
5. Acquire local zoning maps and visit areas (or have learners observe on the way to or from school). Attend city council meetings to determine how zoning laws are established and modified. Analyze whether zoning laws seem appropriate for land formation, resources available, long-term community interest.

Even if the teacher's goal is simply to develop a notion of the physical characteristics of ghettos, one would still have to ask whether the bus trip is the most efficient method. One of the principles of concept development is generalization; viewing a single ghetto may not assist the learner in developing a notion of what characteristics ghettos outside of eastern urban centers exhibit. Perhaps several movies or even color slides of various types of ghettos would be as effective as well as more efficient. In addition, the alternatives may be more feasible, because the teacher will always labor under constraints imposed by a rather limited financial reserve. Thus although direct experiences are

There is one blanket statement which can safely be made about the world's schools: the teachers talk too much.

Martin Mayer

excellent facilitators of concept attainment, such activities are too often unavailable.

The potential of vicarious experiences as facilitators in concept attainment are too often overlooked by teachers—particularly the potency of models and simulations. Virtually all disciplines have such resources available, and often substitutes can be constructed if the teacher lacks the financial resources to purchase such items. The skeleton, the human model that can be disassembled, the clear plastic internal-combustion engine, representations of cell structures, miniature pulleys, levers, and flywheels, scaled-down replicas of slave ships or Conestoga wagons, plastic chips that can be arranged in various geometric shapes, and a myriad of other materials are examples of vicarious experiences that can be profitably employed in various content areas.

Another vicarious experience that is most potent in the social and biological sciences is the moving picture, or movie. Though often overlooked as a teaching tool, movies offer a number of benefits unavailable through either models or still pictures. If the teacher wished to develop the concept of *revolution* in social studies class, then several popular movies might be employed. Scenes depicting the mood and dialogue that accompanied the French, American, and Russian Revolutions could exert powerful influences toward shaping the notion of *revolution*. Similarly, a television program such as *Roots* effectively developed the concept of *slavery,* among many others. Time-lapse photography presented in a movie format allows the learner to see a seed germinate, sprout, extend, leaf, mature, blossom, seed, and die. Many movies have been produced for educational purposes with development of specific concepts as the goal. The teacher should become aware of collections of such films developed for their content area and attempt to identify films that can be effectively employed.

The use of slides or still pictures is yet another way for the teacher to provide experience. In this case, the assigned textual material often has a variety of illustrations that might be expanded upon. There is a lot of truth in the oft-heard phrase "A picture is worth a thousand words." The teacher should not overlook this readily available resource for facilitating concept attainment.

Finally, if all levels of direct and vicarious experiences are exhausted without identifying a manageable teaching strategy, the teacher can turn to talking, or the verbal symbolic level. Here, as at the other levels, the teacher must carefully consider how to present the concept. The first step might be to present the learners with a definition followed by verbal descriptions of examples relating the known to the unknown whenever possible. Elicit from learners hypotheses about the dimensions of the concept under study and provide feedback about the correctness of these.

By providing a description and examples, the teacher hopes to reduce the number of hypotheses the learner might generate concerning the characteristics of the concept to be attained. The addition of instructions to identify attributes of the concept or to list features or examples also facilitates concept attainment. The learner is typically assisted by cues or instructions to recall previously acquired information that might aid in identifying attributes. The teacher should attempt to build on the learner's prior knowledge.

Recognizing Problems in Concept Learning

The student with no idea of a concept's attributes is generally not difficult to identify. However, partial learning and even erroneous learning can at times make identifying those learners who have not fully mastered a concept difficult. Markle and Tiemann (1969) list three error patterns that often appear in concept learning:

1. **Overgeneralization**—the learner simply identifies nonexamples as examples. This pattern simply indicates that the learner has not been exposed to a sufficient variety of examples or has not identified key attributes. An example of this was offered earlier when we discussed the difficulty small children may have in distinguishing horses and cows.
2. **Undergeneralization**—the learner identifies true examples as nonexamples. Again an insufficient exposure to a variety of examples underlies these errors. The small child who fails to classify a small Shetland pony as a horse or a Texas longhorn as a cow illustrates undergeneralization.
3. **Misconception**—the learner classifies examples as nonexamples and vice versa. Typically, in this case the learner has not had a sufficient variety of either examples or nonexamples; as a result, the learner classifies on the basis of an irrelevant attribute. A person who labels any bovine with horns as a bull exemplifies this error pattern, because bulls may or may not have horns and the same is true of cows.

By eliciting responses from learners, the teacher can often identify whether learners fall into one of the above error patterns and modify instruction accordingly. Some instructional modifications seem most effective in eradicating these error patterns. **Matching** requires presenting an example and a nonexample that have the same irrelevant attribute and differ on the relevant attribute. Thus if the learner were overgeneralizing and thus confusing cows and horses based on the attributes of color and size, the teacher would present an example of brown, similarly sized horses and cows and attempt to direct attention to the relevant attributes.

Given the error patterns described by Markle and Tiemann (1969), label each example following as *overgeneralization, undergeneralization,* or *misconception*.

- John argues that the moon has no gravity because you can jump so much farther than on earth. _____
- John points to South America on the map and states that it is a large island. _____
- John labels a snake a mammal and a duck an amphibian. _____
- John says 99 is a prime number because the numerals are identical. _____
- John points out that a particular work under study cannot be a sonnet because it has more than thirteen lines. _____
- John says spiders cannot be crustaceans because they do not live under water. _____

A second strategy is **divergent pairing,** in which two examples that differ radically on the irrelevant attributes are presented together. In the case of the learner who is undergeneralizing and failing to label Shetland ponies as horses, the teacher would present examples of horses ranging in size from Shetlands to Clydesdales, which pull the Budweiser wagon in television ads.

For the learner who exhibits misconception errors, a combination of the above strategies is called for. Markle and Tiemann (1972) reported that presenting examples seems primarily to improve generalization of concepts, whereas presenting nonexamples seems to improve discrimination. Thus both examples and nonexamples seem necessary instructional strategies to ensure full concept attainment.

In all stages of instruction the teacher must remember that acquiring concepts is a complex cognitive activity. The level of learner prerequisite knowledge, the number of concepts to be presented, the type of concepts to be attained, and the quality of instruction all interact to either facilitate or hinder learning from the assigned textual materials. However, the teacher can—through judicious selection of key concepts and vocabulary, informal assessment, and effective instruction— build in learners the repertoire of concepts necessary for learning effectively and efficiently from textual material. Rather than assume that reading the textual material will be sufficient for full development of concepts and vocabulary, the teacher should attempt to build the key concepts and vocabulary prior to assigning textual material.

THE LOGICAL PROCESS OF CONCEPTUALIZATION

1. *The act of joining* (bringing together, comparing, generalizing, classifying). Its logical operator is *and (moreover, furthermore)*. Its grammatical form is the coordinating conjunction and the connective adverb.
2. *The act of excluding* (discriminating, negating, rejecting). Its logical operator is *not* (this . . . *not that*). Its grammatical form is *neither* . . . *nor* (exclusive, dichotomous).
3. *The act of selecting* (one or the other or both). Its logical operator is *some (part, few)*. Its grammatical form is *either* . . . *or*; quantitative pronouns.
4. *The act of implying* (*if* not *this* . . . *then that*; cause-effect, result, necessity, proof, condition). Its logical operator is *if* . . . *then*. Its grammatical form is the subordinating connective adverb and the subordinating conjunction.

Source: W. H. Henry, *Teaching Reading as Concept Development*, © 1976 by International Reading Association (Newark, Delaware). Reprinted by permission of W. H. Henry and International Reading Association.

Summary

1. Words, whether printed or spoken, are simply the symbols assigned to represent a concept. In a sense, then, developing vocabulary is concept learning, particularly learning the technical vocabulary of the content areas.
2. Conceptual learning is typically the intended outcome of content area instruction. By identifying a unit's key concepts or vocabulary, the teacher can focus instruction. Teaching, or facilitating the attainment, of concepts, then, is the primary task of the content area teacher.
3. Concepts vary along a number of dimensions that affect their "teachability." Learners vary in interest, motivation, intellect, the

type of previous knowledge available, all of which affect concept attainment. These factors interact to produce the need for different amounts and types of instruction.

4. Concepts seem to be developed through the processes of differentiation and generalization; at times one process works independently, and at other times the processes work interdependently.

5. There are different levels of concept attainment ranging from concrete to formal. Certain concepts cannot be attained until the learner reaches the appropriate state of cognitive development.

6. Three general levels of experiences are available for facilitating concept attainment. These range from the most effective (direct purposeful experience) to vicarious experiences (such as models, simulations, and pictures) to the least effective abstract experiences (the verbal symbolic [talking] and visual symbolic [reading]).

7. Developing concepts prior to presenting assigned textual material is often necessary in content area teaching, because comprehension and learning depend on the learner's attaining an understanding of the technical vocabulary of the content area. Unlike more general reading materials, content area textual materials often presuppose knowledge of concepts or fail to adequately cue the learner as to the relevant attributes of a new concept.

8. Four types of error patterns are common in concept learning: (1) the "I have no idea" pattern in which the learner has no basis for a judgment; (2) overgeneralization, in which the learner identifies nonexamples as examples; (3) undergeneralization, in which the learner identifies examples as not belonging; and (4) misconception, in which the learner misclassifies both examples and nonexamples.

Providing Organizational Assistance for Learning

IN THIS CHAPTER, we try to provide a general framework for assisting content area teachers in their attempt to provide organizational structure for the textual materials to be employed by the learner. Although virtually all texts have a coherent structure, a diversity of structural patterns exists. Furthermore, the inability of the learner to identify the organizational pattern can serve as an effective barrier to learning. Thus providing learners with assistance in identifying the organizational structure of textual material enhances the probability of learning from text.

In text learning there are two major considerations for the teacher: the learner and the textual material. Each plays a separate role, but it is the interaction of the two that results in learning. We have discussed similar points in earlier chapters, but now we hope to bring these together in order to provide a workable system assisting learners.

The Learner

In Chapter 3 we discussed learners in terms of considering their ability to read assigned textual material. However, each learner brings much more to a text-reading assignment than simply the ability to read the words appearing on the page. Learners have successfully existed for a number of years in a very complex environment, the world. Based on this existence, they have developed concepts, ideas, opinions, attitudes, and so forth, that Smith (1975) aptly labels "a theory of the world in the head." The use of this theory allows learners to evaluate, predict, infer, and conclude—in short, to understand new information. Smith (1975) points out that learning takes place at the point of contact between the individual's theory of the world and the information to be learned. This means that if new information cannot be related to what is already known, little, if any, learning will take place.

This is certainly not a revelation, but it serves to reinforce the importance of assuring that learners do have sufficient readiness to handle new information.

Much of the basis for our understanding of how this "theory of the world in the head" works comes directly from the work of various researchers in the field of artificial intelligence—that is, computer intelligence. Early computers were restricted to answering questions for which the answers had been previously stored. In other words, these early models were able to remember what they had been given. If we were talking about reading comprehension, this ability would probably be labeled literal recall of stated fact or recall of text-bound information. The early computers were unable to go beyond the information given, unable to make inferences. In other words, they did not have stored concepts that could be used to generalize or reorganize information in order to apply it to new situations or events.

Script Theory

Recently, researchers have developed a method for providing computers with concepts; Schank (1973) labels these **scripts**. A script is essentially a stereotype about a situation or an event. Pearson and Johnson (1978) apply this notion of scripts to reading-comprehension theory in the following manner: a script is useful to a reader in that it provides an organizational framework into which new information can be assimilated and which also provides a basis for judging the description, actions, or outcomes of an episode. For instance, suppose a student is required to read a short story that involves the relationships among family members during the great depression. In order to understand the story, the learner probably would have to call up the following scripts: (1) mother role, (2) father role, (3) sibling roles, (4) family patterns, (5) economic depression, (6) unemployment. Each of these scripts would contain essential attributes of the label. The short story is filtered through the existing scripts, and the new information is examined in terms of the stored attributes. If perceived as useful, interesting, or important, new information will be added to the existing scripts, which results in an elaboration of the attributes assigned. In some cases the information may be in conflict with existing scripts, in which case the learner may decide to modify the existing script to accommodate new information; create a new script separate from the existing script; or perhaps reject the information as incomprehensible, irrelevant, or untrue.

The authors of most textbooks assume that the learners have available existing concepts, or scripts, that can be employed during reading and learning from that textbook. Difficulties in this area can arise from at least three different perspectives: (1) The learner is unsure about which concepts or scripts to apply when reading the text. (2) There is a mismatch between the learner and the author about the nature of the concept, as in the difficulties that arise when sociocultural mismatches occur. Racism, for instance, may be seen from quite different perspectives by persons from different backgrounds. (3) The learner simply lacks the necessary concepts or scripts to understand the situation, event, or information presented (see Chapter 8).

Each of these types of difficulties should be considered in the planning stages of instruction rather than only at the point of delivery. The actual treatment supplied to ameliorate the difficulties can occur prior to assigning the reading of textual material, or it may occur concurrently with the reading.

If the difficulty is caused by a mismatch between the level of prior knowledge expected by the author and the existing knowledge of the learner—in other words, by a lack of the necessary concepts—learning from text can be facilitated by providing appropriate readiness experiences. For instance, many of the techniques provided in Chapter 8 would serve to develop an appropriate conceptual base for learners whose available knowledge was inadequate for the task. One of us recalls struggling with the concept of oxidation in a high-school chemistry class. The author of the assigned textual material presupposed that a fundamental understanding of the concept was available to the reader—that it existed within the reader—and thus discussed this phenomenon without providing examples or adequate definition. The instructor therefore supplied *rusting* as an example of an oxidation process, which provided sufficient understanding that this concept could be elaborated by completing the assigned reading. The crucial point is that the instructor initially assumed existing knowledge, as did the author of the text. The absence of such prior knowledge rendered the text incomprehensible because there was no framework into which the new information could be assimilated. This **assumptive teaching**, as Herber (1978) calls it, along with the mismatch about students' prior knowledge and the actual level of that knowledge between the author's presupposition effectively prevented learning until the appropriate background knowledge had been obtained.

Schema Theory

Difficulties caused by not knowing which concepts or scripts to employ can be handled by developing adjunct aids such as study guides; several of these strategies are discussed later in this chapter. A second way to deal with this type of difficulty is by applying what has become known as **schema theory.** The notions of schema and scripts are highly related and may, in fact, simply be different labels for the same construct. The work of the schema theorists, however, dramatically points up the importance of the reader's orientation to the reading task. For many years teachers have been encouraged to provide purposes for reading prior to directing learners to complete assigned textual material because, whenever one reads, some conclusions must be drawn about what information is important and, more critically, how to integrate such information. When teachers provide purposes for reading, they are simply cueing or orienting the learner as to which scripts or schemas seem most appropriate for achieving the desired outcome and, in addition, assisting the learner in identifying a strategy for integrating the new information with existing knowledge. Providing such purposes for reading textual material is directly related to setting instructional goals, as discussed in Chapter 7, because the purpose provided for reading should be congruent with the stated goals of instruction.

We can develop purpose-setting activities that range from the very simple to the quite complex. Following are three purpose-setting strategies that seem to run the gamut from easy and simple to more time consuming and complex.

1. The teacher simply provides a single explicit purpose for reading an assigned textual material.

   - "Tonight you are to read pages 221–226 and discover (list, or identify) the four major battles of the French and Indian War."
   - "Read these four paragraphs and find the most probable cause for the deterioration of the ozone layer."

2. The teacher provides a set of key words from the unit and has learners generate questions that become the purpose for reading.
3. The teacher develops a reaction guide and uses it as a device to facilitate learner purpose setting.

Match the characteristics in Column B with the characters in Column A.

A. Characters

_____1. Dr. Grimsby Royloff
_____2. Helen Stoner
_____3. Mrs. Hudson
_____4. Dr. Watson
_____5. Sherlock Holmes

B. Characteristics

a. precise, observant, somewhat eccentric
b. helpful, unobtrusive, domestically inclined
c. erratic, cruel, intelligent
d. sensitive, fearful, genteel
e. logical, trustworthy, excels at narration

Basically, what we are suggesting is that the teacher exerts a powerful influence on what is remembered, what material is integrated into existing scripts and schemas, and what type of new structures will be created from reading textual material. Several researchers have shown that, by simply suggesting that subjects attend to different features of text, one can largely manipulate the amount and type of information recalled. Probably the earliest demonstrations of this effect were done with simple recall of word lists in which it was demonstrated that categorizing the items facilitated recall. Recently, several researchers (for example, Mistler-Lachman, 1974; Mosenthal, 1977; Spiro, 1977) have demonstrated that subjects can be rather easily influenced to remember some features of text but not others, depending on the type of orientation provided. Virtually all recent work in this area assumes that the reader does not begin with letters and sounds and move in linear progression ultimately to meaning, but rather that subjects begin reading with a script, schema, or notion about what is to be read. Further, researchers argue that, although one can induce subjects to read to remember exact sentences, for instance, most skilled readers more often read for "gist" and actively evaluate information in relation to their existing knowledge (Anderson, Reynolds, Schallert, Goetz, 1977). Thus individual differences in existing scripts and schemas will lead to different integrations and interpretations of new information in the text.

Thus the teacher can play a significant role in facilitating learning from text by providing orienting tasks that cue the learner as to which scripts and schemas to draw upon when reading the assigned textual material. By using such cueing, the teacher can direct learning toward the instructional goals developed for that unit of study.

Selected Strategies for Orienting Learners to Tasks

There are a variety of strategies the teacher can employ to facilitate learner comprehension of assigned textual material. The strategies presented in this section deal primarily with orienting the learner to the goals of the lesson and activating existing scripts to facilitate understanding.

In Chapter 8 we discussed strategies for developing concepts important to understanding a particular assigned text. The strategies suggested there can be considered useful prerequisites to providing an orientation to the task for the learner. That is, knowing that one is going to study the relative merits of Ayrshire versus Brown Swiss is of little use without the basic understandings of dairy cow and milk production. Thus, to a large extent, learners must have an adequate conceptual base before the teacher can facilitate learning through the use of orienting strategies. With this in mind, we first consider the possibility of providing an advance organizer (Ausubel, 1960) as one form of an orienting strategy.

> As Ausubel (1968) points out, clarity of content is not the only factor that precludes meaningful learning. That content must be available within the cognitive structure of the learner. Specifically, the reader must be able to hold information in abeyance and bring his/her experience to it in order to successfully sift out and simplify information.
>
> Source: J. Sullivan, "Comparing Strategies of Good and Poor Comprehenders," *Journal of Reading*, 8: (1978), 710–715. Reprinted by permission of J. Sullivan and the International Reading Association.

Advance Organizer. Ausubel (1960) argued that "learning and retention of unfamiliar but meaningful verbal material could be facilitated by the advance introduction of relevant subsuming concepts" (p. 271). He was able to demonstrate that providing learners with a brief introductory statement to the assigned textual material effectively increased both acquisition and retention of new information. This advance organizer is a statement of the topic under study and the general concepts dealt with in the assigned text. If the assigned material did in fact deal with the relative merits of Ayrshire versus Brown Swiss in terms of milk production, the advance organizer would present sent this information and perhaps basic information on the criteria employed in the argument by the author of the text. By directing learner attention to the general nature of the information given and to the particular concepts to be presented, the teacher provides an organizational framework for reading the text. This type of orienting strategy induces the learner to call up existing knowledge about the topic to be studied and directs cognitive attention to the relevant aspects of the information presented. Without such a statement, learners are left to deduce for themselves not only the general nature of the task but also the particular concepts to be called into play. Although some learners find this process relatively easy, many process textual material without discovering either the general framework or the important aspects of the information presented.

A primary purpose of all orienting strategies is to develop in learners an awareness of the task to be completed. The use of advance organizers facilitates learning from text by providing such an awareness to the learner as long as the learner possesses some basic information about the concepts to be presented. That is, in order for learners to incorporate new information into a script or to incorporate subordinate concepts, they must have available the general attributes of the topics discussed.

EXAMPLES OF ADVANCE ORGANIZERS

Bats, Cats and Sacred Cows portrays the characteristics of animals and their relationship to man. It traces some of the superstitions that have arisen about animals, amusingly and informatively recounts some stories which show the instinct and feeling of animals, and gives a small insight into the worship of animals by humans.

• • •

Introduction to selection from *The Hobbit*, by Tolkien:

You might mistake a hobbit for a dwarf except that hobbits are a little smaller and have no beards. Hobbits hate adventures, and Bilbo Baggins, a hobbit, wonders how he ever allowed himself to be tricked into this one. For Bilbo finds himself being official burglar for Thorin and his band of 12 dwarves.

• • •

Idea Direction

This chapter explores ways to meet the reading achievement needs of individual students in content classes without jeopardizing the substantive part of the courses. Ideas presented are illustrated by materials designed for adult use. The chapter will have more meaning if you use the materials as suggested.

Reading Direction

Look for information presented and problems posed in previous chapters as you read this chapter. You will have to switch roles as you read various sections—sometimes you will read about a procedure, other times you will actually experience the procedure yourself.

Sources: Tamara Wilcox, *Bats, Cats and Sacred Cows* (Milwaukee: Raintree Children's Books, 1977).

The Literature Sampler (New York: MacMillan, 1971).

H. Herber, *Teaching Reading in Content Areas* (Englewood Cliffs, N.J.: Prentice-Hall, 1970), p. 61.

Using Prequestions.   A second orienting strategy is the use of questions prior to reading the assigned material. This seems to be a modification of the advance-organizer strategy (Rickards, 1976), one that evolved as researchers sought to improve on the original technique. In this instance, the teacher would examine the goals of instruction and develop a small number of questions to guide the learner's reading of the assigned material. These questions would be rather general in nature, much like the advance organizer, and attempt to give the learner a purpose for reading. The prequestions may focus learner attention on the information the teacher has decided is important to attaining the goals of the instruction. One criticism often directed at prequestions is that the learner may only skim the material to find the answers to the questions provided and therefore not develop any in-depth understanding of the information in the assigned material. This is most likely to be the case if the questions ask only for recall of explicit information or reproduction of text-based information. The simplest way to avoid such behaviors is to develop questions that require the learner to reorganize presented information—to evaluate, synthesize, compare, or apply the new knowledge to a novel situation.

Initiating the Use of Prequestions

In order for learners to appreciate the potential impact of prequestions on learning from text, the teacher may want to follow this strategy:

1. Have the learners read a passage silently, directing them to read it as they normally read their assignments.
2. When the learners have finished reading, present several questions about the information without allowing them to refer to the material.
3. Prior to reading a second passage, present the learners with several questions to guide their reading. Direct learners to read to develop answers to these questions.
4. When the learners have again finished, present the questions from #2 above and elicit either oral or written responses.
5. Have learners compare their performances on the two selections and discuss with them whether the prequestions facilitated the desired learning.

There is a second type of purpose-setting question, one designed to facilitate acquisition of strategies by the learner that enable him or her to learn independently of the teacher. Jarolimek and Foster (1976) suggest that these questions, which focus on the learning process, are best designed to draw the learner's attention to facts, ideas, and conclusions that will lead to formulating generalizations and inferences. By learning to apply such generalizations, learners can transfer these skills to reading outside of that particular content area.

> Self-monitoring questioning behavior is most directly traceable to the theoretical stance taken by Frank Smith in his book *Comprehension and Learning* (1975). Smith defines comprehension as the condition of having your cognitive questions answered. The term *cognitive* here implies that the questions asked by good readers are generally implicit rather than explicit. If we can accept the possibility that some readers may fail to comprehend because they either did not ask or asked the wrong questions during reading, then an instructional strategy which encourages self-initiated questioning is supportable. (Chodos, Falope, Gould, Lavato, Schullstrom, and Wheeler, 1977)

The use of numerous questions is not recommended, because the learner can only possibly remember four or five. Questions concerning specific information should also be avoided, unless the information is particularly important to attaining instructional goals, because these items may serve to draw learner attention away from more important aspects of the text. The prequestion strategy seems quite powerful in focusing learner attention, but questions that focus on trivial aspects of the information presented typically result in the acquisition and retention of that trivial information. Thus the teacher should strive to develop items that require the learner to evaluate and integrate information.

Both the advance organizer and the prequestion strategies are teacher-controlled orienting methods: that is, the teacher decides how to structure the advance organizer and what aspects of the textual information to highlight. Similarly, the teacher develops prequestions intended to focus the learner's attention on particular aspects of the information presented. Although both strategies facilitate learning from text, neither involves the learner in the process of organizing the task. We note this because, in order to become effective and independent learners from textual material, students must develop an independent purpose-setting strategy, one that can be called on in the absence of teacher-provided orienting strategies. The following two strategies are designed to involve the learner in this process, in order to develop independent purpose setting.

The SQ3R Strategy.   The SQ3R strategy (Robinson, 1961) has been widely discussed in educational literature, and a variety of adaptations have been offered. Basically, this strategy involves students in developing a purpose for reading by requiring them to create a set of guiding questions to be answered while reading textual material. The teacher can present this strategy without examples and experience using it, but generally such a technique fails to generate any substantial change in learner reading behaviors. Instead, the teacher could simply walk through the steps with the learners, demonstrating the process, eliciting responses, providing evaluative comments, listing the questions developed, and demonstrating the general usefulness of the technique. This **walk-through** is more effective if it is repeated over several assignments because, just as in most other human behaviors, the process must be practiced until it becomes genuinely natural. The success of the strategy for individual students is the single most important feature of the demonstration. If learners only see it as busywork and identify no positive payoff, then the strategy will not be incorporated into their text-reading repertoire. The teacher, then, should make every attempt to demonstrate the facilitating effect of the strategy.

THE SQ3R METHOD

The content area teacher should have learners follow the steps described below and attempt to demonstrate the usefulness of each step and the process as a whole.

- *Survey*—Look through the whole assignment. Read the headings if there are any. Read the summary if there is one. Try to get a general idea of the content of the whole lesson. Later you can piece the details into the framework you have in mind, and the whole lesson will mean more to you.
- *Question*—Think of the questions likely to be answered in the lesson, and your reading will have much more purpose. Write these questions when you are first learning this method of study; later you may merely keep them in mind. The headings can easily be turned into questions. Use them!
- *Read*—Read the lesson carefully. Read to find the answers to the questions you have raised.
- *Recite*—Go back over the lesson immediately. Check the headings and also your own questions. Ask yourself: "Do I remember what this section was about?" or, "Can I answer this question?"

Put your ideas into actual words. Write out your answer in short form. Later you may say them to yourself or aloud. This step in study is *very* important. Don't kid yourself into believing that you understand what you have studied unless you can put your ideas into words. This will also help you remember what you have read.

● *Review*—Sometime later, and also before an examination, go back to your headings and questions. Quiz yourself. Reread those parts you have forgotten. This is the more efficient kind of review.

Source: Adapted from "Steps in the SQ3R Method" pp. 32–33, in *Effective Study*, 4th ed., by Francis P. Robinson. Copyright © 1941, 1946 by Harper & Row, Publishers, Inc. Copyright © 1961, 1970 by Francis P. Robinson. Reprinted by permission of the publisher.

The SQ3R strategy works because it activates existing frameworks of knowledge. Again, however, the teacher should remember that it is difficult to create meaningful questions about a generally unfamiliar topic. If the learner has little or no knowledge of the basic concepts to be studied, then this strategy, like most others suggested, will not be effective. The teacher must remember that the goal is to *teach* the purpose-setting process, which is not the same goal as *providing* the purpose-setting framework for the learner.

Learner-Generated Questions. Another orienting strategy that develops independent purpose-setting strategies in children has been suggested by Duffy, Sherman, Allington, McElwee, and Roehler (1973). This particularly appealing technique also requires learner-generated questions but in a somewhat different manner from the SQ3R process. To induce generation of questions prior to reading, Duffy et al. (1973) suggest presenting students with key words from the textual material. These key words are then used to generate questions following the basic theme: What do you think this selection will tell you about _____? or, What is one question you have about _____? Allington (1975) suggests the use of a **teaser sentence** from the text with directions to the learners to develop the questions necessary to accept the statement as true.

Because it seems that (1) learners progress only as far as is necessary to achieve their purposes, and (2) participation increases motivation (Watson, 1964), learner-generated questioning facilitates acquisition of knowledge, because learners are setting purposes beyond merely "getting through" the text, and because this strategy, more than any other, actively involves them in developing these purposes. Because the focus is on developing a strategy in the student, the teacher must attempt to build and refine student abilities over time. The first attempt may be frustrating for teachers, particularly with under-achievers, because for many this type of independent orienting is unfamiliar. Thus the teacher should not be disappointed if few truly good questions are generated in the initial attempts; only through experience will the learners develop the abilities necessary to pro-duce effective questions efficiently.

The SQ3R and learner-generated-questions strategies are based on an active processing model of reading. That is, when reading one is constantly evaluating, inferring, and extending the new information with the existing knowledge. These strategies work for those learners who either do not typically process textual material actively or who have few effective independent strategies for setting a purpose for reading. However, once this active behavior has been established in learners, the teacher should continue to refine the strategies by aiding learners in formulating better questions more easily.

ELICITING LEARNER-GENERATED QUESTIONS

Duffy, et al. (1973) suggest presenting key words from a passage to elicit learner-generated questions. For instance, they present examples from a social studies unit on ancient Egypt by offering the words *mummy, pyramid, pharaoh,* and so forth, to the learners, eliciting pos-sible questions about each item in turn.

Allington (1975) suggests using a teaser sentence such as "The leaders of the American Revolution were simply a bunch of criminals and profiteers who cared little, if at all, about the concept of democ-racy." From such sentences, the teacher directs the learners to develop questions that will provide information to prove or disprove the statement.

Chodos, et al. (1977) suggest using the title of a book or selection or a picture from the text to elicit learner questions prior to reading. Basically, from this information the student is asked, "What questions do you think this story will answer for you?"

In each strategy, the learner-generated questions are listed on the chalkboard and categorized by topics. Rephrasing and revising ques-tions can also become part of these sessions.

Visualization Skills. A final orienting strategy to be developed in learners is the ability to **visualize** or, to use Levin's (1972) term, to **image.** A variety of research studies have examined the effects of train-ing students to visualize while reading text. The strategies employed have generally been quite simple, with the most common merely directing students to close their eyes and to attempt to picture in their minds the scene, setting, characters, or sequence. The ability to create an image seems to be strongly tied to both acquisition and retention of information from text. Most skilled readers seem to do this naturally, but again, to construct a mental image the student must have basic familiarity with the information presented. The ability to image is basically the ability to call up existing scripts from memory; if no script exists, then creating an image is difficult, unless some type of assistance is provided. The experienced-based strategies for developing concepts discussed in Chapter 8 are ideal for facilitating the development of images and scripts.

DEVELOPING VISUALIZATION SKILLS IN LEARNERS

Use content area material that is particularly rich with "imageable" concepts. The best beginning is using descriptive passages that present familiar scenes, settings, and characters. Direct the learners to attempt to "see the scene (setting, or character) in their minds while they read." After reading, ask them to draw or describe the mental image they created and compare these visualizations.

In later stages use less familiar settings, scenes, and characters, drawing from learners information about why they created an image in a certain way. This allows the teacher to identify what type of sifting and categorizing the learner is doing.

Each of these orienting strategies is designed to facilitate learning from text by providing the learner with a clearer notion of what aspects of the information to attend to. Each strategy also encourages a more active processing of text by providing a framework for reacting to the information presented. These strategies are usually easy to implement into content area instruction because they are simply extensions of either instructional planning or learners participating in the knowledge-acquisition process. Thus the content area teacher has to expend less time and effort than would be required to implement the text-based organizational assistance discussed in the next section.

Imagine a panda. For most people a mental image of a cuddly, black-and-white teddybear-like representation appears. However, most people have a difficult time creating a mental image of a panda that is explicit in terms of size, weight, length of hair, color of eyes, much less an image of a panda eating his favorite food. The difficulty stems from a lack of experience or script for panda. However, as long as the general representation of a panda is available, new information can be incorporated. However, the relative validity of such information is difficult to assess. For instance, did you know that carrots are the favorite food of pandas? Can you judge the validity of that statement? Probably not, because few Americans have such detailed knowledge of pandas. You could check what you consider to be more reliable sources for confirmation; however, because you are generally familiar with pandas and carrots, you can visualize a panda eating a carrot without much effort. But what does a puffin look like?

The Text

Many content area teachers have observed that some learners who seem to have adequate reading abilities still have difficulty in learning from their textbooks. In Chapter 6 we discussed ways to evaluate textual materials, but teachers should consider additional difficulties.

One area of difficulty is the difference in the writing patterns that most children learn to read in and the writing patterns that they read to learn in. The primary writing pattern found in the readers used by elementary schools for reading instruction is narrative—materials that tell stories. Because this pattern is common in materials found outside of schools, it seems defensible to use such in developmental-reading programs. There is one problem though: content area textual material is seldom written in a narrative pattern. Thus, much reading instruction does not truly prepare students for the writing patterns found in most secondary-school reading materials.

Most content area textual materials are written in expository pattern, which is primarily used to communicate information. This pattern is most useful for presenting organized information to the reader. Paraphrasing *Webster's*, expository writing is writing designed to clear up that which is difficult to understand. However, if the pattern used to clarify a difficult concept causes difficulty in its own right, the problem for the learner is compounded.

In order to learn efficiently and effectively from expository writing, students must use skills that may not have been stressed while they were learning to read, skills that because of the narrative pattern found in elementary reading materials, they have probably had little experience using. This weakness in the reading curriculum is only now receiving the attention of publishers, curriculum developers, and classroom teachers, and it seems that an increased emphasis on reading expository materials is occurring. Even if this emphasis is increased greatly, the teacher can expect to find learners experiencing difficulty, because different content areas require different types of skills, and often these skills are best developed in the content area class by the content area teacher. It will always be necessary, then, for teachers to be prepared to offer some assistance in developing the specific skills most useful in their particular content area.

Examining Organizational Schemes within Texts

A major task in learning from texts is discovering the point of a piece of material. Typically, in talking about reading, discovering the point is referred to as **getting the main idea.** Authors often develop a discernible pattern for presenting the main idea, or **superordinate structure,** and the supporting details. Thankfully, many are consistent in maintaining the same pattern throughout the text.

The first pattern for presenting the main idea might be called the **pyramid.** In this pattern the superordinate structure is presented in the first sentence, and the remaining sentences serve to support or prove it. A second pattern is the **inverted pyramid.** In this type of paragraph, a set of related details are presented at the beginning of the paragraph and the final sentence serves as a logical conclusion tying all the details together. Another type is the **hourglass pattern,** in which supporting information is presented first, to set the stage for a synthesis statement, which is in turn followed by further details presented as reinforcement. Yet another common pattern might be referred to as the **diamond.** In this type, the superordinate statement is presented first; it is then followed by a set of details that reinforce or support it. The final sentence often qualifies the first or is a paraphrase of it. Finally, many paragraphs will have no identifiable superordinate statement; each sentence will be of equal or near-equal weight. The reader's task is to synthesize the elements and arrive at a general statement.

PYRAMID STRATEGY FOR IDENTIFYING PARAGRAPH STRUCTURES

1. Football can be dangerous to players who do not know enough about the game. In "pickup" teams the young men have rarely had any training or real experience. They seldom wear protective equipment, and there is no well-informed referee to prevent fouls. Even though the game begins as a friendly struggle, the excitement and the desire to win may soon turn it into a tough scrimmage. A tackle made without skill may result in a serious injury to

either the tackler or the runner. That is a heavy price to pay for what starts out in a spirit of pleasant competition.

2. You begin with some wood shavings or small dry twigs. On top of that you place wooden pieces; use a crisscross pattern. That leaves plenty of air space for the fire to come through. <u>There is really nothing complicated about building a campfire.</u>

3. When he was only three years old, Mozart could pick out melodies on a clavichord, and at five he was already beginning to compose. <u>It was evident that he was a prodigy and a musical genius.</u> He learned to play the violin and organ without instruction. He published his first composition when he was seven. By the time he was a young man, he had played at concerts in most of Europe's great cities.

4. <u>Penicillin is one of the greatest of the wonder drugs.</u> It has saved thousands of lives already and will save many more in the future. But it has no effect whatever on the bulk of the ills of man and of beast. <u>Good as it is, it is certainly not a cure-all.</u>

5. The range of the mule deer is usually east of the Sierra Nevadas. It is the largest of the North American deer, sometimes weighing almost 400 pounds. The name has been given to the species because of the long ears and the mule-like tail. Owing to its rather large antlers, it is a valuable game animal.

In addition to organizational style, authors usually rely on certain common relationships to present information. The four most common are: (1) listing, (2) chronological sequence, (3) cause and effect, and (4) comparison and contrast. Often these relationships are signaled by particular words or phrases. Teachers can assist students greatly by making them aware of the relationships these markers signal.

Within particular content areas certain organizational patterns are fairly recurrent. Nila Banton Smith (1973) has identified common types for the following content areas:

Science

1. CLASSIFICATION: In this pattern, living things, objects, liquids, gases, forces, and so forth, are first classified under a general heading. This heading, in turn, contains subdivisions, each of which has an element or elements in common which vary in certain respects from one another.

In reading this pattern the student who identifies it concentrates on grasping the subdivisions and the chief characteristics of each one.

2. EXPLANATION OF A TECHNICAL PROCESS: In this pattern the text is usually accompanied by diagrams, thus necessitating very careful reading of text, with continuous reference to diagrams. The diagrams, in themselves, require the student to use special skills in addition to those needed to grasp the text explanations.

3. CAUSE AND EFFECT: In this pattern the student is given information to explain why certain things happen. In reading this type of pattern, the student first reads to find the causes and effects, then carefully rereads to determine why the causes had the effects they did.

4. INSTRUCTIONS FOR AN EXPERIMENT: This pattern consists of explicit directions that must be carried out exactly and that call for careful observation, an explanation of what happens, and the drawing of a conclusion.

5. STATEMENT OF FACT: This pattern in science differs from fact-giving text in other subjects in these respects: the facts are more dense, and they frequently lead to or embody a definition or a statement of a principle.

Social Studies

1. CAUSE AND EFFECT: Every major event in history or geography comes about as the result of some cause or set of causes, and when the event occurs, its effect or effects are felt. The student who is adept at identifying the cause-and-effect pattern and who gears his reading toward ascertaining causes and effects will find this to be one of his most valuable assets in studying social studies.

2. COMPARISON AND CONTRAST: This pattern is most frequently encountered in a discussion of such topics as differences in the theories of government or policies of different leaders) physical features; products or industries of different countries; the past and present condition of peoples in certain countries; and so on.

   If the student is aware that he is about to read a comparison and-contrast chapter or section, he can approach it with the purpose of noting likenesses and differences.

3. PROPAGANDA: One of the most important reading skills in social studies is that of teaching students to recognize and interpret propaganda. It can be intricate and subtle and not always easily detectable. There are, however, seven techniques which are generally considered to be basic among the tricks used by the propagandist. These tricks make use of "glittering generalities," "unpleasant

words," "transfer," "testimonials," "plain-folks implications," "bandwagon techniques," and "stack the cards."

Mathematics

1. VARIETY OF SYMBOLS: One pattern in math is that text composed of words alone is at a minimum. Students could read number symbols alone and word symbols alone, but when the two kinds of symbols appear in the same sentence, confusion can result.
2. GRAPHS AND CHARTS: Another distinctive pattern found in math is the use of graphs and charts. Although these visual aids are used in other contents, they represent mathematical concepts.
3. EXPLANATIONS: The explanatory pattern in math constitutes difficult reading. Sections are comparatively short, contain a variety of symbols, and usually are accompanied or preceded by a series of exercises or questions designed to guide the student in discovering the principle or process.

Literature

Special analysis is not necessary in discerning patterns of writing of literature. Patterns in this field have been established for years. There are the story, exposition, essay, drama, fable, biography, and poetry. Each of these patterns requires a different approach.

Since, traditionally, teaching reading has fallen to the English Department, a general approach on detecting organizational patterns could be taught as part of the language-arts curriculum.

KEY WORDS THAT SIGNAL RELATIONSHIPS IN TEXT

Listing		Sequence	
the following	also	first	subsequently
then	in addition	second	until
another	furthermore	third	while
finally	likewise	last	meanwhile
moreover	as well as	soon	already
besides	and	at last	next
next	many	then	after
first	much	now	during
second	some	immediately	in the meantime
third	several	ago	afterwards
	lastly	at that time	

Cause/Effect		Comparison/Contrast	
for this reason	hence	even though	on the contrary
in order to	thus	but	nevertheless
since	consequently	however	notwithstanding
because	accordingly	yet	rather
so that	as a result	otherwise	not
therefore	so	although	in spite of
on account of	so that	despite	in comparison
	it follows that	still	conversely
		on the other hand	

Identifying Specific Skills Necessary to Read in Various Content Areas

Just as there are difficulties caused by the switch from narrative to expository materials, there are also difficulties caused by the patterns of materials for particular content areas. It is foolish to assume that learners should read a math text in the same fashion they would read social studies materials. One of the factors too often overlooked by content area teachers is identifying reading skills unique to the textual material of their content area. Examine the content area material that follows and attempt to identify any unique skills required to read and understand that page. Keep in mind the patterns identified by N. B. Smith (1973), which are common to the various content areas.

SINE AND COSINE

1. Refer to each triangle below.
   a. Compute the ratio of the measure of the side opposite the 30° angle to the measure of the hypotenuse.

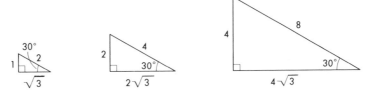

   b. What did you notice about each of your answers in a?

> The ratio of the measure of a side opposite a given angle in a right triangle to the measure of the hypotenuse depends on the measure of the angle and *not* on the measure of the sides.
>
> This ratio is called
> *sine of the measure of the angle*
> and is abbreviated *sin*.

   c. What is sin 30° equal to?

2. Continue with the three triangles in 1 above.
   a. Compute the ratio of the measure of the side adjacent to the 30° angle to the measure of the hypotenuse. Leave the square root sign in the answers.
   b. What did you notice about each of your answers in a?

> The ratio of the measure of a side adjacent to a given angle in a right triangle to the measure of the hypotenuse depends on the measure of the angle and *not* on the measure of the sides.
>
> This ratio is called
> *cosine of the measure of the angle*
> and is abbreviated *cos*.

   c. What is cos 30° equal to?

Source: E. D. Nichols et al., *Elementary Mathematics Patterns and Structure 8*, (New York: Holt, Rinehart & Winston, 1966), p. 156.

Mathematics

One of the first things teachers should notice in the mathematics sample is the technical vocabulary required to understand the directions, because many of the words are unique to mathematics texts. The first thing to do would be to determine which words represent a special mathematics vocabulary—*triangle, ratio, angle, hypotenuse, right triangle, sine, square root, cosine.* Because most of these words represent mathematical concepts, the content area teacher should have taught these concepts in an earlier lesson. The only new concept words for this lesson would be *sine* and *cosine.* Besides understanding the meanings of the words, the student must also learn that *sine* equals *sin* and *cosine* equals *cos.*

Some words that are not unique to mathematics are necessary in this lesson—*refer, compute, measure, opposite, given, depends, abbre-*

viated, continue. These words would probably not have been taught by the teacher in any systematic manner prior to this lesson. The teacher assumes that the students already know the meanings of these words; this assumption is often faulty. Learners may have some meanings for these words, but specific meanings in this context may not be available. Take, for example, the word *measure*. Normally, if learners encounter this word, it is a verb that tells one to do something. In this case, it is a noun and thus the meaning is subtly changed. *Given* is another example, because students often have a meaning for this word but perhaps not the one implied here. The same is true for *continue,* which generally means "go on with what you're doing" but here means "refer to."

Finally, there is the symbol vocabulary used in mathematics: $\llcorner$ = right angle, ° = degrees, $\llcorner$ = angle, $\sqrt{}$ = square root. These specialized notations communicate meaning just as words do, and learners must have access to their meanings.

The poor reader might experience trouble with any one of the three types of vocabulary on the sample page. The one least likely to produce confusion is the technical vocabulary, because that generally is the one best taught. The common vocabulary (for example, *refer, compute,* and so forth) constitutes the structure words for this selection; unless the learner understands the specific meanings of these words, it would be impossible to follow the author's logic. If these words were taught at all, it was probably in a general vocabulary lesson in an English class. However, the meanings for these words taught in English class would not be sufficient for math class. The symbol vocabulary may have been taught earlier in the year, but perhaps it has not been reviewed since and thus may also produce confusion.

Another facet in the sample is the syntax of the sentences. Generally, material in mathematics is written in a style that attempts to pack as much meaning into a sentence as possible. Students who have trouble understanding simple narrative prose would be at a severe disadvantage if faced with the following:

> The ratio of the measure of a side opposite a given angle in a right triangle to the measure of the hypotenuse depends on the measure of the angle and not on the measure of the sides.

A good reader attempting to read that sentence can probably understand it only by slowing down the reading rate and thinking carefully about each proposition in the sentence. The poor reader probably lacks this flexibility and thus is at a double disadvantage.

Social Studies

The sample selection (*Citizenship*) is not overly difficult, yet it still causes problems for the reader, and again one might first consider vocabulary difficulties. Most of the vocabulary problems in this selection represent concept words—*amendments, provision, immunities, naturalized, jurisdiction.* However, it is not safe to assume that these words have been previously taught. Because concepts in social science are fairly abstract, giving a capsule definition of *amendments,* for example, may prove rather difficult—not to mention *immunities.*

4   CITIZENSHIP

So far this chapter has dealt with the rights guaranteed by the Constitution itself, by the Bill of Rights, and by other *amendments* to the Constitution. But between 1 and 2 *percent* of the people in the United States today are not citizens. Do these non-citizens *possess* all the rights, some of the rights, or none of the rights of American citizens? How can a non-citizen become a citizen? And, *conversely,* can a citizen ever lose his citizenship?

The Fourteenth Amendment defines citizenship.

The men who wrote the Constitution took it for granted that most people living in the original thirteen states had been British subjects before the War for Independence. For this reason, they were citizens of their *respective* states and hence citizens of the United States. In the original Constitution, therefore, there is no *specific* definition of citizenship; nor is there a *provision* guaranteeing the privileges of citizenship. The Constitution simply assumes citizenship. For example, Section 2 of Article I states that "no person shall be representative who shall not have . . . been seven years a citizen of the United States." Similarly, Section 3 of the same article states that "no person shall be a senator who shall not have . . been nine years a citizen of the United States." Section 1 of Article II states that "no person except a natural born citizen . . . shall be eligible to the office of President." And Section 2 of Article IV asserts that "the citizens of each state shall be entitled to all privileges and *immunities* of citizens in the several states."

Not until the Fourteenth Amendment was adopted in 1868, however, was citizenship clearly defined. At the conclusion of the Civil War an important question confronted the American people: Were former slaves citizens? The Fourteenth Amendment answers yes, and gives a general definition of citizenship: "All persons born or *naturalized* in the United States, and subject to the jurisdiction thereof, are citizens of the United States and of the State wherein they reside."

Birthplace and parentage determine native citizenship.

Any person born in the United States and subject to its *jurisdiction* — that is, its *authority* — is a citizen of the United States. Citizenship in this case is determined by the place of birth. It makes no difference whether a child's parents are citizens. As long as the child is born within the United States, he is a citizen.

Immigration 1820–1970

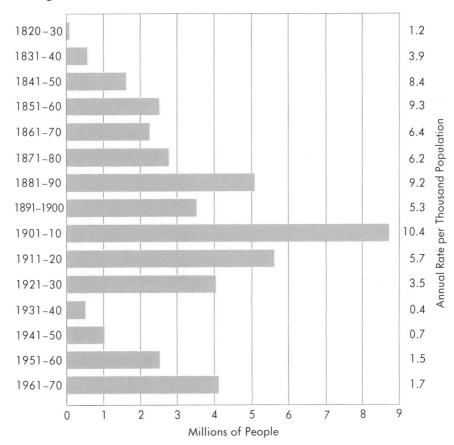

Source: S. Schick and A. R. Pfister, *American Government*, page 59. Copyright © 1975 by Houghton Mifflin Company. Used by permission. (Italics added.)

The common vocabulary is also rather difficult to understand—*percent, possess, conversely, respective, specific, authority*. These are words many people use daily in their speech, but many poor readers probably do not. A failure to appreciate this and plan for it can cause difficulty for the poor reader.

The syntax may again cause some difficulty for the poor reader. For example, failure to realize that the second paragraph includes a list of propositions from the Constitution causes the greater portion of the paragraph to be unintelligible. Or consider the dilemma of the learner who misses the cause-and-effect relationship implied in the third paragraph.

Another difficulty in social studies is the liberal use of charts, graphs, maps, and so forth. Very little, if any, instruction is given in how to read these aids. Therefore, many learners ignore them in their reading, unless their attention is drawn to them by the teacher, and the skills necessary for interpreting such information are either available or developed by the teacher.

Referring back to the discussion of concepts, scripts, and schema earlier in this chapter, the learner must at least be able to call up the concepts for *constitution, citizenship,* and *rights.* If students are unable to do this, they will have some difficulty understanding this material. Along these lines, the concept for *rights* may prove most difficult, because minors do not have full rights of citizenship. Thus students may not be aware of which rights aliens are denied.

Science

The most important consideration in understanding the sample page for science is the learner's previous knowledge. Care should be taken to establish that students understand the differences and similarities between ionic and covalent bonds as well as the concept of *molecule.* These can be considered readiness concepts for this sample page. Without this knowledge, the page under consideration becomes meaningless.

The major vocabulary problem for this sample is not the technical concept vocabulary but rather the common vocabulary. Some of these difficult words are *discussion, confined, numerous, simultaneously, transfers, stable, dissolved, dissociates, furnished, solutions, composed, previously,* and *mentioned.* One of the problems these words present is simply their length. The poor reader is apt to look at them and conclude that the page is too difficult.

The technical concept vocabulary in this sample is not terribly difficult. The biggest problem is represented by the names of the elements and compounds. However, these words are not critical to understanding what is being explained and could, for all practical purposes, be nonsense words.

COMPOUNDS WITH BOTH IONIC AND COVALENT BONDS

So far in our *discussion* of bonding, we have *confined* ourselves to molecules in which there are *only* ionic bonds or *only* covalent bonds. There are, of course, *numerous* substances in which bonds of both types exist *simultaneously*.

Potassium hydroxide is an example. The molecule, KOH, contains one ionic bond and one covalent bond. First the hydrogen atom is bonded to the oxygen atom by a covalent bond to form the unit:

$$\boxed{\cdot}\; O \;\boxed{\cdot\cdot}\; H$$

Then the potassium atom *transfers* an electron to form the *stable* molecule:

$$K^{\oplus}\quad \boxed{\vdots}\; O \;\boxed{\cdot\cdot}\; H^{\ominus}$$

Thus, when potassium hydroxide is *dissolved* in water, it *dissociates* into potassium ions (K^+) and hydroxide ions:

$$\boxed{\vdots}\; O \;\boxed{\cdot\cdot}\; H^{\ominus}$$

A second example is *furnished* by silver nitrate, whose formula is $AgNO_3$. The three oxygen atoms are bonded to the nitrogen to form the unit NO_3, to which a silver atom transfers an electron to form $NO_3{}^-$:

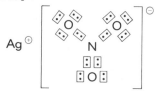

Solutions of silver nitrate are thus *composed* of silver ions (Ag^+) and nitrate ions $(NO_3{}^-)$. Many other common substances exhibit this kind of dual bonding, some of which have been *previously* mentioned. For example, calcium sulfate $(Ca^{++}SO_4{}^=)$, potassium carbonate $[(K^+)_2CO_3{}^=]$, and sodium azide $(Na^+N_3{}^-)$.

Source: R. Johnson and E. Grunwald, *Atoms, Molecules, and Chemicals Change,* Reprinted by permission of Prentice Hall, Inc., Englewood Cliffs, New Jersey, 1965. (Italics added.)

The visual aids on the page provide difficulty if the learner does not clearly understand the meanings of the symbols. What, for instance, is the critical difference between $\cdot O \cdot H$ and $\cdot O \cdot$, H^-, the extra dot in $\vdots$ or the $^-$?

Another difficulty of this type may be understanding the role of the [ ] and ( ) in $[(K^+)_2 \ CO_3 \ ^=]$. By the way, what do those $_2$'s and $_3$'s and $^+$'s and $^-$'s mean?

The materials presented here are neither the worst nor the best textual material available. They do fairly accurately represent textbooks in general use in secondary schools. The point we are trying to make is that there are difficulties inherent in the materials used by students. To overcome these problems, it is necessary for content area teachers to become familiar with them and begin to deal with them in the context of the students they are to teach.

Text-Organizing Strategies

The strategies presented thus far have dealt primarily with assisting the learner by providing extra-text assistance in setting purposes for reading assigned material. These strategies are usually generalizable across all content areas, because the primary goal is enhancing the active processing of textual material in general. However, many learners need more than simply to have a purpose for reading identified—many require more extensive assistance in developing strategies for processing the information presented in textual materials. Assigning textual materials without identifying a particular purpose for reading assumes that each learner will be able to sort out what is important and how to organize that information. Assigning textual material and providing a purpose for reading assumes that the learner can read to meet those purposes without any further assistance. Unfortunately, just as many students have inadequate abilities for identifying a purpose for reading, many also cannot read for a particular purpose once it is identified for them. Thus, in this section we present several strategies intended to assist students who may know how to learn from textual material. The learners may have the ability to deal with one type of textual material, but not another; this problem occurs because of the unique demands of different styles of writing.

Post-Reading Questions

Although we have discussed a rationale for using pre-reading questions and provided general guidelines for developing them, the formulation and delivery of good questions to follow the reading of assigned textual material is a particularly important facet of effective content area instruction. The use of pre-reading questions is intended

Postman and Weingartner (1969) proposed that all existing curricula and available textual material be eliminated from secondary schools in an attempt to reform the educational process. In place of these traditional frameworks for education, they suggested that questions provide the framework. These questions would simply reflect a larger question: What's worth knowing? The questions were to be evaluated on the following eight criteria. If every classroom question you ever ask were to meet at least one-half these criteria, think what a difference it would make.

1. Will the question increase the learner's will as well as capacity to learn?
2. Will the question provide the learners with confidence in their ability to learn?
3. In order to get the answer, will the learner be required to make inquiries? (ask additional questions, clarify terms, observe, classify, record, etc.)
4. Does the question allow for alternative answers?
5. Will the answers help the learners to sense and understand the universals in the human condition and so enhance their ability to draw closer to other people?
6. Would the question produce different answers if asked at different stages of the learner's development?
7. Will the question help provide a sense of joy in learning?
8. Will the process of answering the question tend to stress the uniqueness of the learner?

Source: From *Teaching as a Subversive Activity,* by Neil Postman and Charles Weingartner. Copyright © 1969 by Neil Postman and Charles Weingartner. Reprinted with permission of Delacorte Press.

to facilitate purpose setting in learners prior to reading, but post-reading questions often serve a similar purpose, especially in identifying the purpose for reviewing material prior to examination. The quality and quantity of post-reading questions often provide learners, rightfully or not, with an indication of the depth of understanding desired by the content area teacher. With this in mind, then, the teacher should carefully develop post-reading questions that reflect the goals of instruction and, if used in conjunction with pre-questions, should extend and refine the type of processing indicated by those.

Constructing Questions. The versatility of questions is the primary reason for attempting to develop expertise in constructing and delivering them. Although teachers commonly employ questioning to evaluate the reading of assigned textual material, this use of questions is

Aulls (1978) offers the following scheme for classifying or creating questions:

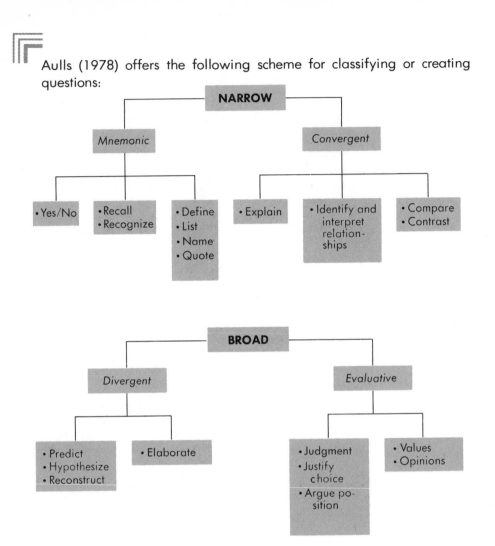

Source: From Mark W. Aulls, *Developmental and Remedial Reading in the Middle Grades.* Copyright © 1978 by Allyn and Bacon, Inc., Boston. Reprinted with permission.

often not done well. Teacher-questioning strategies can be improved by focusing on both developing a variety of question types and improving the delivery of questions in the classroom.

Many teachers present far too many questions, asking only for a reproduction of text-based information. These are generally called **literal-level questions.** Although reproducing text-based information is often crucial, in most instances students would profit from questions requiring reorganization or reconstruction of information or embellishment on the text-based information.

Questions that ask for **reproduction** of information, such as requesting a specific date, distance, character, action, or event, put demands primarily on the memory of the learner. This type of question does not tap understanding (Allington and Strange, 1978). For instance, read sentence (1) below and then answer questions (2) and (3).

(1) The bandicoot ate 12.163 liters of nizzle.
(2) Who ate the nizzle?
(3) How much nizzle did the bandicoot eat?

Most readers have no difficulty providing the correct answer to items (2) and (3). However, because few know what a bandicoot is or what nizzle is or how much 12.163 liters is, there can be no true understanding. For instance, consider questions (4), (5), and (6):

(4) Could a bandicoot eat that much nizzle in a single feeding?
(5) Why would a bandicoot eat nizzle?
(6) Of what food value would nizzle be to a bandicoot?

Each of these items requires **reconstruction** of text-based information and, therefore, cannot be answered using simple reproduction of text-presented information. In order to answer (4), (5), and (6), the learner would need a script for bandicoots, particularly including eating habits, knowledge of liter as a measure, and some idea of what nizzle might be. The learner would not have to know specifically about how much nizzle a bandicoot could eat, if he would, because with an adequate script for bandicoot the learner could judge the validity of (4), create a rationale for (5), and infer a logical response for (6). Each item requires manipulation of information that is not necessary to answer (2) or (3).

Embellishment is the least related to reproduction of text-based information. In embellishment the learner extends or predicts from given information, but generally the sole judge of the response's validity is the learner. For instance, (7) asks for embellishment on the information given in (1).

TYPES OF QUESTION STEMS

Reproductive Response Required:

1. Most who, what, why, and when questions.
2. Any item asking only for reproduction of text information.

Reconstructive Response Required:

1. How was the _____ similar to _____?
2. How did the _____ cause the _____?
3. What made the _____ react so _____?

4. What might have happened if _____ had _____?
5. Which _____ seemed most _____?
6. Why did the _____ respond _____?
7. Was _____ right in doing _____?

Embellished Response Required:

1. What else could the _____ have done?
2. What might the final results of _____ be?
3. What other possible choices about _____ could have been made?
4. What might have happened if _____?

(7) If you were a bandicoot, do you think you would like nizzle?

The point of these examples is to demonstrate that (1) content area teachers can develop items that go beyond reproduction of text, and (2) although questions calling for reproduction are not inherently bad, they do have their limitations, particularly for evaluating learner understanding of information presented in textual material. In developing post-reading questions for evaluation of learning, the teacher should analyze the demands placed on the learner with each question. Developing questions that require reconstruction or embellishment of information serves to foster a greater depth and permanency of information presented in text.

Delivering Questions.   The second facet of questioning that can generally be improved is **delivery.** There are several critical variables in the effective use of questions. One of the first issues to resolve is whether the question is best used (1) to establish purpose as a pre-reading question, (2) as a technique to stimulate a particular type of reconstruction of text-based information, or (3) as an evaluative tool for assessing learner understanding after reading assigned material. Questions that serve one purpose well may not be appropriate for another. The teacher must examine the question and ask, "What learner behaviors are best served by this question?" That is, what behaviors will this question induce in learners? As noted previously, some questions serve only to require the learner to reproduce, whereas others stimulate reconstruction or embellishment of text-based information. After deciding what type of cognitive activity the question should elicit, the teacher can decide whether the items match the instructional goals and whether each serves better as a pre-reading purpose-setting tool or as a post-reading evaluation item.

Wait Time.   Delivery of post-reading questions is often poorly done. A crucial but often overlooked variable influences the quality of learner response. This variable—**wait time**—can easily be controlled by the teacher who is aware of its importance. For instance, if the average wait time between asking a question and selecting a student to respond is about one second, the student has almost no time for reconstruction or embellishment. By simply increasing the wait time to even three seconds, the teacher allows learners to formulate responses, responses that are generally of a higher quality than those generated with a one-second wait time. The questions most easily answered with the typical one-second wait time are those that call only for reproduction of text. However, if the teacher wishes to encourage other cognitive behaviors through the use of questions requiring reconstruction or embellishment, then wait times must be increased.

WAIT TIME

Identifying Average Wait Time in the Classroom

Wait time is simply the amount of time between uttering a question and identifying a respondent.

> Teacher: Describe the impact of the First Battle of Bull Run on the economic base of the Confederacy.
>
> (wait time)
>
> Teacher identifies learner to respond.

To calculate average wait time, simply record the interval between the end of an utterance and identifying a respondent for at least ten questions, then compute the average. Generally, a stopwatch is needed, but to gather an estimate of wait time, simply use the traditional "one thousand one, one thousand two" strategy.

Strategies for Increasing Wait Time Following Questions

1. Simply count slowly to five before identifying a respondent.
2. Scan up and down each row of students.
3. Take a deep breath and check your fingernails for hang-nails.
4. Look up at the wall clock and wait for five seconds to pass.

Another facet of short wait times is that the teacher often ends up answering the question. Usually this occurs when no learner attempts to respond quickly. The teacher becomes uncomfortable and, ultimately, to alleviate this provides the sought-after response, often adding a tag question such as "Isn't that right?" Teachers can easily suppress these behaviors if they are conscious that the behaviors are occurring.

Effective use of questions can immeasurably enhance learning from text. Whether used prior to reading or following it, whether teacher-imposed or learner-generated, questions serve to stimulate cognitive activity. By implementing an effective questioning strategy and shaping learner responses within it, the teacher can induce greater understanding of textual material in any content area.

The following small-group format, which allows for participation, or active manipulation of textual material, can be employed for a variety of purposes:

1. Assign a segment of text, usually between three and five pages. You may also want to use an especially prepared selection that would be distributed in mimeograph form.
2. Break the class up into groups, each with three to six members. You may wish to attempt a heterogeneous grouping to ensure some equal distribution of academic abilities.
3. Have learners attempt to list all the facts or propositions presented in the material. Learners would simply underline or list them.

At this point, several options are available. Several of these, which could be used individually or sequentially, are listed below:

4. Compare the number of facts identified by the various groups. Attempt to determine, with your students, which is the correct number of facts. This will entail discussions of how to identify "facts."
5. Direct learners to classify facts as major, minor, or inconsequential. Attempt to determine which are the important facts. Force learners to defend selections.
6. Direct learners to identify proof of the facts presented. Does the author support the facts?
7. Classify the facts by topics. Again, force learners to defend groupings.

Reading Guides

Another text-organizing strategy that offers more guidance to the learner is the **reading guide.** A reading guide is material that aids students in learning from text by literally guiding them through textual material. Learning to use them should build strategies for learning from text that can be used independently later. The concept of a reading guide is certainly not new. It masquerades under many different labels: study guides, text aids, reasoning guides, text supplements, and so forth, but the basic idea is to provide learners with assistance toward reaching an instructional goal. We prefer to use the term *reading guide* to cover all such devices because the term suggests generalizability to many different forms and goals.

Constructing any reading guide requires essentially four steps:

1. determining the goal for the reading assignment
2. identifying the barriers to the goal
3. determining how to overcome the barriers to the goal
4. constructing the guide

Rather than try to explain the process, we feel it is more helpful to trace the development of a reading guide in a content area. Read the material on women activists and then the explanation of building a study guide for the material.

WOMEN GAIN A MORE IMPORTANT PLACE IN AMERICAN LIFE

From the earliest days women worked together with men in the development of America. They shared the loneliness, the dangers, the desperately hard work involved in settling the wilderness and transforming it into a land of prosperous farms and thriving towns and cities.

The status of women

But there was this difference: even as late as the 1830's, women had legal rights hardly better than those of children. These rights varied from state to state. In some states a married woman had almost no right to own property. When a woman married, all the property she owned went to her husband. If she earned money or inherited property after marriage, it too belonged to her husband.

Moreover, a married woman had almost no legal claim to her own children. The husband controlled his sons and daughters while he lived. He, not both parents, decided what the children should do. Indeed, if a man wished, he could leave a will placing his children under a guardian after his death, even though their mother was still alive. However, men rarely used their full legal rights over their wives and children.

As for the practice of politics, that was entirely a man's job. Women often exercised a large influence over husbands and friends, but the right to vote and hold office was a man's right.

A declaration of women's rights

Even during colonial days a number of women had protested against the limitations on the rights of women. In 1774, for example, Abigail Adams sent a letter to her husband John, who was in Philadelphia attending the First Continental Congress: "We are determined to foment a rebellion," she wrote, perhaps with a twinkle in her eye, "and will not hold ourselves bound by any laws in which we have no voice or representation."

The rebellion Abigail Adams warned her husband about did not come in her lifetime. By the 1820's and 1830's, however, women were raising their voices in defiant protest against their lowly place in society. Leaders appeared, women with deeply rooted convictions.

In these years women frequently tried to force their way into men's meetings, even into political conventions. The men, astonished at this unladylike conduct, usually turned them away.

A few of the leaders came from Europe, where a similar women's rights movement was under way. Among the Europeans who traveled across the Atlantic to help the American women in their struggle for equal rights with men were Ernestine L. Rose of Poland, Frances Anne Kemble of England, and Frances Wright of Scotland.

But American women bore the brunt of the struggle. Among the American leaders were Lucretia Mott and Elizabeth Cady Stanton. These two women were in large part responsible for organizing the first women's rights convention, held at Seneca Falls, New York, in July 1848. At the convention the women adopted a Declaration of Sentiments, which said, "All men and women are created equal . . ." and went on to list demands for political, social, and economic equality with men. But decisive gains in these fields did not come until the latter half of the 1800's. Most of the early victories were confined to the field of education.

LIVING AMERICAN DOCUMENTS

*The Seneca Falls Declaration of Sentiments
and Resolutions (1848):*

*WE HOLD THESE TRUTHS to be self-evident: that all men and
women are created equal. . . . Now, in view of this entire dis-
franchisement of one half of the people of this country, their
social and religious degradation—in view of the unjust laws
above mentioned, and because women do feel themselves
aggrieved, oppressed, and fraudulently deprived of their most
sacred rights, we insist that they have immediate admission to all
the rights and privileges which belong to them as citizens of the
United States. . . .*

Education for women

Back in the days when Abigail Adams was warning her husband that women might rebel if they did not receive a larger
share of rights, a Boston clergyman wrote to a friend: "We
don't pretend to teach the female part of the town anything
more than dancing, or a little music perhaps."

By the 1820's, however, education for girls and women
was getting well started. Emma Hart Willard opened the Troy
Female Seminary in 1821 at Troy, New York, and began to
teach mathematics, science, history, and other subjects. During the next few years Catharine Esther Beecher, Mary Lyon,
and other dedicated women opened schools for girls.

The movement grew most rapidly in the Middle West. The
first college to open its doors to women was Oberlin Colle-
giate Institute in Ohio, which admitted women four years
after it was founded in 1834. This action, and the fact that
Oberlin also admitted Negroes, led many Americans to look
upon the institution as "radical." But other colleges in the
Middle West also began to admit women students. In 1856
the University of Iowa attracted attention as the first state
university to open its doors to women.

Early achievements

Slowly, and against strong opposition, women began to win
places for themselves in what, until this time, had been con-

sidered a "man's world." Dr. Elizabeth Blackwell, the first woman to win a medical diploma in the United States, began to practice medicine in New York City in 1850. She founded the first school of nursing in the United States and in 1875 became a professor in the London School of Medicine for Women. Her sister-in-law, Antoinette Louisa Blackwell, the first fully ordained female minister in the United States, became minister of the Congregational Church at South Butler, New York, in 1852.

Other women won distinction as writers and editors. Louisa May Alcott was the author of a number of children's books, among them *Little Women,* which was translated into several languages. Harriet Beecher Stowe wrote *Uncle Tom's Cabin.* Margaret Fuller preceded Ralph Waldo Emerson as editor of *The Dial,* a philosophical and literary magazine. She also served for a time as literary critic for the *New York Tribune.*

Dorothea Lynde Dix

Another woman who exerted an enormous influence was Dorothea Lynde Dix. For a number of years, Miss Dix ran a boarding school in Boston, and during these years wrote a highly successful textbook, *Conversations on Popular Things.* Ill health forced her to close her school, but in 1841, after inspecting the East Cambridge jail near Boston, she began a new career of institutional reform that made her famous at home and abroad.

Miss Dix was horrified by conditions in the jail. It was cold, bare, and filthy. The sane and the insane lived side by side. Determined to do something about the situation, she laid the facts before the Massachusetts legislature, but the men were indifferent to her remarks.

Goaded to further action, Dorothea Dix made up her mind to visit every jail and poorhouse in Massachusetts, to collect an overwhelming amount of data, and to present them to the legislature. She packed notebook after notebook with records of horrors almost beyond belief. In all of the jails and poorhouses, she found old men, young girls, the poor, and the mentally ill thrown together in cold, dirty prisons. Some were chained to walls, beds, or floors. Some wore iron collars or strait jackets. Some were confined in cages for years.

Finally, Miss Dix went again to the Massachusetts legislature with her evidence. This time the legislators listened. They

Ernestine Rose,
Battler for Human Rights

Ernestine Louise Potowski (1810-1892), the daughter of a learned rabbi, was born in the ghetto of Piotrkow, Poland. Even as a young child she began to rebel against injustice. At seventeen she left home to avoid a marriage that had been arranged for her. Given the times and the environment, this was an act of rare courage and an extraordinary assertion of independence. The young girl traveled to London. There she met Robert Owen, a successful manufacturer who was devoting his life to improving the condition of the working man. Through Owen, she met and fell in love with a young jeweler and silversmith named William Rose. They were married, and in 1836 left England for America.

In America, Ernestine Rose made a career of her battle for human rights. She traveled widely, and wherever she went, interested audiences gathered to witness the novel sight of an attractive young woman with an appealing foreign accent lecturing against injustice. In her lectures—for which she refused to accept any payment—she pleaded for equal rights for women, emancipation of the slaves, better pay and working conditions for wage earners, freedom of religion, and free public education.

Ernestine Rose was sharply criticized for many of her views. But with her eloquence as a speaker, her brilliant intellect, her intense enthusiasm, and her unquestionable sincerity, she became one of the most influential women of her time.

began to pass laws to improve conditions in jails and poorhouses.

Other states watched these developments with interest. During the next few years Miss Dix repeated her reform work in Connecticut, New York, Pennsylvania, and Kentucky. Moreover, her efforts to improve the treatment of the poor and the insane attracted the attention of European reformers and helped to improve conditions in European jails and institutions for the poor and insane.

By the 1850's, in large part as the result of the work of Miss Dix and others who shared her views, important reforms had been made in the United States. The death penalty had been abolished for a number of crimes, and a growing number of people were demanding the "complete abolition of capital punishment." Most states had outlawed the whipping of prisoners. Imprisonment for debt had been ended. Men and women were confined in separate sections of prisons, and the mentally ill were separated from other prisoners. More attention was given to the individual criminal, and more effort was made to reform rather than to punish.

Dorothea Dix lived to the age of eighty-five. When she died in 1887, a famous English doctor said, "Thus has died and been laid to rest in the most quiet and unostentatious way the most useful and distinguished woman that America has ever produced."

SECTION SURVEY

1. Even as late as the 1830's, women had legal rights far inferior to those of men. Discuss.
2. What was the significance of the Seneca Falls Convention of 1848?
3. How do you explain the fact that the first victories of the women's rights movement were in the field of education?
4. Describe three notable accomplishments by women during this period.
5. What important reforms did Dorothea Lynde Dix help to introduce?

IDENTIFY: reformer, capital punishment; Lucretia Mott, Elizabeth Cady Stanton, Emma Hart Willard, Elizabeth Blackwell, Antoinette L. Blackwell, Louisa May Alcott, Margaret Fuller, Ernestine L. Rose; 1821, 1848.

Developing a Reading Guide for "Women Gain an Important Place in American Life"

Step 1: Determining the Goal.   The overall purpose for reading this section might be for learners to realize that although the United States professed democracy for all, the "all" did not include women. A secondary purpose might be to trace the changes in the rights of women through the eighteenth and nineteenth centuries. A third purpose could be to have learners compare the status of women in the nineteenth and twentieth centuries.

Step 2: Identifying Barriers to Learning. To achieve the primary goal the learner must sense the irony that at the same time the United States was trying to guarantee freedom and rights for its citizens, it was systematically denying freedom and certain rights to its female population. This is not explicitly stated in the selection and only implied in the quote from Abigail Adams.

To achieve the secondary purpose the learner needs to attend to the dates, because historical events seldom are isolated incidents. The passages relating to time are generally well sequenced, but there is some confusion because when education for women is considered the text does not faithfully follow a chronological sequence.

To achieve the third goal students must be aware that they are expected to make this comparison concerning the status of women because it is not alluded to in the selection.

Certain other elements might cause learners some difficulty. Because the second section, "A declaration of women's rights," has no stated main idea, learners may need assistance to arrive at organizing statements such as "the increasing militancy of women." The third section's main idea has to do with increasing education for women, but learners are led to this with a quote from a Boston clergyman. This quote, however, implies the main idea through contrast and some students might miss this.

The section on Dorothea Dix is designed as an example of the increasing influence of women. It is not necessary to the achievement of any of the three purposes we identified earlier. In fact, it may distract the learner's attention from the primary goals.

Finally, a few vocabulary terms may present problems: *sentiments, decisive, radical, reforms* and *abolition.*

Step 3: Determining How to Overcome the Barriers. We will deal first with the barriers that will cause difficulty regardless of the goal. Usually these will be problems of syntax and vocabulary. In this case the difficulty is of vocabulary. This can be handled in one of two ways: (1) in the reading guide or (2) by preteaching the pronunciation of key vocabulary and the concepts represented. If there are few words (five or less), it is most efficient to preteach using strategies presented in Chapter 8. For purposes of illustration, however, we will treat these in the reading guide. Three of the words—*sentiments, radical,* and *reforms*—should not cause serious pronunciation problems; therefore, the reading guide should focus on developing their meaning. The words *decisive* and *abolition* may present problems both in terms of meaning and recognition; therefore, the guide should focus both on developing meaning and pronunciation. We feel that the most efficient way of handling word-meaning problems in a reading guide is by providing learners with a familiar synonym appropriate to the context and handling pronunciation problems through respellings.

In helping the learner achieve the primary purpose (detecting the contradiction between the principles of democracy and the reality regarding women), all that may be necessary is a purpose-setting question focusing attention on the contradiction. To reach the secondary goal (tracing the changes in the status of women), we would ask the learners to respond by completing a time line of some sort. Finally, to reach the third goal (comparing the rights of women in the past and present), we could choose to have the learner complete a table designed to illustrate major changes. This table might also include the rights of men to reinforce the primary goal.

Step 4: Constructing the Guide.   Examine the accompanying reading guide for "Women Gain a More Important Place in American Life," which illustrates how the guide might look as it is supplied to the learners prior to reading the selection.

READING GUIDE FOR "WOMEN GAIN A MORE IMPORTANT PLACE IN AMERICAN LIFE"

1. Below are some words you may not know. Review them before reading the assignment.

   sentiments = feelings   radical = rebel
   reforms = changes   abolition (ăb-ōh-lĭsh-ŭn)
   decisive (dēē-sī-sĭv) =   to get rid of
       important

2. Read the section entitled "The status of women", on p. 201. Be prepared to discuss the following question:

   The Declaration of Independence states that all men have certain unalienable rights, such as life, liberty and the pursuit of happiness. Did these rights apply to women?

3. Read the sections on pp. 202–204 entitled "A declaration of women's rights," "Education for women," and "Early achievements." Complete the following time line by filling in the important event that occurred in each of the years listed.

   1774 _____

   1821 _____

1838 _____

1856 _____

1850 _____

1852 _____

1875 _____

4. Complete the chart below by writing Yes or No in each box if the rights had been granted by that time.

	1800		1900		1980	
	Women	Men	Women	Men	Women	Men
Right to vote						
Right to hold office						
Right to own property						
Right to inherit						

Other Types of Reading Guides

Reading guides can have many other formats (for a number of examples, see Herber, 1978). Some reading guides are designed to elicit different types of information reorganization. For instance, the reading guide might consist simply of a series of true and false statements purposefully written in an ambiguous fashion. The task for the learners might be to clarify the statements so that they could be answered as true or false. Another type of reading guide might require learners to complete analogies or perhaps to identify appropriate analogies based on textual information. Reading guides may also require learners to infer actions, beliefs, or descriptions. The point is, reading guides can be developed in many different formats for many different purposes. They can be employed to assist the learner in a basic understanding of textual information or to extend and reorganize text information with existing knowledge. Reading guides should be varied in format so as to not become tiresome and should be supplemented with instruction on how to accomplish the manipulation of information they require.

SCIENCE READING GUIDE

Following is a reading guide developed by Herber (1970) for a ninth-grade general science unit on weather. Note how it requires the learner to translate principles into real-world situations or vice versa.

Directions

Below are five principles and nine statements. In front of each statement, write the number of the principle which applies to that statement.

Principles

1. Warm air holds more moisture than cold air.
2. Altitude affects temperature.
3. Humidity affects man's comfort.
4. Warm air is lighter than cold air, and is often forced upward by cooler air.
5. It takes much longer for a large body of water to become warmed by the sun than it does for the land.

Statements

_____A.   In the winter, moisture often appears on the inside of the windows of the classroom.

_____B.   It is usual on a hot summer day for clouds to form some distance above the earth's surface.

_____C.   A 90° temperature in the desert would be more comfortable than a 90° temperature in the Mohawk Valley.

_____D.   If the air in a room is perfectly still, the smoke from a cigarette will usually rise.

_____E.   On a hot humid June evening, air from over the land moves over the ocean. A fog occurs.

_____F.   You come into a warm room from outside on a cold winter's day, and moisture condenses on your glasses.

_____G.   In the winter months, moist air from the Pacific is carried over the mountain ranges of the Northwest coast. These winds are deflected upward. Clouds form and rains are frequent.

_____H.   Thunderclouds are likely to form on hot humid summer afternoons. They may grow upward and become thousands of feet high. Hail, as well as rain, often falls from these clouds.

_____I.   You can see your breath when you exhale on a cold winter day.

Source: H. Herber, _Teaching Reading in Content Areas_ (Englewood Cliffs, N.J.: Prentice-Hall, 1970), p. 271.

    Although reading guides require more effort by the teacher, the potential benefits outweigh the costs. In addition, a useful feature of reading guides is their relative permanency. Once constructed, these guides can be employed time after time. In addition, eliciting the cooperation of other teachers who use the same textual materials reduces the effort necessary to develop the reading guides.

HISTORY READING GUIDE

Following is another example of a reading guide. It requires learners to identify cause-and-effect relationships and chronological sequence in a unit on European exploration of the Americas in a social studies text.

_____1. Monopoly of Asia by Italian merchants
_____2. Columbus seeks a shorter route to Asia
_____3. Magellan's voyage
_____4. Search for the Northwest Passage
_____5. Vasco da Gama's voyage
_____6. The explorations of Ponce de Leon and Francisco Vasquez de Coronado
_____7. Travels of Sir John Mandeville
_____8. Samuel de Champlain fires on a party of Iroquois

A. fear of the unknown
B. decline of the Italian trading cities of Genoa and Venice
C. European search for an all-water route to Asia
D. North and South America rediscovered by Europe
E. true size of the world is finally realized
F. eventually caused the French to lose all land claims in North America
G. resulted in the exploration of North America by France and Great Britain
H. gave Spain land claims in the southwestern and southeastern United States

    List the following events in the order they occurred. Use the number 1 for the first event, 2 for the second, 3 for the third, etc.

___1. Columbus reaches America
___2. The English settle in Jamestown
___3. The Vikings settle in Finland
___4. Jaques Cartier claims Canada for France
___5. Vasco da Gama reaches India

Summary

Many learners need assistance in organizing information from textual materials. In this chapter, we discussed the difficulties experienced by many learners in terms of both extra-text and in-text strategy deficiencies. We explored a number of possible routes for facilitating learning from text by providing organizational assistance in a variety of formats. The central themes of the chapter were:

1. Understanding and learning are basically the process of finding answers to one's questions. Without personal questions, neither understanding nor learning occurs easily, nor is any degree of permanency of stored information achieved.

2. To facilitate learning, the teacher should identify for learners the purposes for which they are to read. However, to ensure adequate independent learning strategies, the teacher should attempt to develop purpose-setting strategies in learners.

3. Questions, either teacher-generated or learner-generated, used either prior to or following reading are effective in enhancing learning from textual material. Too often, teachers spend too little time on this aspect of instruction. Several types of questions should be developed, and these should be congruent with instructional goals.

4. Questions serve as orienting devices for learners, cueing them as to either (a) what information is to be attended to, or (b) what type of information reorganization is called for.

5. Orienting strategies will not be particularly effective if the learner has little existing knowledge of the content to be developed. The teacher must ensure that, if available, existing knowledge is activated.

6. Some learners need assistance beyond orienting strategies, because they have difficulty recognizing and coping with the organization of information in text. Reading guides can help these learners to process information in text. Reading guides can take many forms but are primarily elaborate extensions of the other orienting strategies.

7. There are different recurrent patterns of text organization in the various content areas. Learners may learn quite readily from the

textual material of one area but may find the organization of information in another area a barrier to learning.

8. Learners need different text-learning abilities for different content
   areas. Many will have to be taught how to identify and learn from
   the organizational patterns found in various content area texts.

Differentiating Instruction

THROUGHOUT THIS BOOK, we have presented a number of arguments, strategies, and goals for differentiating instruction in the content area classroom. Virtually every topic addressed reflects in some way the notion of improving instruction by differentiating on the basis of instructional goals, learner abilities, and textual difficulty. Although teachers can use many other media in content area instruction, this text has focused on printed material primarily because (1) its use is pervasive, and (2) there are other resources for learning the effective use of nonprint media. In this final chapter differentiating text-based instruction is again the primary topic, but the focus is on effective use of available resources to facilitate instructional differentiation. Or, to put it another way, this chapter presents strategies for easing the burden on the individual content area teacher. This facet is too often overlooked by the various experts, be they professors, assistant superintendents, curriculum directors, inservice consultants, or reading specialists.

There are only so many hours in a day and not all of them should be spent on work related to teaching. The plans presented in this chapter should allow the teacher to more effectively meet the needs of learners within the limits of a typical eight-hour day. A primary goal of this text has been to present both a basic understanding of the complexities of learning from text and strategies for meeting the needs of learners. However, knowledge that is not applied is of little more use than no knowledge at all. Thus the primary goal of this chapter is not to convince teachers that differentiation *should* be done (though we will argue that briefly), but rather that it *can* be done and that by differentiating, both the teaching and the learning tasks become easier.

There are various levels of differentiated instruction. Using different textbooks in classes of different ability or age levels is differentiating, although quite minimally. Purely individualized assignments are differentiated instruction carried to an extreme, in our view. Thus the teacher can choose to apply instructional differentiation at a variety of intensities. The plan proposed in this chapter suggests beginning at a rather minimal level of differentiation and steadily moving along until instructional differentiation is well developed, although not to the point of complete individualization.

> A central and persisting problem of our schools resides in the necessity to design and provide environments that adapt to individual diversity. Commitment to the realization of individual potential, equality of opportunity, and social justice demands that the process of education consider individual differences along all the various dimensions in which they are manifested—differences in needs, interests, abilities, talents, and styles of learning and living.
>
> The fundamental educational task is to design settings for education that are flexible and adaptive enough to handle these differences which derive from an individual's cultural milieu and his or her own uniqueness among other human beings. An educational environment that is not capable of adjusting to these differences inhibits the development of individual potential, becomes elitist and selective, is heavily biased toward the mainstream culture, and perpetuates inequality. (Glaser, 1977)
>
> Source: From *Adaptive Education: Individual Diversity and Learning* by Robert Glaser. Copyright © 1977 by Holt, Rinehart and Winston. Reprinted by permission of Holt, Rinehart and Winston.

A Rationale

It should be obvious that no matter how hard one might try, it will never be possible to gather together twenty-five content area learners with identical abilities, traits, experiences, intentions, and motivations, much less a whole class of, say, ninth-graders with a similarity in such areas. Yet one complaint often heard in content area classes is "He (or she) shouldn't be here if he cannot read the material." Well, unfortunately they will never all be able to read the material (as illustrated in Chapter 3), and the content area teacher will have to accept that as fact. The implementation of Public Law 94-142 mandates that learners with special needs or handicapping conditions (mentally retarded, deaf, learning disabled, physically handicapped, emotionally disturbed, behaviorally disordered, and so forth) be placed in the "least-restrictive environment" and provided with a detailed individual educational program (IEP). The least-restrictive environment is often the regular classroom, and whether or not the content area teacher feels equipped or willing to provide instruction, federal law mandates the learner's right to such educational instruction. These learners will be exceptional cases in most classrooms but the point is that learners, even those whose only deviation is underachievement, have a right to be educated. Teachers, then, have a responsibility, in some cases a legal responsibility, to provide differentiated instruction.

> The purpose of teaching is to help students learn. You should, therefore, create conditions that will make learning easy. This seems obvious when it is stated this way, but some teachers do not act as if they believe in facilitating learning. They present material in ways that make it seem more difficult than it is, perhaps to "impress" the students, or perhaps because they want to scare off the ten less capable students, or maybe because they think hard work is good for students. But, for whatever reason it is done, it has the effect of damaging learning and turning off students. Others make up tests that are extremely hard so that they will have a perfect normal distribution of grades. None of these practices is coexistent with good instruction. (Lahey and Johnson, 1978)

However, there are better reasons for providing instruction that more closely matches student abilities. A primary reason is that learning improves—the ultimate goal of education. Even mastery of the content material improves with learners grasping new ideas, concepts, and relationships that would have been missed had instruction not been modified.

A second reason is that both teaching and learning become easier if instruction is differentiated. The teaching is easier because learners operating nearer their own ability level are not as aggressive and need less extrinsic motivation to complete tasks. Thus the teacher's role becomes less one of policeperson and more one of educator. Learning is easier because task demands are more realistic, and if learning is facilitated, more is learned.

> Robert Glaser (1977) describes several principles of learner-centered education, education that tries to take into account the distinctive needs, capabilities, and abilities of individual learners. These educational principles attempt to provide a learning environment that makes equality of educational opportunity more than a nice-sounding phrase:

1. The human and material resources of the school are flexibly employed to assist in adapting educational practice to meet the needs of learners.
2. Curricula are designed to provide realistic sequencing and multiple options for learning.
3. Alternative learning options are openly displayed and access to information and instructional materials are provided.
4. Testing and monitoring procedures are designed to provide information for decision making to teachers and learners.
5. Emphasis is placed upon developing abilities in learners that assist them in guiding their own learning.
6. The role of teachers and other school personnel emphasizes individual learners.

Source: From *Adaptive Education: Individual Diversity and Learning,* by Robert Glaser. Copyright © 1977 by Holt, Rinehart and Winston. Reprinted by permission of Holt, Rinehart and Winston.

None of this is to say that differentiation will solve all the ills burdening our schools, but rather that it is one step that can be accomplished by teachers individually or in cooperation with each other. It is our hope that by providing what we feel is a workable model for instructional differentiation, the content area teacher will venture onto the path and rather effortlessly be led to improved content area instruction.

A Beginning

Probably the first step the teacher should take is to examine the goals for instruction. Often content area goals are textbook imposed—that is, the teacher relinquishes authority for what is to be taught to the authors of the text. The goals are simply to learn the information presented, with no goals independent of the mandated or selected textual material. Whenever the goals of a content area class are restricted to information in a single text, differentiation becomes a bit more difficult. Whenever a single text is the primary source of instructional goals, several types of differentiation may be completely ruled out.

Another reason for examining the goals of instruction is to assess their appropriateness for given learners. Because most goals have a variety of prerequisites—both strategy and content—the teacher should assess whether the intended learners have acquired the necessary prerequisite abilities that would enable them to achieve the goals. Without a general knowledge of learner abilities, this is a difficult task, so the teacher often should explore several sources of pertinent information typically available within the school.

For instance, because most content areas are taught at different levels of schooling (such as science, math, and social studies), simply discussing the earlier curricula with teachers at those levels provides some general notion of the adequacy of content area knowledge. Similarly, these teachers can also provide a general notion of the academic aptitudes of learners in comparison to other groups. Although this sort of information is less reliable than more standardized assessments, it is usually more readily available.

Another source of information concerning general learner academic abilities is the formal achievement data collected by school systems. These achievement tests generally provide a feeling for the existing achievement levels of groups of learners. Even though many schools do not necessarily test such abilities yearly, data from earlier assessments as old as two years can provide an indication of whether the group is of about average ability. Ideally, recent standardized test data are available for teachers, but realistically we know that too often these data are outdated and at times nonexistent. Even with the limitations of such data (as discussed in Chapter 5), there are useful reasons for knowing whether a group of learners seems generally at, above, or below grade level and whether there are wide variations in performances particularly in general reading achievement. In a model program, teachers would have such data provided in the form of group profiles prior to planning instruction segments, say, at the end of the previous school year. Although these data will not be adequate to differentiate beyond a modest level, if available they do require the least amount of teacher time commitment.

With a set of goals for instruction and a notion of the general level of learner academic abilities, especially text-learning abilities, the teacher can begin to identify suitable texts to provide learners with the desired goals. At this point, then, the content area teacher should begin evaluating available textual materials along several lines. The most important criterion is whether the textual material will allow the students to meet the intended goals. The two primary factors to consider here are (1) the appropriateness of a text to the desired goals, and (2) its appropriateness to learner ability levels. Thus a text might be rejected because it failed to provide the means to meet the goals, although it was of appropriate difficulty. Another might be rejected because it was too difficult, even though it was suitable as a means of attaining desired goals. Evaluating the appropriateness of content to goals is left to the teacher trained in that subject matter area, but assessing textual difficulty in terms of readability can be done by virtually any teacher or trained aide.

Although there are numerous weaknesses in calculating structural readability estimates, the formulas provided in Chapter 4 can be profitably employed as long as the limitations are noted. The teacher should examine materials and attempt to estimate their difficulty in relation to learner abilities. Textual material that ranks several levels above average learner abilities will be of no use in imparting knowledge of the content area to be studied. Similarly, material that is far too easy will not produce the maximum learning. Thus the teacher must search for textual material that strikes a happy medium—just about right for the majority of the learners.

This, then, is the beginning of instructional differentiation. Those learners who are advanced or lagging have not yet had their needs met, but by simply attempting to match learners, materials, and goals, the teacher has begun the differentiation process and learning will be facilitated. Far too often the textual material assigned in content area classes is several levels above the abilities of the learners, sometimes even if the learners display average achievement, because the material used in a freshman earth science class may have been of college-level difficulty. Consistent selection of textual materials of a difficulty level appropriate to the majority of learners facilitates and enhances learning in all content area classes.

In a model program the available textual material for various content areas is preanalyzed and the readability levels of these materials distributed to teachers much in the way learner achievement data are. Unfortunately, not all programs are model programs, and half are below average. The programs near the bottom of the pile generally have the fewest available resources; hence textual materials are limited, learner data are limited or nonexistent, and there is no staff or aides to assess the difficulty level of textual material. It is in these programs that instructional differentiation generally requires the greatest effort and where it is needed the most desperately.

STATEMENTS THAT SHOULD NOT BE HEARD IN CONTENT AREA CLASSROOMS

- "Read Chapter 11 tonight—you'll have a test tomorrow."
- "O.K., John, you read the first paragraph on page 256 aloud; then you read the next paragraph, Heidi, and so on."
- "Sound it out, Bo. You should know that word; my fourth-grader could get it."
- "What was the song the British band played when Cornwallis surrendered to Washington at Yorktown?"
- "You figure out what you're supposed to do."
- "If you can't read it, you shouldn't be in this class."
- "Only a dummy would ask that question."
- "Why on earth would you think that, Tinker?"

- "I don't want your opinion, Maggie, just tell me what the book said."
- "Forget it, Jay, you'll never figure it out."
- "It's important because I said so."
- "Think! What year was Michigan granted statehood?"

A case in point is an urban district visited recently in which the majority of the sophomores read at or below fifth-grade level. Although there were over a thousand pupils in this secondary school, only one reading teacher was available, providing small group instruction to less than seventy-five pupils. The instructional staff had little professional preparation for assessing text-learning abilities, text difficulty, or for interpreting available test data. In addition, because of limited funds, no in-service training monies were available, and in virtually all content area classes only a single text was available for use.

The content area teachers in this situation were hard-pressed to differentiate instruction, even though a severe need for such action existed. The initial steps taken were small: First, text difficulty was assessed, and those that were obviously too difficult were eliminated for instructional purposes. Second, alternate avenues for presenting the information necessary to meet content area goals were explored. The use of lectures, guided discussions, movies, audio-tapes, and teacher-made materials was examined, and, depending on the content area and the teacher, various options were selected. The situation, which had earlier seemed hopeless, had been improved but was still far from desirable. However, through awareness of strategies and options, the staff was able to differentiate minimally and enhance learning. The effort also brought a number of issues to the fore and resources were found or reallocated to correct the most glaring deficiencies. Although it would be nice to say that all turned out well, it has not, because tremendous disparities between needs and available resources still exist. Although not a model program, or even an average program, the situation has greatly improved and continues to improve slowly.

The point we would like to make is that even though a content area teacher may have an inordinate number of underachievers and virtually no available resources, an understanding of the processes of learning from text and a desire to enhance learning are the primary ingredients necessary to enhance learning in the content areas.

Further Differentiation

For the content area teacher who has selected a text appropriate to the goals of instruction and of a difficulty level appropriate for the majority of learners, further differentiation is not only possible but desirable because, whereas some learners will be faced with material that is too difficult, others will not be challenged and will attain only some of the goals possible. For this stage of differentiation, the teacher usually has to begin to think in terms of using multiple textual materials.

At the beginning of differentiation, the teacher might attempt to match the difficulty of textbooks to groups or classes of learners across grade and achievement levels. Thus one would surely find different texts for social studies in seventh grade at a lower difficulty level than texts in a tenth-grade social studies class. One might also expect to find different texts assigned within a grade if groups of learners differed significantly in achievement levels. Thus, if one tenth-grade social studies class had an eighth-grade average reading-achievement level and another had an eleventh-grade average reading-achievement level, one could expect different texts to be employed in each. This may seem "commonsensical" to many readers, but in practice one can still find discrepant groups of learners using a common text. At times this common text will be of college-level difficulty and therefore too difficult for both groups! That is why we have suggested the strategies discussed earlier (see the section entitled "A Beginning," p. 220); providing more appropriate-level texts across groups would in itself do much to ease the text-learning demands placed on many students in the content areas.

QUESTIONS TO EVALUATE THE DEGREE OF INSTRUCTIONAL DIFFERENTIATION

Materials:

- Does all instruction depend on text-based learning?
- Do learners use maps, models, slides, films, tapes, and so forth?

Instruction:

How frequently are learners required to:

- figure out what the task demands are?
- listen to a full-period lecture?
- cognitively manipulate information?
- reorganize information?
- complete assigned readings?

- answer questions calling for reproduction of text-based information?
- construct models, dioramas, charts, and so forth?
- write reports?
- interact with each other on an issue presented in class?
- complete a ditto?
- study the same text regardless of ability?
- set personal goals for learning?

Evaluation:

Do you require:

- all learners to complete identical assignments?
- all learners to take the same tests?
- a single correct answer reproducing text information?
- a rationale for an answer?

However, as noted earlier in this chapter, adopting different-level texts across groups will still leave some learners with a text of inappropriate difficulty. To rectify this the teacher should consider further differentiation by means of within-class differentiation. In this case, several texts are used within one class in an attempt to provide more adequately for the needs of all learners. This strategy will be particularly important in content area classes with a great deal of heterogeneity of reading achievement, because differentiation is based on an attempt to match learner abilities with textual difficulty more appropriately.

It is here that developing individual goals for content area instruction is particularly important. In using multiple texts within a single content area class, the teacher must coordinate textual information to meet the learning-from-text goals. When examining textbooks for appropriateness, the teacher must take both content and level of difficulty into consideration. Although exact matches on either variable will be virtually impossible, it is important to attempt to find sources of appropriate levels of difficulty that allow for attainment of text-learning goals. Remember also that we identified two types of text-learning goals—content-related goals and strategy goals. Because most textual materials for content area classes exhibit similarities across texts within a content area, it is generally not a major problem to find different-level texts in which similar strategies can be developed. However, it is more difficult to find textbooks of different levels of difficulty that are appropriate for meeting similar content-related goals.

Again, in our model system teachers would be supplied with a bibliography of available materials identified by specific content area curriculum level with an estimate of the difficulty level of each. In this instance, then, the teacher would be able to peruse a listing and select texts of different difficulty levels that fulfilled the content area goals for a particular grade. In the typical middle or secondary school, however, the teacher must seek out such material and hope that funds will be made available to purchase the texts identified.

Although using multiple-level texts within a content area class requires more effort than differentiating across content area classes, it is still manageable, especially if more than a single teacher can be mustered to carry out the search. It is also less difficult if the search is carried out over the period of, say, a year rather than attempting to find appropriate materials within ten days. These two factors should be kept in mind. We will return to them later in discussing a model for implementing instructional differentiation.

There is another type of multiple-text differentiation that may be meshed with, or independent of, attempts to match abilities and textual difficulty. This multiple-text strategy is primarily designed to evoke discussion and learning by eliminating the single source of information—the assigned text. In this strategy the teacher might purposely select materials of differing levels, but the primary goal is to provide multiple information sources for learners to draw from. Goals are identified, assignments are made, and learners use various materials to attempt to meet the goal. After reading, the information and points of view expressed in the various information sources are brought out through questioning and discussion (Allington, 1975). Such a strategy works well to develop in learners the realization that content area learning is more than memorizing the information presented in a single text. Unfortunately, this type of multiple-text approach is seldom found in content area classrooms.

At any point in the process of implementing differentiated instruction, the many other activities and strategies suggested in this text could be employed, regardless of the appropriateness of textual material to learner abilities. For instance, instruction designed to develop concepts presented in text or key vocabulary can be expected to enhance learning even for those learners for whom the text is too difficult. Strategies such as those presented in Chapter 8 can then be used to better meet learner needs, or in other words, to differentiate instruction.

It must be noted that in some content area classes some learners have virtually no text-learning abilities or have abilities so low as to make it impossible to find suitable content area textual material at an appropriate level of difficulty. In these cases, oral presentation of information, such as the development of concepts, should be a primary method of instructional differentiation.

The intermediate stages of instructional differentiation move from across-class to within-class differentiation strategies. Even in these intermediate stages, though, each content area teacher has a fair amount of leeway in deciding how fully to differentiate or how much energy to expend. The point to remember, though, is that any effort toward differentiation accrues benefits in enhanced learning from text.

The Final Stages of Instructional Differentiation

The intermediate stages are marked by the initiation of within-class instructional differentiation. Moving on to the final phase of differentiated instruction involves more attention to within-class differences in learner abilities. At this point the teacher will need to complete more detailed assessments of learner abilities—to gather information beyond general text-learning abilities and estimates of textual difficulty. The more intense informal assessment techniques detailed in Chapters 5 and 6 will be necessary to achieve the final phase of instructional differentiation.

> It has not been a contention of this study that the teachers observed could not or would not teach their students. They did, I believe, teach quite well. But the high-quality teaching was not made equally accessible to all students in the class. For the students of high socioeconomic background who were perceived by the teachers as possessing describable behavioral and attitudinal characteristics, the classroom experience was one where the teacher displayed interest in them, spent a large proportion of teaching time with them, directed little control-oriented behavior towards them, held them as models for the remainder of the class and continually reinforced statements that they were "special" students. (Rist, 1970)

At this point the teacher would have completed the activities necessary to achieve the lower levels of differentiation, and thus would have attempted (1) to identify the general reading-achievement levels of groups of learners, (2) to identify the difficulty level of the textual material, and (3) to match learner abilities more closely with textual difficulty both across and within classes. Having completed the various activities associated with these efforts, the teacher has probably become even more aware of the heterogeneity of learner abilities.

To further explore these differences and to develop instructional plans that ensure a learning environment in which all learners can achieve to their potential, the teacher might begin by attempting to sort out the difficulties of those learners with the least-developed text-learning abilities. The most useful assessments for this stage are those such as the cloze procedure, the word test, and the Group Informal Screening Test (GIST) or Group Informal Diagnostic Test (GIDT).

In our model-school situation, much of this screening would be accomplished by, or with, the reading teacher or content area reading specialist. In this case, the text-learning abilities of the poorest learners, particularly, would be assessed by the school reading staff with suggestions for differentiation presented following such screening. In addition, these learners would also receive daily instruction, separate from their content area classes, directed at developing improved text-learning strategies. The nature and focus of this instruction would be discussed with the content area teacher, and an instructional environment in the content areas would be designed to support and extend the remediation being provided. Again, however, few schools have such a procedure in operation, even though many have resources adequate to implement this model. Too often, the reading staff is shut off in a deserted room somewhere to work autonomously, rather than cooperatively with content area teachers. Perhaps this is because far too many reading personnel seem to want everything changed now and will settle for nothing less than full differentiation. Perhaps content area teachers want no part of differentiation and expect the reading staff to solve all the woes surrounding insufficient text-learning abilities. In any case, in the model program the reading and content area instruction would be mutually supportive. Such instruction is not developed without cooperative efforts on the part of both parties.

Ultimately, in a content area class in which full differentiation is provided, each learner is receiving instruction that enhances the acquisition of information important to content area goals and is also provided instruction that facilitates the development of strategies for learning from text, strategies designed to create more independent learners. The teaching strategies discussed in Chapters 8 and 9 would be fully evident. The content area teacher would provide instruction for the full and rich development of a conceptual base for understanding the content area information. Various strategies would be used to orient learners to the learning tasks to ensure that the information presented in content area texts is reconstructed, reorganized, manipulated, and incorporated into the existing scripts, knowledges, and concepts. Many other activities that aid the learner in dealing with the structure of the textual material itself would be evident. Strategies to assist the learner in recognizing and understanding the various ways in which bodies of knowledge are organized in texts would be offered. Finally, at the highest levels of differentiation, different content area goals and different learning-from-text goals would be established for individual learners. Thus the content area teacher would work more closely with individual learners to assess abilities in both areas and to set goals and plan instruction.

At this point we end our discussion of instructional differentiation. It is not that we feel fully individualized instruction is dangerous, wrong, or silly. Rather, it seems to us that many conditions mitigate against implementing individualized instruction in the situations most commonly found in content area classrooms. Content area teachers who teach from 90 to 150 students a day, often in different content areas, are hard pressed, to say the least, to ever implement a fully individualized program. Further, many of the so-called individualized programs we have seen in operation in content area classes were paper-and-pencil shuffling exercises. That is, little teacher-provided instruction in either content or learning-from-text strategies was visible. Learners spent far too much time waiting for assistance from the teacher and far too little instruction occurred, from our point of view. Finally, most of the learning from text was reproductive, with little or no reorganization, reconstruction, or embellishment of textual information.

In our model content area class, then, the instruction is differentiated and attempts are made to maximize learning from text by matching learner abilities appropriately with text difficulty and by developing goals and plans that require the learner to move beyond reproducing text-based knowledge to the reorganization, integration, and reconstruction of new information with existing knowledge. This will require no small effort on the part of the content area teacher, but the improved learning atmosphere and improved outcomes outweigh the necessary expenditure of effort. However, to ease the transition into differentiated instruction, we present several strategies in the remainder of this chapter.

A Time Frame for Differentiating Instruction

To allay some of the doubts that may have arisen in the previous section, it would be well to keep in mind that, although we consider fully differentiated instruction an ideal, two factors can effectively hinder the implementation of this process even for those teachers who desire it: available time and available resources.

The First Year

The primary task of a beginning content area teacher is to survive the first year. That is not to say that the process of differentiating instruction should not begin, but rather that the first year is, in the main, a time to learn and to adjust to the real world. Thus during the first year of teaching, we suggest that the teacher primarily focus differentiation efforts toward gathering information about the general level of learner text-learning abilities and assessing the difficulty of available material. In addition, the teacher should investigate the available resources—finances, personnel, and materials. Thus the content area teacher can identify any available standardized test information and explore the adequacy of such. Some schools have no data and others have much, but most fall somewhere in between—for example, data only on reading-achievement levels of freshmen. In most cases these data are not readily accessible in a format useful for the purposes of the content area teacher. However, if data exist, usually a format can be found to display results effectively and efficiently. If data do not exist, one might politely question why.

Assessing the difficulty level of available textual material is relatively straightforward using either a readability formula or sample cloze passages. In some schools this information is available, but generally it is not. Storing this information once it is generated is useful because it will eliminate the necessity of recalculating later. For teachers who find gross disparities between abilities and text demands, the process of within-class instructional differentiation, or at least the initiation of differentiation between groups of learners in separate content area classes, may have to begin in the first year.

Basically, though, we suggest that in the first year the content area teacher begin to establish the groundwork for beginning instructional differentiation by completing assessments of the availability of financial, personnel, and material resources. In addition, estimates of the congruence between learner abilities and text difficulty should be developed. Completing these activities gives the teacher a base from which to operate with some idea of the feasibility of implementing differentiated instruction.

The Second Year

Prior to beginning the second year the content area teacher should have identified general levels of learning from text abilities and any between-class differences, and possibly attempted to match across classes based on abilities and text difficulty. The next step is to fully implement between-class differentiation by selecting materials that seem appropriate for a majority of learners in each class. This may be difficult if financial resources are so constrained that no funds are available to purchase even small quantities of additional texts. However, in this case the content area teacher can explore the possibility of using texts meant for lower grade levels—texts that perhaps the learners had assigned to them before but for which they had inadequate text-learning abilities at that time. The hazard in this approach is identification of these as "baby books" by the learners, but such resistance can be overcome with adroit efforts by the teacher. Another option that provides satisfactory results, but only through great effort, is rewriting important segments from the difficult textual material to be distributed to the learners. This final option, though, should only be considered if the available textual material is too difficult for the majority of the learners and no other materials can be purchased or located.

EVALUATING A CONTENT AREA LESSON

	Yes	No
1. Are goals specified with regard to:		
a. content to be learned?	___	___
b. text-learning strategies to be used?	___	___
2. Do plans exhibit congruence with goals?	___	___
3. Do learners have textual material of an appropriate level of difficulty?	___	___
4. Are prerequisite concepts and vocabulary fully developed?	___	___
5. Are orienting tasks that establish purpose for reading provided?	___	___
6. Do orienting tasks require the reconstruction or reorganization of text-based information?	___	___
7. Are post-reading tasks congruent with orienting tasks required?	___	___
8. Do post-reading tasks require an understanding of text-based information as opposed to simply remembering?	___	___
9. Are learners actively engaged in generating hypotheses from text-based information?	___	___
10. Is an evaluation of goal attainment provided the learner?	___	___
	Totals*	

* At the very least, a content area lesson should have more checks in the Yes column than in the No column.

Once between-class differentiation is accomplished, though if all classes are roughly equivalent this step would be omitted, the content area teacher should begin to collect data on the range of individual text-learning abilities within each class. The techniques suggested in

Chapter 4 and 5 can be employed here. The use of the GIST, cloze, word tests, and so forth, all provide information about such individual abilities. An assessment of this sort should identify the range of abilities encountered, in terms of both level of content knowledge and learning-from-text abilities. Instructional differentiation, based on the information gathered in this phase, should follow. The integration of goals, plans, and instruction with knowledge of learner strengths and weaknesses is accomplished through the use of well-constructed orienting tasks, reading guides for some lessons, and multiple-level texts.

At this point, however, such practices are just being initiated and the content area teacher does not necessarily differentiate all or even most of the time. Rather, differentiation is implemented somewhat cautiously whenever time and other resources allow. If only one-third of the instruction is differentiated during this year, it is one-third that will be readily differentiated in the following years. As these lessons are differentiated and implemented, the materials, questions, and procedures should be filed for future use.

> Because most of us do not understand the hidden needs of our students or the effects that the mass media and their peer culture have upon them, we institute innovations in our schools that only accentuate the alienation of students . . . recent evidence suggests the crucial educational determinants of a student's development are the humanistic climate or atmosphere of the school, the student's sense of participant involvement, and the student's identification with the purposes of the faculty. (Heath, 1970)

The Third Year

At this point the teacher should have identified an efficient strategy for estimating the general reading-achievement levels of learners and the difficulty levels of available materials. Thus, an estimate of the disparity, if any, between abilities and text difficulty would be available. To further explore this issue, the teacher would again administer the GIST and the GIDT. From this information, the final phase of differentiation can be developed. Using the products of the previous two years, the teacher should now be able to complete and sustain full differentiation without an extraordinary effort. Again, however, note that instruction is not fully individualized and may not even be fully differentiated at all times.

High school teachers can draw these implications: (1) they have something to contribute to the whole reading program, but they need not become reading specialists themselves; (2) even though emphasis on direct instruction decreases, it does not disappear; (3) the responsibility for this direct instruction is not theirs but the reading teachers'. Making a dual program work in reality, not simply on paper, requires expert teachers of reading and subject-matter specialists who understand and respect each other's goals, and can agree upon the means of achieving them.

Source: Margaret J. Early, "The Meaning of Reading Instruction in Secondary Schools," *Journal of Reading*, 1964, 8, 25–29. Reprinted by permission of Margaret J. Early and the International Reading Association.

Why a Three-Year Plan?

As noted earlier in this chapter, the time demands involved in developing fully differentiated instruction are quite severe. However, by spreading the process over a three-year period, these demands can be met without undue sacrifice. Moving slowly toward full differentiation also allows the teacher the opportunity to experiment, reflect, and modify those best-laid plans that went astray. The time commitment necessary to fully differentiate instruction may seem impossible, but an hour here and an hour there do in fact make a difference. Attempts to differentiate fully in a short period (such as a semester) have, in our experience, been too often unsuccessful. Thus for those we have been able to convince of the value of differentiation, we offer the three-year plan and encouragement.

Other Resources for Easing Differentiation

Probably the most valuable and available resources are other teachers. If possible, the development and implementation of differentiated instruction is best conducted by two or more content area teachers who share the workload. Two teachers cuts the workload by half (*almost* by half, because each may create unique materials or strategies). Ten teachers cooperating also cuts the workload, but not by 90 percent; unfortunately, spending much time with such large groups seems to be rather unprofitable. Enlisting two or three teachers lightens the workload considerably.

A PLAN FOR DIFFERENTIATING INSTRUCTION

First-Year Goals:

- Identify available sources of achievement data
- Identify range of general learner text-learning abilities
- Identify available textual resources
- Identify range of textual difficulty
- Identify available support personnel (such as reading teacher or curriculum director)
- Identify between-class differences in text-learning abilities
- Attempt to match textual material across classes.

Second-Year Goals:

- Initiate between-class differentiation based on textual difficulty
- Identify within-class differences in text-learning abilities
- Initiate differentiation based on orienting tasks
- Initiate differentiation through multiple-level texts within classes

Third-Year Goals:

- Initiate within-class differentiation for both content and strategy goals

Another staff resource that may be available is the reading teacher. Unfortunately, too often reading personnel only provide tutorial or small-group instruction to underachieving readers, and the number of learners taught effectively precludes spare time to work with content area teachers. However, some in-school reading personnel are assigned part time and some full time to work with content area teachers, primarily to provide support for the process of differentiating instruction. Should such personnel be available, the content area teacher should identify what types of assistance are provided.

Finally there are the administrators. Though in most cases these personnel cannot be expected to provide any direct assistance to the process of differentiating instruction, they hold the key to allocating funds and other resources that can ease the transition. If instructional differentiation is not a current practice, if assessments of text-learning abilities are not conducted, or if multiple-level materials are not available, then a plan outlining proposed changes should be drawn up to be presented to the administrators. Such a plan, including a rationale, does not have to be detailed, but it should include the needs estimates for materials, time, personnel, and so forth, and data delineating the discrepancies between learner abilities and text difficulty. How such discrepancies affect attainment of the goals set should also be presented. Administrators are charged with managing the learning plant and usually are open to ideas and programs that enhance learning. However, they are more aware than anyone else of the financial constraints on the school system and therefore must be convinced of the need for any such changes. With this in mind, the content area teacher should submit a plan and take care that each need is documented. Remember, even if the needs are great, a plan cannot be outrageously lavish and one must always be prepared to face rejection.

Summary

To enhance learning in the content areas, instruction must be differentiated. Several levels and types of differentiation can be implemented, depending primarily on one's level of commitment and resource availability. Therefore, content area teachers must consider the extent to which they are willing to differentiate, and at what rate. The use of the strategies, ideas, and techniques presented in this book should lead to instructional differentiation and enhanced learning.

1. Differentiation is simply the modification of instruction in response to learner characteristics. This may occur across classes, between classes, or within classes.
2. The initial phase of differentiation is primarily one of data gathering. The content area teacher should know the general learning-from-text abilities of learners and the difficulty level of available textual materials. If discrepancies are found, the teacher must identify and assess possible avenues that might be followed to alleviate the mismatch.
3. In order to implement instructional differentiation, the content area teacher must identify the financial, personnel, and textual resources available in the school. With this information, a feasible plan for implementing differentiated instruction can be developed.
4. Rather than attempting to resolve all difficulties immediately, we suggest a three-year plan for implementing instructional differentiation. This allows the content area teacher time to create, reflect, and evaluate. The amount of effort necessary is spread out over the three-year period.
5. Usually, available sources of assistance are other content area teachers, reading personnel, and administrators. Each of these resources should be considered, because additional assistance further reduces the level of effort necessary from any individual.

6. The initiation of any level or type of instructional differentiation is preferable to no differentiation at all. The goal of teaching is the production of learning, and such is the goal of instructional differentiation.

Epilogue

Our purpose in creating *Learning Through Reading in the Content Areas* was to attempt to provide content area teachers with an introduction to how students learn from texts. We will be pleased if even one-tenth of those who read this work implement one-quarter of the suggestions. As we noted in the first chapter, the use of textbooks is pervasive in American education, especially in the content area classes. Unfortunately, teacher-preparation programs have too often overlooked providing effective training in how to facilitate learning from texts. It is our belief that one of the primary goals of content area instruction should be to develop and refine the learner's ability to learn from textual material. We hope this book has provided a basic understanding of the complexity of learning from text and, in addition, has provided a basic set of skills for facilitating learning from text.

In summary, the content area teacher who chooses to use textual material as a learning resource has a responsibility to consider the various barriers to learning that may be operating and to take some steps to ease the acquisition of knowledge. Learning in the content areas should not be a "Twenty Questions" game, in which the learner is in doubt about what is important and relevant. Nor should content area teaching reward only those who arrive with well-developed abilities, strategies, and knowledge. Rather, content area teaching and therefore content area teachers must always strive to improve both the learner's understanding of the content and the ability to learn effectively and independently from text.

Bibliography

Allington, R. L. "Improving Content Area Instruction in the Middle School." *Journal of Reading,* 18 (1975): 455–61.

Allington, R. L. "Communities and Schools: Compensatory Reading Instruction." Paper presented at The International Reading Association, Anaheim, Cal., 1976.

Allington, R. L. "Teaching, Learning, and Reading in the Middle Grade Content Areas." In Welle, D. (ed.), *New Directions in Meeting Special Needs in Reading.* Union, N. J.: Kean College, 1976.

Allington, R. L. "The Visual Confusability of High-frequency Words." *Journal of Learning Disabilities,* 10 (1977): 444–49.

Allington, R. L. "Are Good and Poor Readers Taught Differently? Is That Why Poor Readers Are Poor Readers?" Paper presented at The American Educational Research Association, Toronto, 1978.

Allington, R. L., Gormely, K. G., and Truex, S. "Poor and Normal Readers' Achievement on Visual Tasks Involving High-Frequency, Low-Discriminability Words." *Journal of Learning Disabilities,* 9 (1967): 292–96.

Allington, R. L., and Strange, M. "Effects of Grapheme Substitutions in Connected Text upon Reading Behaviors." *Visible Language,* 11 (1977): 285–97.

Allington, R. L., and Strange, M. "Remembering Is Not Necessarily Understanding in Content Areas." *Reading Horizons* (in press).

Anderson, R. C. "Control of Student Mediating Processes during Verbal Learning and Instruction." *Review of Educational Research,* 4 (1970): 349–69.

Anderson, R. C., Reynolds, R., Schallert, D., and Goetz, E. "Frameworks for Comprehending Discourse." *American Educational Research Journal,* 14 (1977): 367–81.

Aukerman, R. C. *Beginning Approaches to Reading.* New York: John Wiley & Sons, 1971.

Aulls, M. *Developmental and Remedial Reading in the Middle Grades.* Boston: Allyn and Bacon, 1978.

Ausubel, D. "The Use of Advance Organizers in the Learning and Retention of Meaningful Verbal Material." *Journal of Educational Psychology,* 51 (1960): 267–72.

Ausubel, D. *Educational Psychology: A Cognitive View.* New York: Holt, Rinehart and Winston, 1968.

Berliner, D. C., and Rosenshine, B. "The Acquisition of Knowledge in the Classroom." In Anderson, R. C., Spiro, R. J., and Montague, W. E. (eds.), *Schooling and the Acquisition of Knowledge.* Hillsdale, N. J.: Lawrence Earlbaum Associates, 1977.

Bloomfield, L. "Linguistics and Reading." *Elementary English Review,* 19 (1942): 125–30.

Bormuth, J. "Cloze as a Measure of Readability." In Figurel, J. A. (ed.), *Reading as an Intellectual Activity.* Newark, Del.: International Reading Association, 1963.

Bormuth, J. "Factor Validity of Cloze Tests as Measures of Reading Comprehension Ability." *Reading Research Quarterly,* 4 (1969): 358–65.

Bormuth, J. "The Cloze Procedure: Literacy in the Classroom." In Page, W. (ed.), *Help for the Reading Teacher.* Urbana, Ill.: National Conference on Research in English, 1975.

Bransford, J. D., and Johnson, M. K., "Considerations of Some Problems of Comprehension." In Chase, W. G. (ed.), *Visual Information Processing.* New York: Academic, 1963, 383–438.

Brady, B. H. "To Test or Not To Test?" *American Educator,* 1 (1977): 4.

Braun, C., and Froese, V. *An Experience-Based Approach to Language and Reading.* Baltimore: University Park Press, 1977.

Brigham, B. "Standardized Tests: Use and Misuse." In Wilson, R., and Geyer, J. (eds.), *Readings for Diagnostic and Remedial Reading.* Columbus, Oh.: Merrill, 1972.

Brophy, J., and Good, T. "Teacher Communication of Differential Expectations for Children's Classroom Performance." *Journal of Educational Psychology,* 61 (1970): 365–74.

Bruner, J. S. "Human Problem Solving." *Educational Review,* 31 (1961): 167–91.

Bruner, J. S., Goodnow, J., and Austin, G. *A Study of Thinking.* New York: John Wiley & Sons, 1956.

Burmeister, L. *Reading Strategies for Secondary School Teachers.* Boston: Addison-Wesley, 1974.

Carpenter, P., and Just, M. "Models of Sentence Verification and Linguistic Comprehension." *Psychological Review,* 83 (1976): 318–22.

Carroll, J. "Defining Language Comprehension." In Carroll, J. and Freedle, R. (eds.), *Language Comprehension and the Acquisition of Knowledge.* New York: John Wiley & Sons, 1972.

Carver, R. "Speed Readers Don't Read; They Skim." *Psychology Today,* 6 (1972): 22–30.

Carver, R. "Further Research on the Reading-Storage Test as a Measure of Gain During Reading." *Journal of Reading Behavior*, 1 (1975): 404–14.

Carver, R. "Word Length, Prose Difficulty, and Reading Rate." *Journal of Reading Behavior*, 6 (1976): 193–204.

Carver, R. "Toward a Theory of Reading Comprehension and Rauding." *Reading Research Quarterly*, 13 (1977): 8–63.

Chodos, L., Falope, C., Gould, S., Lavato, J., Schullstrom, F., and Wheeler, D. "Comprehension: An Active Process Strand-Student Generated Questioning." Paper presented at the New York State Reading Association, Kiemesha Lake, N.Y., 1977.

Chodos, L., Gould, S., and Rusch, R. "Effect of Student Generated Pre-questions and Post-statements on Immediate and Delayed Recall of Fourth Grade Social Studies Content." Paper presented at the National Reading Conference, New Orleans, La., 1977.

Coleman, E. "Developing a Technology of Written Instruction: Some Determiners of the Complexity of Prose." In Rothkopf, E. Z., and Johnson, P. E. (eds.), *Verbal Learning Research and the Technology of Written Instruction*. New York: Teachers College Press, 1971.

Collins, A. "Processes in Acquiring Knowledge." In Anderson, R. C., Spiro, R., and Montague, W. (eds.), *Schooling and the Acquisition of Knowledge*. Hillsdale, N.J.: Lawrence Erlbaum Associates, 1977, 96–136.

Compayre, G. *Herbart and Education by Instruction*. New York: Crowell, 1907.

Conklin, K. "Wholes and Parts in Teaching." *Elementary School Journal*, 73 (1973): 165–70.

Cromer, W. "The Difference Model: A New Explanation for Reading Failure." *Journal of Educational Psychology*, 61 (1970): 471–503.

Cunningham, P. "Investigating a Synthesized Theory of Mediated Word Identification." *Reading Research Quarterly*, 11 (1976): 127–43.

Dale, E. *Audio-Visual Methods in Teaching*. New York: Holt, Rinehart and Winston, 1969.

Dale, E., and Chall, J. "A Formula for Predicting Readability." *Educational Research Bulletin*, 27 (1948): 11–20.

Davis, F. B. "Research in Comprehension in Reading." *Reading Reserach Quarterly*, 3 (1968): 499–545.

Davis, F. B. "Psychometric Research on Comprehension in Reading." *Reading Research Quarterly*, 1 (1972): 628–78.

Dick, W., and Carey, L. *The Systematic Design of Instruction*. Glenview, Ill.: Scott, Foresman, 1978.

Doyle, W. "The Practicality Ethic in Teacher Decision Making." Paper presented at the Milwaukee Curriculum Theory Conference, November, 1976.

Drucker, P. F. *The Age of Discontinuity: Guidelines to Our Changing Society*. New York: Harper & Row, 1969.

Duffy, G., and Sherman, G. *Systematic Reading Instruction*. New York: Harper & Row, 1976.

Duffy, G., Sherman, G., Allington, R., McElwee, M., and Roehler, L. *How to Teach Reading Systematically.* New York: Harper & Row, 1973.

Early, M. "The Meaning of Reading Instruction in Secondary Schools." *Journal of Reading,* 8 (1964): 25–29.

Elkind, D. "We Can Teach Reading Better." *Today's Education,* 9 (1975): 35–38.

Farr, R. *Reading: What Can be Measured?* Newark, Del.: International Reading Association, 1969.

Farr, H., and Waller, T. "Mathemagenic Behaviors and Efficiency in Learning From Prose Materials: Review, Critique, and Recommendations." *Review of Educational Research,* 46 (1976): 691–720.

Fleming, J. T., Ohnmacht, F., and Niles, J. "Effect of Selected Deletion Strategies and Contextual Constraints on Reading Performance." Paper presented at the National Reading Conference, New Orleans, La., 1972.

Fraser, C., Bellugi, V., and Brown, R. "Control of Grammar in Imitation, Comprehension, and Production." *Journal of Verbal Learning and Verbal Behavior,* 2 (1963): 121–35.

Fries, C. *Linguistics and Reading.* New York: Holt, Rinehart and Winston, 1963.

Fry, E. "Fry's Readability Graph: Clarifications, Validity and Extension to Level 17." *Journal of Reading,* 3 (1977): 242–52.

Gagne, R. M., and Briggs, L. J. *Principles of Instructional Design.* New York: Holt, Rinehart and Winston, 1974.

Gentner, D. *On Relational Meaning: The Acquisition of Verb Meaning.* Technical report no. 78, Center for the Study of Reading, University of Illinois, 1978.

Gibson, E. J., and Levin, H. *Psychology of Reading.* Cambridge, Mass.: MIT Press, 1975.

Glaser, R. *Adaptive Education: Individual Diversity and Learning.* New York: Holt, Rinehart and Winston, 1977.

Golinkoff, R. "A Comparison of Reading Comprehension Processes in Good and Poor Comprehenders." *Reading Research Quarterly,* 11 (1975): 623–59.

Goodlad, J. I. "What Goes on in Our Schools." *Educational Review,* 3 (1977): 3–6.

Goodman, K. "A Linguistic Study of Cues and Miscues in Reading." *Elementary English,* 42 (1965): 639–43.

Goodman, K. "Reading: A Psycholinguistic Guessing Game." *Journal of the Reading Specialist,* 6 (1967): 126–35.

Goodman, K. "Do You Have to be Smart to Read? Or Do You Have to Read to be Smart?" *Reading Teacher,* 28 (1975): 625–31.

Goodman, K., and Goodman, Y. "Learning About Psycholinguistic Processes by Analyzing Oral Reading." *Harvard Educational Review,* 47 (1977): 317–33.

Goodman, Y. "Reading Comprehension—the Redundant Phrase." *Michigan Reading Journal,* 9 (1975): 27–36.

Goodman, Y., and Burke, C. *Reading Miscue Inventory*. New York: Macmillan, 1972.

Greene, E. "Effectiveness of Various Rates of Silent Reading of College Students." *Journal of Applied Psychology*, 15 (1931): 214–27.

Guthrie, J. "Models of Reading Ability and Disability." *Journal of Educational Psychology*, 65 (1973): 9–18.

Hackney, B., and Reavis, C. "Poor Instruction: the Real Cause of Dropouts." *Journal of Secondary Education*, 43 (1968): 18–25.

Hammill, D., Goodman, L., and Wiederholt, J. "Visual-Motor Processes: What Success Have We Had in Training Them?" *Reading Teacher*, 27 (1974): 469–78.

Harris, A. J., and Sipay, E. R. *How to Increase Reading Ability*. New York: McKay, 1975.

Hart, L. A. "The New 'Brain' Concept of Learning." *Phi Delta Kappan*, 59 (1978): 393–96.

Heath, D. "Student Alienation and School." *School Review*, 79 (1970): 515–28.

Henry, G. H. *Teaching Reading as Concept Development*. Newark, Del.: International Reading Association, 1976.

Herber, H. *Teaching Reading in Content Areas*. Englewood Cliffs, N.J.: Prentice-Hall, 1970.

Herber, H. *Teaching Reading in Content Areas*, 2d ed. Englewood Cliffs, N.J.: Prentice-Hall, 1978.

Horton, R. "Construct Validity of the Cloze Procedure." *Reading Research Quarterly*, 10 (1975): 248–52.

Howlett, N., and Weintraub, S. "Instructional Procedures." Paper presented at the International Reading Association, Anaheim, Cal., 1976.

Jarolimek, J., and Foster, C. *Teaching and Learning in the Elementary School*. New York: Macmillan, 1976.

Jenkinson, M. "Selected Processes and Difficulties of Reading Comprehension." Unpublished doctoral dissertation, University of Chicago, 1957.

Jensen, M. "Humanistic Education: An Overview of Supporting Data." *High School Journal*, 56 (1975): 341–49.

Johnson, D., and Pearson, P. D. "Skills Management Systems: A Critique." *Reading Teacher*, 28 (1975): 757–62.

Johnson, P. "Some Psychological Aspects of Subject-Matter Structure." *Journal of Educational Psychology*, 58 (1967): 75–83.

Katz, I. "A Critique of Personality Approaches to Negro Performance." *Journal of Social Issues*, 25 (1969): 13–27.

Katz, J., and Fodor, J. "The Structure of a Semantic Theory." *Language*, 39, (1963): 170–210.

Kintsch, W. "On Comprehending Stories." In Just, M., and Carpenter, P. (eds.), *Cognitive Processes in Comprehension*. Hillsdale, N. J.: Lawrence Erlbaum Associates, 1977.

Kintsch, W., and Van Dijk, T. "Comment On Rappelle et On Résume des Histoires." *Languages*, 9 (1975): 98–116.

Klausmeier, H. J., Ghatala, E. S., and Frayer, D. A. *Conceptual Learning and*

Development: A Cognitive View. New York: Academic, 1974.

Koenke, K. "Reading Evaluation by the High School Teacher: A Plan." *Journal of Reading,* 16 (1972): 220–27.

Lahey, F., and Johnson, M. *Psychology and Instruction.* Glenview, Ill.: Scott, Foresman, 1978.

Lehmann, I.; Mehrens, W. *Educational Research.* New York: Holt, Rinehart and Winston, 1970.

Levin, J. "Comprehending What We Read: An Outsider Looks In." *Journal of Reading Behavior,* 4 (1972): 18–27.

Lindberg, M., and Smith, L. "Teaching Vocabulary as an Introduction to New Material: Is It Worthwhile?" In Johason, N.A. (ed.), *Current Topics in Language.* Cambridge, Mass.: Winthrop, 1975.

Mager, R. *Preparing Instructional Objectives.* Palo Alto, Cal.: Fearon, 1962.

Markle, S., and Tiemann, P. *Really Understanding Concepts: Or in Furious Pursuit of Jabberwock.* Champaign, Ill.: Stipes, 1969.

Markle, S., and Tiemann, P. "Some Principles of Instructional Design at Higher Cognitive Levels." Paper presented at the International Congress for Educational Technology, Berlin, 1972.

Masters, G. "Reading Tests Don't Really Tell It Like It Is." *New England Reading Journal,* 8 (1972): 29–33.

McNeill, J. "False Prerequisites in the Teaching of Reading." *Journal of Reading Behavior,* 6 (1974): 421–27.

Menzel, E. "The Pronunciation of the First Vowel in VCV Words." Paper presented at The International Reading Association, New Orleans, La., 1973.

Meyer, B. J. F. *The Organization of Prose and Its Effect on Memory.* Amsterdam: North-Holland Publishing, 1975.

Miller, G. *Linguistic Communication: Perspective from Research.* Newark, Del.: International Reading Association, 1973.

Mistler-Lachman, J. "Depth of Comprehension and Sentence Memory." *Journal of Verbal Learning and Verbal Behavior,* 13 (1974): 98–106.

Mosenthal, P. "Children's Metacognitive Reproductive and Reconstructive Comprehension in Listening, Reading Silently, and Reading Aloud: A Problem of Psychosocial Development." Paper presented at The National Reading Conference, New Orleans, La., 1977.

Mosenthal, P. "Three Types of Schemata in Children's Recall of Cohesive and Non-cohesive Text." Paper presented at the American Educational Research Association, Toronto, 1978.

Neimark, E. D. "Intellectual Development During Adolescence," In Horowitz, F. D. (ed.), *Review of Child Development Research.* Chicago: University of Chicago Press, 1975, 541–94.

Nelson, K. "Cognitive Development and the Acquisition of Concepts." In Anderson, R. C., Spiro, R., and Montague, W. (eds.), *Schooling and the Acquisition of Knowledge.* Hillsdale, N. J.: Lawrence Erlbaum Associates, 1977.

Niles, O. S., and Early, M. J. "Adjusting to Individual Differences in English." *Journal of Education,* 138 (1955): 2–16.

Olson, D. "From Utterance to Text: The Bias of Language in Speech and Writing." *Harvard Educational Review,* 47 (1977): 257–81.

Pearson, P. D. "The Effects of Grammatical Complexity on Children's Comprehension Recall, and Conception of Certain Semantic Relations." *Reading Research Quarterly,* 10 (1975): 155–92.

Pearson, P. D. "Some Practical Applications of Psycholinguistic Research." In Samuels, S. J. (ed.), *What Research Has to Say About Reading Instruction.* Newark, Del.: International Reading Association, 1978.

Pearson, P. D., and Johnson, D. *Teaching Reading Comprehension.* New York: Holt, Rinehart and Winston, 1978.

Pearson, P. D., and Studt, A. "Effects of Word Frequency and Contextual Richness on Children's Word Identification Abilities." *Journal of Educational Psychology,* 67 (1975): 89–95.

Penty, R. "Reading Ability and High School Drop-outs." Reprinted in R. Karlin (ed.), *Teaching Reading in High School.* Indianapolis: Bobbs-Merrill, 1969.

Petrosko, J. "The Quality of High School Reading and Vocabulary Tests: Implications for the Researchers." Paper presented at The American Educational Research Association, New York, 1977.

Piaget, J. *The Theory of Stages in Cognitive Development.* In Green, D., Ford, M., and Flamer, G., eds., *Measurement and Piaget.* New York: McGraw-Hill, 1971.

Piercey, D. *Reading Activities in Content Areas.* Boston: Allyn & Bacon, 1976.

Postman, N. "The Politics of Reading." *Harvard Educational Review,* 40 (1970): 244–52.

Postman, N., and Weingartner, C. *Teaching as a Subversive Activity.* New York: Delta, 1969.

Preston, R. *A New Look at Reading in the Social Studies.* Newark, Del.: International Reading Association, 1969.

Ramanauskas, S. "The Responsiveness of Cloze Readability Measures to Linguistic Variables Operating over Segments of Text Longer than a Sentence." *Reading Research Quarterly,* 8 (1972): 72–91.

Rankin, E. "The Cloze Procedure: a Survey of Research." In Thurstone, E. L. (ed.), *The Philosophical and Sociological Bases of Reading.* Clemson, S. C.: National Reading Conference, 1965.

Rickards, J. "Processing Effects of Advance Organizers Interspersed in Text." *Reading Research Quarterly,* 11 (1976): 599–622.

Rist, R. C. "Student Social Class and Teacher Expectations: The Self-fulfilling Prophecy of Ghetto Education." *Harvard Educational Review,* 40 (1977): 411–50.

Robinson, F. *Effective Reading.* New York: Harper & Row, 1961.

Rogers, C. R. *Freedom to Learn.* Columbus, Oh.: Merrill, 1969.

Rosenthal, R., and Jacobson, L. *Pygmalion in the Classroom.* New York: Holt, Rinehart and Winston, 1968.

Rothkopf, E. "The Concept of Mathemagenic Activities." *Review of Educational Research,* 40 (1970): 325–36.

Rothkopf, E. "Structural Text Features and the Control of Processes in Learning from Written Materials." In Freedle, R., and Carroll, J. (eds.), *Language Comprehension and the Acquisition of Knowledge*. Washington, D.C.: V. H. Winston, 1972.

Rumelhart, D. "Notes on a Schema for Stories." In Bobrow, D., and Collins, A., eds., *Representations and Understanding: Studies in Cognitive Science*. New York: Academic, 1976.

Rystrom, R. "Reflections of Meaning." *Journal of Reading Behavior*, 9 (1977): 193–200.

Sacks, H., Schegloff, E., and Jefferson, G. "The Simplest Systematics for the Organization of Turn-Taking in Conversation." *Language*, 50 (1974): 696–735.

Saucier, W., Wendel, R., and Mueller, R. *Toward Humanistic Teaching in High School*. Boston: D. C. Heath, 1975.

Schank, R. "Conceptual Dependency: A Theory of Natural Language Understanding." *Cognitive Psychology*, 3 (1972): 552–631.

Schumacher, E. F. *Small is Beautiful: Economics as if People Mattered*. New York: Harper & Row, 1973.

Shepard, David. *Effective Reading in the Social Sciences*. New York: Harper & Row, 1961.

Shores, H., and Husbands, K. "Are Fast Readers the Best Readers?" *Elementary English*, 27 (1950): 52–57.

Silberman, C. *Crisis in the Classroom*. New York: Random House, 1970.

Skinner, B. F. *Verbal Behavior*. New York: Appleton-Century-Crofts, 1957.

Smith, F. *Understanding Reading*. New York: Holt, Rinehart and Winston, 1971.

Smith, F. *Psycholinguistics and Reading*. New York: Holt, Rinehart and Winston, 1973.

Smith, F. *Comprehension and Learning*. New York: Holt, Rinehart and Winston, 1975.

Smith, N. B. *Be a Better Reader Series, 2nd ed*. Englewood Cliffs, N.J.: Prentice-Hall, 1973.

Spache, G. "Is This a Breakthrough in Reading?" *Reading Teacher*, 15 (1962): 258–63.

Spiro, R. J. "Remembering Information from Text: The 'State of Schema' Approach." In Anderson, R. C., Spiro, R., and Montague, W. *Schooling and the Acquisition of Knowledge*. Hillsdale, N. J.: Lawrence Erlbaum Associates, 1977.

Staats, A. W., Staats, G. K., Schutz, R., and Wolf, M. "The Conditioning of Reading Responses Using 'Extrinsic' Reinforcers." *Journal of Experimental Analysis of Behavior*, 5 (1962): 33–40.

Standal, T. C. "Readability Formulas: What's Out, What's In?" *Reading Teacher*, 31 (1978): 642–46.

Steiner, R., Weiner, M., and Cromer, W. "Comprehension Training and Identification for Poor and Good Readers." *Journal of Educational Psychology*, 62 (1971): 506–13.

Stennett, R., Smythe, P., and Hardy, M. "Hierarchical Organization of Reading Subskills: Statistical Approaches." *Journal of Reading Behavior,* 7 (1975): 223–28.

Sticht, T. G. *Reading for Working.* Washington, D. C.: Hum RRO (Human Resources Research Organization), 1975.

Strang, R. "Secondary School Reading as Thinking." *Reading Teacher,* 13 (1960): 155–61.

Sullivan, J. "Comparing Strategies of Good and Poor Comprehenders." *Journal of Reading,* 18 (1978): 710–15.

Task Force on Educational Issues, "What Do Teachers Think About Tests and Testing." *American Educator,* 1 (1977): 10–12.

Taylor, W. "Cloze Procedure: A New Tool for Measuring Readability." *Journalism Quarterly,* 30 (1953): 414–38.

Thorndyke, P. "Cognitive Structures in Comprehension and Memory of Narrative Discourse." *Cognitive Psychology,* 9 (1977): 77–110.

Tinker, M., and McCullough, C. *Teaching Elementary Reading.* Englewood Cliffs, N. J.: Prentice-Hall, 1975.

Tinker, M. A. *Basis for Effective Reading.* Minneapolis: University of Minnesota Press, 1965.

Tuinman, J. "Determining the Passage Dependency of Comprehension Questions in Five Major Tests." *Reading Research Quarterly,* 9 (1974): 206–23.

Tuinman, J., Blanton, W., and Gray, G. "A Note on Cloze as a Measure of Comprehension." *The Journal of Psychology,* 90 (1975): 159–62.

Veatch, J. *Individualizing Your Reading Program.* New York: G. P. Putnam, 1959.

Walmsley, S. A. "Some Persistent Problems with Objectives and Objective-Item Congruence in Criterion-Referenced Tests." *Improving Human Performance,* 6 (1977): 157–64.

Walmsley, S. A. "The Criterion-Referenced Measurement of an Early Reading Behavior." Unpublished paper, State University of New York at Albany, Albany, N. Y., 1978.

Watson, G. "What Do We Know about Learning?" In DeGrazia, A., and Sohn, D. (eds.), *Revolution in Teaching: New Theory, New Technology.* New York: Bantam, 1964.

Weiner, M., and Cromer, W. "Reading and Reading Difficulty: a Conceptual Analysis." *Harvard Educational Review,* 37 (1967): 620–43.

Williams, J. P. "Learning to Read: a Review of Theories and Models." *Reading Research Quarterly,* 8 (1973): 121–46.

Wiig, E. H., and Semel, E. *Language Disabilities in Children and Adolescents.* Columbus, Oh.: Merrill, 1976.

Wolf, T. "Reading Reconsidered." *Harvard Educational Review,* 47 (1977): 411–29.

Index of Names

Index

Ability, reading, 5, 15, 41–43
Abstraction, in concept development,
  142, 159
Achievement tests, 59, 73
Achieving below potential, 31
Age, and reading ability, 43
Ambiguity, in informal assessment, 95
American Federation of Teachers Task
  Force on Educational Issues, 55
Anthologies, 104
Arithmetic average, 60. *See also* Scores
Assessment
  cloze procedure technique of, 89
  informal, 77–78, 94–96
  of instruction, 138
  of learner attainment of concepts,
    144–48
  of readiness, 89–92
  of reading rate, 84
Assessment strategies, 77. *See also*
  Tests
Association, in concept development,
  157–58
Assumptive teaching, 171
Average
  arithmetic, 60
  below, 31

Basal readers, 27
Behavioral model, of reading process,
  23–24
Bell-shaped curve, 60
Boldface print, 112, 118
Brain, human, 122

Categorization, in concept development, 158

Charts, in text, 115–16
Classification, in learning process, 149
Classrooms
  content area, 222
  specialized-reading, 36
Cloze procedure, 78, 89, 105–111, 118
  administration of, 110–111
Cognitive model, of reading process,
  24
Cognitive process, reading as, 16–17
Complexity, 142
Comprehension, reading, 16, 36
  and cloze procedure, 108
  and reading rate, 45
  skills involved in, 57
Concept attainment, 151
  facilitating, 161
  levels of, 149–52, 165
  problems of, 162–64
Concepts
  assessing learner knowledge of, 144–
    46
  complexity of, 81, 143
  development of, 48, 152–62
  differentiation and generalization of,
    147–48
  facilitating attainment of, 146–47
  planning for development of, 159–
    62
  vicarious experiences in attainment
    of, 161
  and vocabulary, 141–44
Conceptualization, logical process of,
  164
Cone of Experiences, 153–56
Consensus method, of establishing
  criterion, 63

253